To Laurence

Best wishes

Bryn Bray

16.10.12

With The East Surreys in Tunisia, Sicily and Italy 1942–1945

Dedication

For Jack Chaffer, Major Frank 'Peachy' Oram, Harry Skilton,
Major Bob 'Toby' Taylor, Frank Weston, Lieutenant Colonel John Woodhouse
and all the Surreys in the Second World War, who did what had to be done.

In books lies the soul of the whole past time; the articulate audible voice
of the past, when the body and material substance of it has altogether
vanished like a dream.
Thomas Carlyle (On Heroes, Hero-Worship and the Heroic, 1841)

With The East Surreys in Tunisia, Sicily and Italy 1942–1945

Fighting for Every River and Mountain

BRYN EVANS

Pen & Sword
MILITARY

First published in Great Britain in 2012 by
PEN & SWORD MILITARY
An imprint of
Pen & Sword Books Ltd
47 Church Street
Barnsley
South Yorkshire
S70 2AS

ISBN 978-1-84884-762-0

A CIP catalogue record for this book is
available from the British Library.

Typeset by Concept, Huddersfield, West Yorkshire.
Printed and bound by CPI Group (UK) Ltd, Croydon, CR0 4YY.

Pen & Sword Books Ltd incorporates the imprints of Pen & Sword Aviation,
Pen & Sword Maritime, Pen & Sword Military, Wharncliffe Local History,
Pen & Sword Select, Pen & Sword Military Classics, Leo Cooper,
Remember When, Seaforth Publishing and Frontline Publishing.

For a complete list of Pen & Sword titles please contact
PEN & SWORD BOOKS LIMITED
47 Church Street, Barnsley, South Yorkshire, S70 2AS, England
E-mail: enquiries@pen-and-sword.co.uk
Website: www.pen-and-sword.co.uk

Contents

Acknowledgements

So many people have given something to this book, their galvanising interest, encouragement, and helped to shape the result, that to thank everyone would require another chapter. Above all I could have neither begun nor completed the book, without the patience, forbearance, love and support of my wife Jean. I am also hugely indebted to the contributions, interest, encouragement and support of so many others. Of course the most influential have been the East Surreys' veterans and their families, and in particular: Jack and Doll Chaffer, their daughter Jackie and her husband Mick; Linda Standen, daughter of Major Frank Oram, and her husband Alan; Harry and Jessie Skilton's daughters Jean, Carol and Karen; Frank and Doreen Weston; Lieutenant Colonel Tim Rogerson; Frank Gage; Major Bob 'Toby' Taylor; John Mumford; George Wilson; Robert de Gavre, son of Lieutenant Colonel Tommy Thompson; Michael Woodhouse, son of Lieutenant Colonel John Woodhouse, John's sister Anne Sutton and Michael's wife, Lorel.

I shall be always grateful for the trust of Michael Woodhouse in sharing with me his father's unpublished memoirs, his passionate enthusiasm, and for the time he has found despite his demanding flying duties, to encourage and believe in my work.

Many other Surreys' veterans have contributed to the book, through their accounts, diaries, letters, articles and other documents, either sent to me, or researched in the Surrey History Centre. Material held by the Centre is reproduced with their kind permission. To the Imperial War Museum, and various regimental histories and journals of the East Surreys and the Queen's Royal Surreys' Association, I extend my thanks for their contributions and assistance with my research. Damiano Parravano of Piumarola, Italy, a member of the Associazione Linea Gustav, generously allowed the use of photographs he has taken of the battlefields around Cassino and I am most grateful to him.

A special thank you goes to: Major Tony Russell, Secretary of the Queen's Royal Surreys' Association, for his interest, help and support with research, the articles drawn from my research published in the Association's Journal, and to another ex-Surrey for his keen interest and encouragement, Lieutenant Colonel Tim Rogerson. Similar appreciation goes to all the staff of the Surrey History Centre and the Imperial War Museum for their always courteous help and assistance.

I am profoundly grateful to Pen and Sword Books for taking on the publication of this book, and in particular to their publishing manager, Brigadier Henry Wilson, for his sustaining interest, and for encouraging me to complete the book. It was Henry who invited Richard Doherty to be my editor, for whose rich and extensive knowledge of the Tunisian and Italian campaigns, and enthusiastic help, advice and suggestions, I shall be always grateful.

I am of course indebted to all those who have written so much on the Tunisian and Italian campaigns, without which this book would not have been possible. Every effort has been made to fully attribute all sources consulted, and to contact those where material quotations have been used in the text.

I must apologise to those veterans and their families, whom I have contacted, and who have found it too distressing, too painful to recall those times. But for all those who served in the East Surreys in the Second World War, this book is for you and your families. Finally, all my thanks and apologies to my friends and family, for their forbearance and patience in listening to my obsession with this book over recent years. Most of all, for ever my love to my wife Jean, whose insights, intuitions and suggestions made it possible, and gave the Surreys' veterans their voices.

Bryn Evans
Sydney
February 2012

Foreword

There is a popular image of the Second World War as a war of movement, with tanks thrusting forward to open the way for the infantry to follow. That may have been true in some instances but the war was more often fought at the pace of the infantry. As in every war in history, the PBI, the Poor Bloody Infantry, bore the greatest burden and suffered the heaviest casualties on the ground.

Nowhere was this more the case than in the Tunisian, Sicilian and Italian campaigns. Tunisia was a hard campaign, fought in cruel mountains and in mud as bad as that of Flanders in the Great War. Sicily was a short but brutal campaign, fought in harsh mountains under a scorching sun. And Italy? That beautiful and historic peninsula witnessed a long, bitter slog for the Allied soldiery and, above all, for the infantry. Common to all three campaigns was the fact that the armour was restricted seriously in its ability to manoeuvre and assist the infantry. And so the burden on the infantry was very much higher.

Throughout all these campaigns the British 78th Division, the Battleaxe Division, distinguished itself. This splendid formation was never found wanting and earned a reputation for mountain fighting that was unique amongst the Allied armies in Tunisia, Sicily and Italy. Among the units of the Division was the 1st Battalion of The East Surrey Regiment, 1st Surreys. This was a Regular Army unit, one of only three in the Division (that number increased to four in mid-1944) and it showed its mettle in the many engagements in which it fought.

Also involved in both the Tunisian and Italian campaigns was 4th Division, one of the oldest of the Army's divisions, which included a Territorial Army battalion of the East Surreys, 1/6th Surreys. The soldiers of this Battalion also proved worthy of their salt, showing that TA units could reach the same standards of prowess and efficiency as their Regular counterparts. Both Surreys' battalions enjoyed good leadership and a tremendous team spirit that allowed them to endure in the midst of many difficulties. And at the heart of that team spirit was the willingness of individual soldiers to work as a team, to support their mates, and to trust and rely on those mates. Not for nothing has it been said that the soldier does not fight so much for King and Country as for the man beside him in the slit trench, or alongside him in the assault or on the line of march.

And therein lies the great strength of this book. Bryn Evans has captured the humanity of the soldiers of the East Surreys in this narrative and analysis of two Surreys' battalions as they fought for every river and every mountain in Tunisia, Sicily and Italy. Here, in the figures of the individuals who populate this book, are men whom we can admire, men who were prepared to endure and even die for their friends, their Regiment, their King and their Country. Men like Jack Chaffer, Frank Oram, Harry Skilton, George Thornton and Frank Weston, under officers such as John Wood-house, Harry Smith and 'Chips' Louis gave all they could, and often more, in the struggle to defeat Fascism. The author's Epilogue distils what they, and their comrades, gave into raw figures of dead, wounded and missing and it is sobering to reflect that the total casualties of 2,153 in the two battalions was almost equal to the strength of three infantry battalions while the figure of 439 dead represents the bulk of the fighting strength of a battalion. Equally sobering is the thought of the pain caused by all those casualties in the homes of the dead, wounded and missing.

I have been interested in the Italian campaign for many years; my late father served there as did two of my childhood neighbours, and I have walked and studied Sicilian and Italian battlefields. In researching the history of the Irish Brigade, also part of the Battleaxe Division, I have also studied the Tunisian campaign and interviewed many who fought there. The ground these men strove to capture was difficult and favoured the defender far more than the attacker. Thus their achievement was all the greater for they took on and defeated one of the most professional armies the world has ever known. None would ever have claimed to be heroes, or anything other than ordinary men. But these 'ordinary men' achieved the extraordinary and helped make the world a better place. We owe them a great debt of gratitude. And we also owe Bryn Evans our thanks for bringing to life their story and reminding us of what they did.

Richard Doherty
(Author: *Eighth Army in Italy: The Long Hard Slog*)
Co. Londonderry
February 2012

Preface

This is a Mediterranean odyssey, which follows the 1st and 1/6th Battalions of the East Surrey Regiment [the Surreys] in their Second World War campaigns through Tunisia, Sicily and Italy. The Surreys became some of the Allies' finest troops in mountain warfare, through the winter rain and mud of Tunisia's Atlas mountains, the sulphur fumes of Sicily's Mount Etna, the swollen rivers of Italy's Abruzzo, the icy killing grounds of Monte Cassino, and a third winter of snow and ice in the Tuscan Apennines on the Gothic Line.

Time and again the Surreys were called upon to break open German defences, crossing swollen rivers under fire, or climbing to assault an enemy-held peak. Then in the spring of 1945, as if a storm finally burst, the Surreys came down from the Apennines into Eighth Army's dreaded final battle in northern Italy. There they met their inevitable destiny, the impossible battle for the Argenta Gap, and the canals and rivers of the flooded River Po valley.

How did the inexperienced troops of the East Surrey Regiment, many still just teenage boys, become tough front-line infantry? Many were teenagers, and lied about their age in order to enlist. So what turned young recruits, drawn largely from suburban London and Surrey towns, into river land fighters and specialists in mountain warfare, and so often to be a spearhead of an attack?

Perhaps a clue can be gleaned from the post-war reflections of Lieutenant Colonel John Woodhouse, at the time one of the Surreys' most respected young lieutenants, who wrote:

> The saying 'There is no such thing as a bad soldier, there is only a bad officer' is sometimes attributed to Napoleon.
>
> On active service in the Second World War officers and men lived together, and the one knew the other. By an example of personal bravery an officer could quickly win the devotion of his men.
>
> The German Army was very well led, better equipped, and by 1943 more battle experienced than us. We did not believe in the glory of war. Unlike the Germans we were not fighting to enlarge our Empire.

We fought with skill and bravery through pride in our Regiment, just to finish and go home.

I myself was often fearful, but it always mattered greatly to me that I should be well regarded and respected by the soldiers that I commanded. This helped in overcoming fear. However, I was generally cautious weighing the odds carefully.

Good leaders become recognised as such because of their personal touch – that is their contact off duty and unofficially with their men. Good leaders can talk with their men, as well as to them, and they inspire enough confidence for their men to talk to them. They do not forget the value of a smile, and an appearance of cheerfulness.

It may be great leaders are born not made, but by experience and practice, and mixing with their men, good leaders can be made. A good regimental officer knows his job, and has the respect and liking of his men ... although in war he must strive to arouse enthusiasm above respect, devotion above liking.

Respect may be sufficient to secure a soldier's obedience, but a good leader will secure more than obedience from a soldier. He will win enthusiasm, instil pride, and be offered life itself. Men will die for a good leader even in a bad cause. They will never willingly die even for a good cause under a bad leader.

John Woodhouse
Higher Melcombe
Melcombe Bingham
Dorchester
Dorset
(from writings on *Infantry and Soldiers 1949,* and *Memoirs*)

The Surreys' 1st Battalion embarked from Greenock in Scotland in October 1942 in Operation TORCH, with a complement of 796 men. When the Tunisian, Sicilian and Italian campaigns were over, they had suffered a total of 1,311 casualties. It is said by veterans that of those 796 there were only eighteen men still serving at the end in May 1945. In a shorter period from March 1943 to November 1944, the 1/6th Battalion also lost more than their original complement, giving a combined total across the two battalions of 2,153 dead, wounded, and missing. From the voices of those who survived, this is their story.

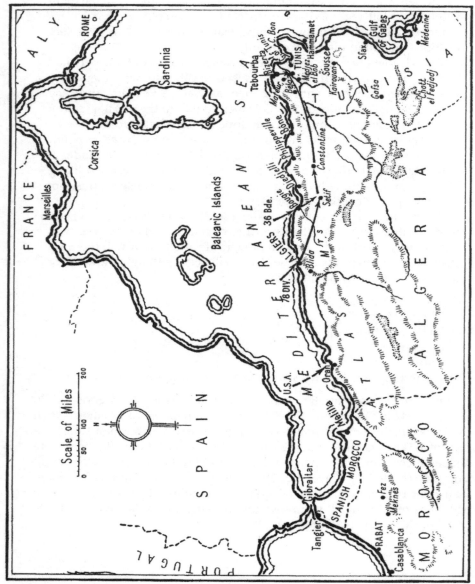

Map 1. Western Mediterranean showing the area in which 78th Division landed and fought during the Tunisian campaign.

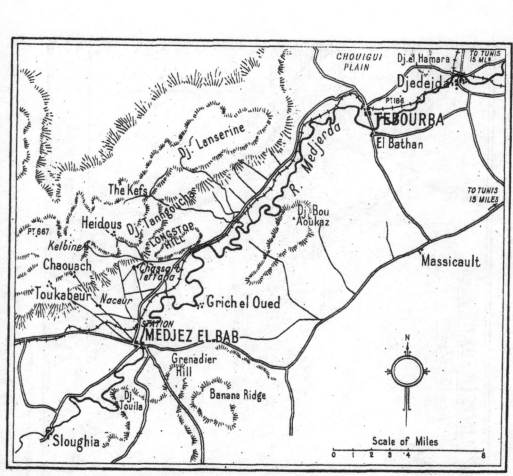

Map 2. 78th Division's main area of operations in Tunisia.

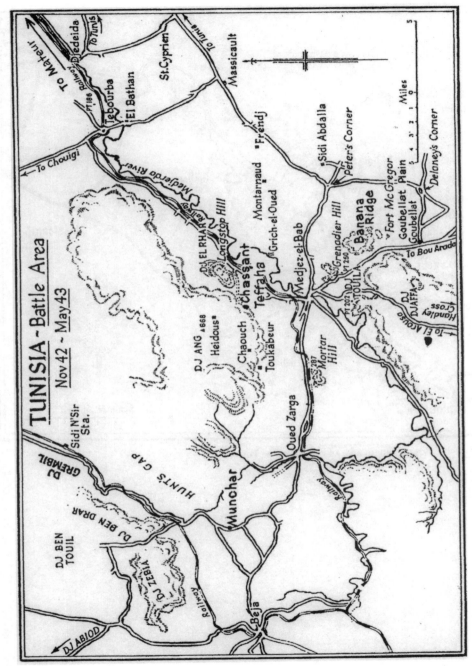

Map 3. The Tunisian battle area between November 1942 and May 1943.

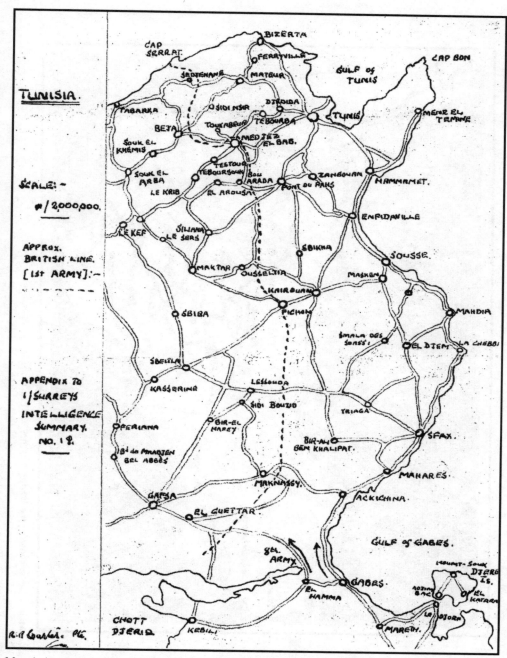

Map 4. A contemporary sketch map of Tunisia from the Surreys' war diary.

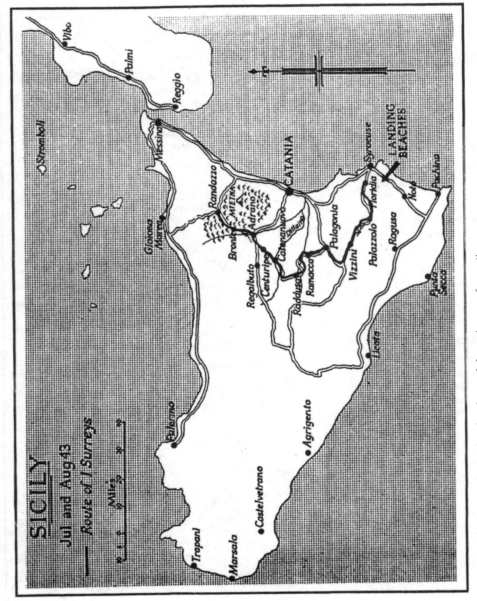

Map 5. Sicily, showing the landing beaches and the main area of operations.

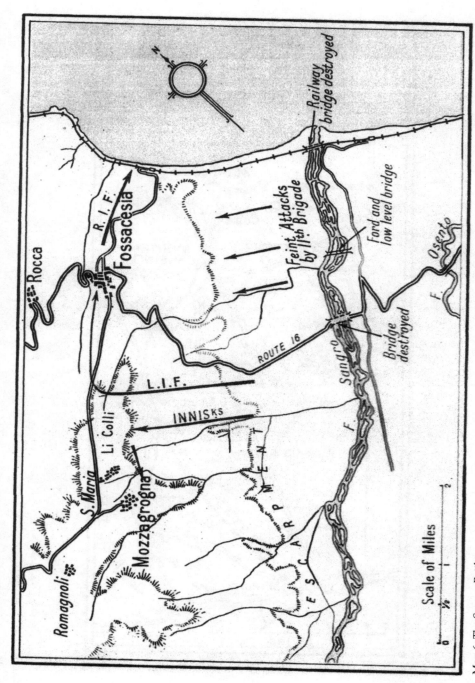

Map 6. The Sangro Battle.

xvii

Map 7. The Cassino area of the Gustav Line in the winter of 1943/44.

xviii

Map 8. Central Italy, showing the Gustav Line, the Hitler Line and Anzio.

xix

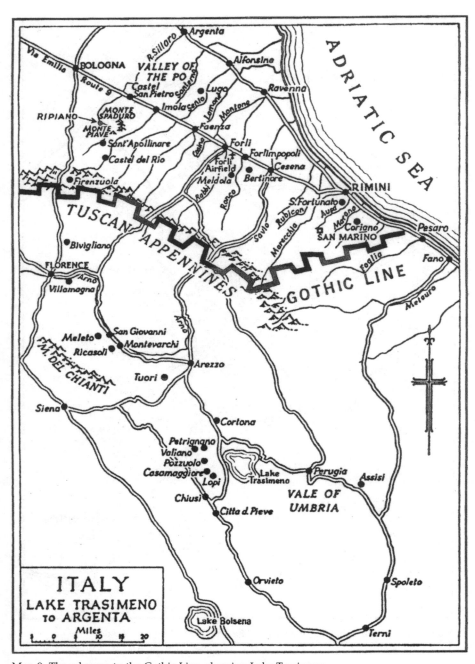

Map 9. The advance to the Gothic Line, showing Lake Trasimeno.

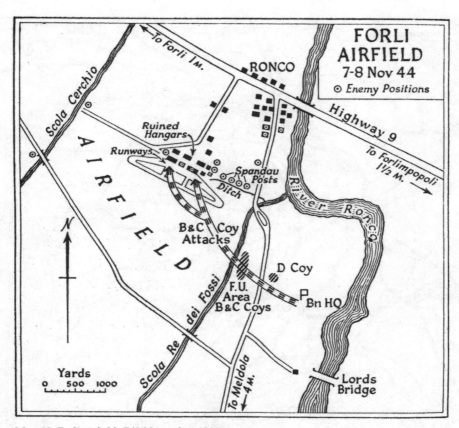

Map 10. Forli airfield, 7/8 November 1944.

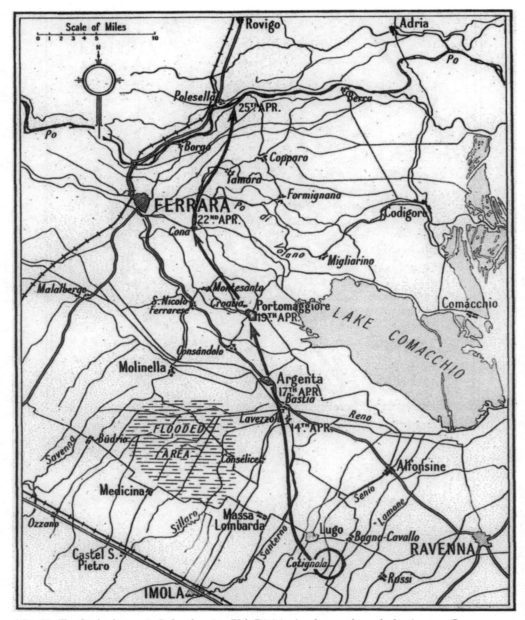

Map 11. The final advance in Italy, showing 78th Division's advance through the Argenta Gap.

Stealing the Dhobi's Donkeys

For the soldier, India was quite unlike anywhere else. All was strange at first and later, nostalgic: the short but vivid vocabulary of native words everyone used; the precise social life and the close family atmosphere of the Battalion; the long columns on the march, with the camels, mules and creaking bullock carts; the solemn native-clerks and the host of servants; the horses and the polo ponies, the dogs and the pet monkeys.

The towns were alive with bustle, especially the colourful teeming bazaars. Away from the towns there was magnificent scenery or sudden glimpses of a mysterious and incomprehensible way of life. Always there were the smells and sounds of India, with early mornings of intoxicating freshness and rich velvet nights, days of stifling heat, dust, glare, and dryness. And against this background was an indefinable romance, the pride and prestige of the British Army in India.

The custom was to serve in the plains during the cool weather, and up in the hills during the hot. When it was necessary to be in the plains in the hot weather, the daily routine was adjusted accordingly. Parades were held early in the morning , and the afternoon was given up to rest in darkened barrack-rooms, with coolies keeping the air moving with punkahs ... until it was cool enough for games and exercises.[1]

From November 1926 to October 1937 the 1st Battalion of the East Surrey Regiment served a continuous tour of duty in India at three stations, Lahore, Fyzabad and Rawalpindi. During these years the Surreys undertook a number of training exercises with the Gurkhas, in mountain warfare in the Murree and Simla Hills.

In the summer of 1930, on the Surreys' Rawalpindi station, school was closed for the holidays. Three boys, Jack Chaffer, Harry Skilton and Frank Oram, all three around eight to ten years of age, sat in the shade on the parched grass and watched the regiment's dhobi wallah walk past with his string of donkeys. The Union Jack hung limp from the flagpole. The boys were bored, and wondering what they could do next.

'What about cowboys and Indians again?' suggested Harry without much enthusiasm.

'It's too hot,' complained Jack. 'In this heat we would need horses like real cowboys.'

While Jack and Harry watched the receding figures of the dhobi and his donkeys, Frank gazed at a bare patch of earth in front of him. A lizard chased two smaller ones under some stones.

'I know!' shouted Frank. 'Maybe we can ride the dhobi's donkeys, like when we did at the fete.'

'Lord O'Reilly!' Jack snapped. 'How the heck do you think we could get hold of the donkeys from the dhobi? He would want us to pay him, like when he sells rides at the annual fete.'

'We can wait until dusk,' said Frank, 'when the dhobi has fed and watered them, and left the base, and gone back to his village. Then we steal them!' He laughed excited. 'Once they have been fed and watered, it will be easy to lead them away out of that compound where they sleep.'

'It's not on,' said Harry. 'A great plan but we would get caught, and into big trouble.'

'And even if we did it and no-one saw us, where would we keep them?' Jack asked, as he thought about it, and got a bit interested. 'Would we be able to ride them without the dhobi leading them like he does at the fete? And where would we ride them, we would be seen surely?'

'Listen, I know how we can do it,' replied Frank quickly, and stood up. 'We put them in that old disused lavatory block, behind the stores sheds, that we explored the other day. It has not been used for a year or more. We get some of that hay from the compound to feed them. And we just keep them for a day to ride them for our game, then take them back tomorrow night. The officers will just blame the dhobi for the donkeys being missing from the compound tomorrow, and tell him he had better find them. Then after we have taken them back tomorrow night, they will just say the dhobi must have been using them for his own jobs for a day. Come on, it's a great wheeze, let's go and check out those old lavatories!'

With that Frank ran off, and as usual Jack and Harry jumped up and ran after him.

They waited until dusk before leading the donkeys out of the compound, then around the back of some stores sheds, and into the disused lavatory block. They had earlier watched as some functions in both the officers' and sergeants' messes, at the far end of the base, seemed to draw everyone, and left the base deserted. Once they had given the donkeys some more hay and water in their new stable, their 'cowboy horses' seemed quite content.

Next day despite the pungent smell by late morning of the donkeys' overnight dung droppings, the boys kept the doors closed to the lavatory block. Frank managed to sit himself astride one of the more docile donkeys, while Harry and Jack tried unsuccessfully to pull or coax it to move. Suddenly the doors burst open, and sunlight flooded in.

'You boys! What do you think you are doing?' In the doorway stood the imposing figure of Provost Sergeant 'Peachey' Oram, Frank's Dad. 'Frank! Get down from that donkey at once. What the hell do you think this is?'

'We were not doing any harm, sir,' replied Harry. 'We just borrowed them to play Cowboys and Indians.'

'Cowboys and Indians! Not doing any harm! I'll give you some harm! You have made me a laughing stock in the regiment, for losing these donkeys. There has been no laundry collected this morning because of this.'

'We were going to put them back in the compound tonight,' said Jack.

'Sorry, Dad ...' tried Frank.

'Shut up, Frank. You should have known better,' his Dad interrupted him. 'It's six of the best for the three of you. You first Frank, come here and bend over.'

The three boys took their medicine without a sound, apart from the thwack of Sergeant Oram's leather baton. They had been caned once before at school, although not six strokes. But it was the shame they felt that was worse.

'Now, I will give you some advice,' said Sergeant Oram, 'always treat donkeys and mules well. Mark my words, one day when you are older and in the Army, your life will depend upon donkeys, and their cousins the mules. Up in the mountains fighting the Afghan tribes, you rely totally on the mule trains to carry your supplies, food, water, guns, ammunition, everything. The mules will even carry you to the hospital when you are wounded. Remember that. Now move! Get them back to the compound.'

As the three boys walked past, gritting their teeth, Sergeant Oram winked at them, and smiled as he said, 'And if you want to hide mules from the enemy, make sure you do not leave a trail of hay all the way to their stables.'

Later when all three served in Tunisia, Sicily and Italy, they would recall this advice.[2]

Notes
1. Daniell, *The History of the East Surrey Regiment*, Vol IV, pp. 27–8.
2. Veterans' Accounts, Chaffer.

Chapter 1

Operation TORCH:
The Invasion of North Africa

It was early morning, 4 December 1942 in Tunisia. Stuka dive-bombers peeled out of the clear morning sky as if it was an air show. With their sirens wailing they screamed down at will to drop their bombs, then turned away back to their base near Tunis to collect a new payload. A few miles away from that attack, and a little to the north of Medjez el Bab, Private George Thornton and other men from A Company of the 1st Battalion of the East Surrey Regiment, sat by the roadside. Exhausted, they waited for some promised transport to continue their forced withdrawal. The 1st Surreys had been just a few miles from Tunis at Tebourba, when they had been driven back by a massive counter-attack of the Germans' 10th Panzer Division.

George Thornton felt the warmth of the morning sun on his back, and relaxed from trench-digging for a moment, the first time since their all night trek south from Tebourba. He could not forget what he saw next.

A 15-cwt truck and an officer pulled in from the opposite direction on the edge of the woods and started to off-load their trucks. They were Guardsmen and unloaded a wicker table, white tablecloth, white mugs and plates, silver cutlery and wicker chairs. It would seem they were going to have breakfast, with Jerry just a few miles away!

He went up to an officer and told him of the threat of German air attack, but he would not listen. When a little later two German fighters flew over, then turned away without firing a shot, George Thornton and his fellow Surreys knew what was coming next. In no time they had finished digging their trenches and jumped in.

Within minutes two Stuka dive-bombers flew over, went to the other end, came back one after the other and dropped bombs right where the Guards were at the end of the woods. The trucks exploded, it was like an inferno. As the Stukas flew off, we approached the area; quite a

4

lot were dead and dying and some severely wounded. Medics tried to have a look at them, but the heat drove them back.[1]

A torn piece of white linen, stained red and still moist, fluttered to the ground. For George and other surviving Surreys it was one disaster after another. Then the bark of a sergeant announced there were more trucks arriving. For now they were getting out of it.

*   *   *

Only four weeks before the defeat at Tebourba, it had been so different. At around midnight on 7 November 1942, by far the largest Allied operation of the Second World War to that time, Operation TORCH, invaded Morocco and Algeria. The enormous Anglo-American task force in excess of 100 ships and more than 107,000 troops, had sailed from the east coast of USA and the west coast of Scotland.[2] In the months leading up to Operation TORCH the 1st Surreys trained with their 78th Division, at first Hoddom Castle near Dumfries, in south west Scotland, and then in the Trossachs bordering Loch Lomond.

In one of the Surreys' training exercises, a Lieutenant only nineteen years old, from the 5th Battalion of the Dorset Regiment, John 'Jock' Woodhouse, acted as a war game umpire. He was quite impressed with the Surreys' efforts.

I joined the 1st Battalion East Surreys in Alloa. They were preparing for a landing in Algeria, a secret of course not known to us at the time. The exercise ran for about ten days in the hills of Ayrshire. These hills were not unlike those in Tunisia, on which the 1st East Surreys were to fight three months later. They were a fine battalion with many pre-war regular officers and NCOs, although I remember their anti-aircraft drill was not as good as ours in Kent, subject as we were to occasional 'live' attacks by the Luftwaffe.[3]

Neither the Surreys nor Woodhouse would have guessed at the prominent role he was to have with the 1st Surreys in the campaigns to come. Nor could anyone have imagined that it would be Woodhouse's first step in a chain of events that would lead him into the journey of his life.

After embarking in the troopship *Karanja* at Greenock, near Glasgow, the 1st Surreys sailed on 26 October 1942 in the invasion fleet of forty-nine ships. Cyril Ray, author of the official history of the 78th Division in 1951, described the Division's departure.

There was a fair lop on the Clyde, and a drab autumn drizzle as the ships left their anchorage at the Tail o' the Bank and filed steadily between the guard-ships into the open sea. The Division must have felt to a man that they were at last committed. Training, leave, letters even, were over. They were the spearhead of Britain's new armies and their selection for this task could mean only one thing – they were Britain's Best. Natural excitement was to be expected, but this was fanned to the deepest intensity by events which, though thousands of miles away, concerned them intimately. For at midday on Saturday, 24 October, the news-boys of Glasgow had gone suddenly wild with the first news of the attack by the British 8th Army at El Alamein, and by evening the whole fleet knew. Dawn on the 27th showed the forty-nine ships ... steaming fast to the west, with Islay and the Mull of Kintyre immediately to the north.[4]

The fleet sailed south with the Ayrshire coast and Culzean Castle to the east. Sealed in a safe on each ship were their orders and destination. No one could have guessed that, after the war, Culzean Castle on the Ayrshire coast would honour General Dwight Eisenhower, the Operation TORCH Commander-in-Chief, by establishing the Eisenhower Museum. The Surreys also could not have known, that they were beginning an odyssey that would take them over ground that had seen Hannibal's campaigns in the Second Punic War in 218–202 BC between the Romans and the Carthaginians. Indeed their first goal was to be Tunis, the site of ancient Carthage itself.

It seems incongruous to connect the names Eisenhower and Hannibal, for they conjure up images of epoch-making wars, some 2,000 years apart in Europe and North Africa. So why speak of them in the same breath? It is well documented that Hannibal was Eisenhower's boyhood hero. In Operation TORCH the 1st Surreys were unknowingly embarking on a series of campaigns through Tunisia, Sicily and Italy to the foot of the Alps, which would link the exploits of these two great generals.

In the Allies' first thrust into Tunisia in the vicinity of Bizerta and Tunis, an assault by paratroopers and seaborne commandos, sought the shock of surprise to gain control of the ports and airfields. Without sufficient numbers, little or no armour or air support, it came to naught.

At the same time Operation TORCH gambled on a land spearhead, that in the main comprised only 11 and 36 Brigades, some light tank units of Blade Force, and an American field artillery battalion. The 1st Surreys, and two other battalions, 2nd Lancashire Fusiliers and 5th Northamptons, made up 11 Brigade, part of the 78th, or Battleaxe, Division of the British First Army. When writing the Surreys' official history, David Scott Daniell described 78th Division as the British Army's cutting edge to rush forward to occupy Tunis.[5]

The strategy of Operation TORCH was first to quickly gain control of the main port of Tunis. The decision not to land at Tunis itself, or even the closest Algerian port of Bone, was driven by a fear of German air attack.

Luftwaffe bombers based in Sicily could easily reach both Bone and Tunis with fighter escorts, whereas the British and American air forces could offer little support to any landings there. Even after air bases were established at Algiers, Allied aircraft would be at the extremity of their range to reach Tunis, which would allow little time over the battlefield to support ground forces.

At the moment of the landings, there were no garrison troops there in Tunis, and the German and Italian High Commands were taken completely by surprise. But Axis reaction was swift, and effectively assisted by the conduct of Admiral Esteva, the French Resident-General. The first German troops arrived by air at El Aouaina airfield, near Tunis, on 9 November, only a day after the Allied landings.

They seized the key points of the cities; they executed or imprisoned the known and suspected Allied sympathizers; they took over the ports of Sousse, Sfax and Gabes and the inland town of Kairouan. Within a week there were 5,000 front-line troops in and around Tunis and Bizerte; they had tanks; and they were still flying in Messerschmitt and Focke Wulf fighters.[6]

It was not known at the time, but by the end of November there would be some 20,000 Axis troops in Tunis, specifically 10th Panzer Division, 334th Infantry Division and the Italian 1st Division, beginning to build up General von Arnim's Fifth Panzer Army. In addition, as had been anticipated, by using mainly all-weather airfields close to Tunis, the Luftwaffe quickly established air superiority. In contrast the Allies' air support was restricted initially to temporary airstrips, while the attacking ground troops of the two brigade groups and Blade Force totalled only 12,300 men.[7]

* * *

'*Nous sommes les Americaines!* – We are Americans!' blared from a hand-held loud-hailer. It was close to midnight on 7 November 1942 as the 1st Surreys' landing craft approached the shore a little to the west of Algiers. Theirs was one of three landings in Operation TORCH, at Casablanca and Oran by the Americans, and at Algiers by an Anglo-American force. Attached to the 78th Division and the Surreys were a few American officers, who had been tasked with shouting a misleading identification claim to give the impression that the whole force was American. Vichy France, the regime established by Petain in collaboration with the Third Reich in July 1940, still controlled North Africa, and it was hoped that they might be more disposed to surrender to US forces.

Algiers was lit up, and its lighthouse flashing. 'There was no moon, but enough light from the town and from the stars for the ships to show as black silhouettes against the grey of the sea and sky. Men were singing on the troop decks, comfortable in the warm air, happy at the news they had heard on the wireless of Eighth Army's advance, speculating about their own future.[8]

Around eight to ten miles offshore the Surreys' troopship, *Karanja*, had anchored, where a rum ration was given out. George Thornton was one of many who struggled to climb down the scramble nets into the Assault Landing Craft (LCAs). 'This was not easy when you are heavily laden. There was a heavy sea running and the LCAs were rising and falling in the swell.'[9]

A submarine then towed the landing craft until they were about three miles from land, where they were on their own. The sickening boat ride into shore heightened a desire in many men to just get on to land and get on with the job. When the ramps were lowered, George Thornton followed his platoon commander into the water. After joining the Surreys at seventeen in 1940, he was just nineteen years old.

Private John Mumford, with his heart racing as he slopped towards the shore, stared at the little clusters of lights: 'I stupidly wondered how many dances were going on! Then a wireless battery I was trying to keep dry, escaped my grip and sank or floated off into the dark. All the time I could hear dogs barking along the beach – a real worry.'

John Mumford was another young recruit from Bisley in Surrey, not long married, and a pay clerk in Headquarters Company.[10] Later the Surreys' A Company did indeed come across a dance hall at Castiglione still in full swing.

Although closer to the shore the sea was calmer, the men staggered in the shoulder-high water. Weighed down by weapons and equipment, it was lucky no-one drowned.[11]

Captain 'Toby' Taylor recalled sensing the menace of the hidden shore:

The night was black and warm, the sea smooth, and in the air was that faint oily smell of Africa. The twinkling lights of Algiers and its sur- rounds made me think of Bridget, and the many past summer's evenings when I had taken her dancing. She was the daughter of General Ken Anderson, who was now in command of [First] Army.[12]

Captain R.C. 'Toby' Taylor was twenty-four, with a trim, spare moustache typical of the times. His chubby cheeks gave the lie to his prematurely receding hairline. After Sandhurst he joined the Surreys in 1938, then served in the Sudan and France before being in action in Belgium in 1940. There he survived wounding to be evacuated from Dunkirk. Now he was hostage to the waves once more.[13]

'I stepped into around five feet of water,' said Private Harry Skilton of Headquarters Company. 'As the water lapped around my neck, I struggled to hold my rifle and other kit above my head.'[14]

Harry Skilton was twenty-one, fair-haired, a career soldier from Kingston-upon-Thames, Surrey, and one of the battalion's top amateur boxers. Following in the footsteps of his father, the 9th Battalion's RSM George Skilton, a veteran of the First World War, he had enlisted in the East Surrey Regiment in 1934 at the age of fourteen.

During the Surreys' pre-embarkation exercises at Hoddom Castle, Harry had managed to get a night off and gone to the fair at the local town of Annan. There he had met a nineteen-year-old Scottish girl, Jessie, and even now she was in his thoughts as he waded towards the beach.

Because of unanticipated sea drift the Surreys made landfall west of Algiers, several miles from their target area. They were exposed, floundering through some 100 yards of sea to the beach. Each man was weighed down by a mass of equipment, weapons, ammunition and rations, which was double what had been used in training.[15] A strong defence could have slaughtered them at the water's edge. However, perhaps the American ruse had caused the withdrawal of some French forces, for even in their wrong landing place the Surreys' luck was holding. Perhaps they could get ashore unchallenged.

Adrenalin and all their training in Scotland kicked in and, hardly conscious of being totally drenched, the Surreys climbed quickly up some unplanned for beach cliffs. When Captain Toby Taylor, with Lieutenant John 'Jake' Saunders and their B Company, reached the top, he found they were quite lost.

'Our company objective did not even appear on our maps and air photographs,' said Taylor. The men were together though, on tenterhooks and ready to go. Taylor had to decide at once which direction to take. He was at a loss, until providence came to the rescue.

> We bumped into an Arab riding a donkey wandering around. He did not seem the least put out by being surrounded by about 100 very wet English soldiers. This Arab understood Jake's French and kindly led us to our objective, the village of Fuka, about three miles away.[16]

It was no accident that Lieutenant Saunders was so fluent in French. Born in 1917 into an eminent banking family, he was educated at Bromsgrove School and in 1937 joined the Hong Kong and Shanghai Bank. Before going out to the bank's operations in the Far East, and in order to learn the financing of the silk trade with Indo-China, he was posted to their Lyons branch in France. On hearing of the outbreak of war in 1939 he resigned immediately, took the train back to London, and enlisted in the Army. After being sent to the OCTU at Sandhurst for officer training, where he was awarded the Belt of Honour, he was commissioned into the 1st Surreys.[17]

The French language skills of officers like Saunders also proved very useful in communicating with the Vichy French forces. As well, by sticking to their rules of engagement, even on one occasion taking fire but not returning it, the Surreys avoided any incidents. Even a Foreign Legion garrison at Kolea offered no resistance. Elsewhere some Vichy French forces resisted the invasion, notably at Oran and in Morocco against American forces. This resulted in needless fighting and casualties, as in places Vichy French troops believed they owed their loyalty to the pro-German, puppet government in France.

Unhindered by any French hostilities, the Surreys then set off from Fuka on a twenty-five-mile march to the Bois de Boulogne area north-east of Algiers. There they took delivery of trucks and troop carrier vehicles, which had been landed in Algiers, and prepared for the advance into Tunisia. Yet while camped in that area for ten days they took their first casualties. While checking out an empty building to assess its suitability for use as the battalion HQ, Lieutenant Geddes the Intelligence Officer was killed by a 'Butterfly Bomb', a German anti-personnel device. It wounded Lance Corporal Barrow, and fatally wounded the Medical Officer Lieutenant Fell.[18]

Those first fatal casualties of Lieutenants Geddes and Fell only accentuated the mounting pressure to get to Tunis and overpower German forces, before they could build up under General Nehring, and join with Rommel's Panzerarmee. Admiral Esteva was allowing German reinforcements to pour in from Italy, by air and sea into Bizerte and Tunis. They were soon in control of other ports at Sousse, Sfax and Gabes.[19] When the Allied command finally made contact with Admiral Esteva on 12 November to urge him to resist the Axis troop influx, it was too late. Esteva replied, 'I have a tutor at my elbow.'[20]

On 17 November after ten days at Bois de Boulogne, the Surreys moved out as part of 11 Brigade, with their sister battalions 2nd Lancashire Fusiliers and 5th Northamptons, to race the 560 miles south-easterly to Tunis. In command of 1st Surreys was Lieutenant Colonel 'Bill' Wilberforce, who had come from The King's Own Yorkshire Light Infantry only a month before. He may have had precisely parted hair and piercing eyes, but he seemed confident and unflappable, and put men at ease.

The Surreys threaded their way through parts of the Atlas Mountains before they crossed the Tunisian border, and began to move down the Medjerda Valley. Their orders were to progressively take the Medjerda Valley towns of Beja, Oued Zarga, Medjez el Bab, Tebourba and Djedeida, as quickly as possible before the final offensive to capture Tunis.

* * *

I began my own journey to follow in the steps of the Surreys in March 2008 in a visit to Tunisia. Like many visitors, my first foray beyond the capital was to the Medjerda Valley. The country's north, with its mountains and river valleys, has been the food basket from the earliest times for its peoples, Numidians, Carthaginians, Romans, Turks, Berbers, Andalusians and Arabs. In Tunis and the north there remains a strong influence of the French language and culture, derived from the many years of a colonial past. To the south lies the Sahara desert, while on the edge of the eastern Sahel coastal plain are the beach resorts around Hammamet, Sousse and Jerba.

Tunisia's rich history can be seen in such places as Phoenician and Roman Carthage, the Punic town of Kerkouane, many Roman ruins such as at Dougga, the carpet manufacturing town and Islamic religious centre of Kairouan, and many other sites. There is even an amphitheatre at El Jem that rivals Rome's Colosseum. Over more than 2,000 years many different cultures have blended their diversity. Tunisian music, known as 'malouf', is a mix of Hispanic and Arab folk music, first introduced in the fourteenth century by refugees from Andalusia. Since Roman times pottery, mosaics and ceramics have absorbed both Andalusian and Italian designs.

Driving through the valley of the Medjerda River in the north, even after having read of its rich fertility, I did not expect the lush green of the landscape, olive groves, orchards, vineyards, and the freshness of early spring corn. Either side are hills and mountains, some forested with pine trees, many bare and rocky, and, sometimes in winter, sprinkled with snow. In his popular accounts of the North African campaign, the war correspondent Alan Moorehead, spoke of wildflowers in the valley's foothills: 'They grow among the brown and red boulders in startling unbelievable shades of vermilion, canary yellow, sky blue, and in mad African luxuriance.'[21]

In November 1942 it was autumn, turning to winter, and the land was dry from the heat of summer. The Surreys, rather than noticing the colour of any surviving flowers, would have scoured the terrain for any evidence of the enemy's presence. Some fifty miles down the Medjerda Valley, the 78th Division's advance came up against Axis forces at Beja. Following an initial assault by British paratroopers of Blade Force, the Surreys occupied the hilltop town for two days and sent out forward patrols. Not far to the south lay the evidence of that much earlier invasion, the extensive ruins of the Roman towns of Bulla Regia and Dougga.

The Medjerda Valley at one time supplied most of Rome's grain, and made Carthage the third largest city in the Roman Empire. I caught a glimpse at Dougga of the startling scale of the Roman colonisation of North Africa. Rome built Dougga into a fortress city, which commanded the Medjerda Valley between Beja and Medjez El Bab. For the Surreys there was no time to appreciate either scenery or archeology as they pressed on towards Tunis.

In the Second World War it was falsely assumed by many of the general public, and remains the popular perception today, that the Tunisian campaign was fought in the desert. In fact the major part of the fighting took place in the mountains and valleys of northern Tunisia. Much of it was in the cold and rain of winter, and the icy winds of the Atlas Mountains.

But while the rain was holding off the Surreys forged on down the Medjerda Valley. Tunis had to be taken before German reinforcements could be fully established there, and merged with Rommel's Panzerarmee Afrika, which was retreating across Libya from Alamein. About half-way between Oued Zarga and Medjez el Bab at dusk, the Surreys came under fire from Mortar Hill, which killed Corporal North. It brought the Surreys' rush to a sudden halt, and threatened them losing pace and contact with the 5th Northamptons, who were advancing through the hills to the north.

Major Tom 'Buck' Buchanan was ordered to lead B Company in a three-platoon assault on the hill, yet he had little intelligence on the strength or positions of enemy forces. The evening twilight was rapidly turning to night, but he knew the Surreys had to keep moving on.

> The company was about a mile from Mortar Hill, it was dark, but the hill's outline could be seen. I decided to make an attack with 11 and 12 Platoons, while 10 Platoon were sent on a detour to attempt to cut off the rear of the enemy. There was a farm at the foot of the hill and I decided to bypass this as it was suspected that dogs were around. Unfortunately the dogs started barking when the company were some distance away.
>
> But we pushed slowly forward up the hill in the dark. It was hard going. Soon automatic fire came from near the top of the hill. Fire was returned and the fire fight had started, but still slow progress was made. The enemy, German paratroops, would fire from one position and then quickly move to another position. It was almost impossible to pin-point them.[22]

When Major Buchanan withdrew his men shortly before dawn, he found there were several casualties, two dead, and Lieutenant Whiffen captured. The Germans may have paid more dearly, for when patrols later reported a lack of enemy activity, Buchanan led B Company in another attack at daylight, and found the Mortar Hill summit deserted.

Major Buchanan was thirty-four. After graduating from London University he became a schoolteacher, and joined the Supplementary Reserve in 1931. When war broke out in 1939 he was posted as a lieutenant to the 1st Surreys in the British Expeditionary Force in France, where he commanded B Company in the retreat to Dunkirk. Buchanan made a huge contribution to the rebuilding of the Surreys from 1940–42, and for a time was Chief Instructor at the 78th Division Battle School.[23]

Further on the Surreys and other 78th Division battalions met more German defences in some strength at Medjez el Bab, an ancient market town and a vital forward defensive outpost for Tunis. In attempts to cross the Medjerda River and take Medjez, the Lancashire Fusiliers and Northamptons were thrown back with heavy losses, and the Surreys' forward patrols also took casualties.

* * *

While 78th Division and the Surreys were being held up at Medjez, some ten miles to the north at Djedeida, two light tank battalions from the British 17th/21st Lancers and the US 1st Armored Division raided a Luftwaffe airfield. They destroyed more than twenty planes, which together with the combined shelling and bombing of Medjez caused the Axis forces to begin a premature withdrawal of their lines. So on 26 November the Surreys led a further attack with a squadron of American tanks, and occupied Medjez.

The same day the Surrey infantry pushed out again some twenty miles north-easterly from Medjez. Many were new to being under fire, but despite the increasing casualties the pace could not be slackened. They approached Tebourba, another small town in the midst of a flat country-side full of orchards and olive groves. It lay on the north side of the steep banked Medjerda River less than twenty miles from Tunis. The town, in ruins from heavy shelling and bombing, and the nearby bridge over the Medjerda at El Bathan, were only lightly defended. By nightfall both were in the hands of the Surreys. The Tunisian capital was only a day's march away.

Some three miles west of Tunis city centre lies a building now visited by nearly every tourist, the Palace of the Husseinite Bey of Tunisia. It would have stood out in the Surreys officers' binoculars, and been well marked on their commanders' maps. Even under the Vichy French Protectorate, the Bey was still the nominal head of state, and his palace served as the parliament.

* * *

That old Palace of the Bey, which had been in the sights and plans of the Surreys, is today probably Tunisia's foremost UNESCO World Heritage site and better known as the Bardo Museum. It houses one of the finest and largest collections of Roman mosaics. You can see that, like today's digital photos, they captured everyday life in Rome's North African colonies. They were predominantly used on the floors of Roman villas,

13

whose owners thought of them not just as decoration, but as a display to impress visitors.

Some scenes show farmworkers herding cows into a stable, while others harvest grapes and olives, catch fish, hunt hares and even spear a marauding leopard. One mosaic shows a group of gladiators feasting and drinking as they gaze at some resting bulls, no doubt shouting how they will kill them in the arena the next day. What brings it to life are the words of the guard, telling them to be quiet and not wake their bovine opponents!

I thought that, on that first night of 26 November 1942 in Tebourba, some of the Surreys may well have been drinking in anticipation of further success to come. I could imagine a lucky few of the Surrey infantry getting hold of some of the local wine and noisily laughing off their tensions and fears, unaware of the German counter-attack that would hit them the next day. For many it would be their last day.

General Nehring, in command of the build-up of German forces in Tunisia, that had already reached about 20,000, had only been in Tunisia ten days. He was not yet fully recovered from being wounded while in Panzerarmee Afrika and it showed in his impulsive decisions to pull his forces back from both Medjez and Tebourba. The steadying counsel of Field Marshal Kesselring in Italy, who even flew over to meet Nehring in Tunis on 27 November, would soon become apparent.[24]

At first light on 27 November 1942 a Surreys' patrol entered an empty police building in the town and found eggs still sizzling in a frying pan – the last of the night had hidden the sudden flight of German troops. Half a mile to the east on Djebel Maiana, a hill renamed Point 186, reflecting its height in metres, the Surreys' A Company had taken up an observation position, from where in the dawn's sun they could see the shimmering minarets of Tunis.[25]

There were no more hills to be seen, only a flat plain that lay less than twenty miles between them and the Tunisian capital. Although the Surreys were now reduced to around 500 men, they hoped to be reinforced very quickly. Major General Evelegh, the 78th Division commander, even had thoughts of entering Tunis on the next day. But there was to be no time. By mid-morning the 10th Panzer Division counter-attacked with some fifty tanks. At the time George Thornton was returning to the Point 186 observation post.

We had just got some blankets from our lorries which were hidden in the olive groves at the base of the hill and were on our way back up when someone shouted, 'Tanks!' Most of us thought they were from our Blade Force, but when they began to open fire we knew otherwise. They shot up all of our lorries, and then came after us, but, luckily, they could not elevate their guns or get up the hill, so we were comparatively safe from them while the raid went on.[26]

So the Battle for Tebourba and its nearby hill Point 186 began. The Surreys' second-in-command, Major Harry Smith, described that first engagement with the German armour:

At about 1030 hours Point 186 reported approximately 50 enemy tanks ... approaching astride the Tebourba – Mateur road ... our medium guns were dive-bombed in relays by three Stuka aircraft ... Our supporting Bofors (light anti-aircraft) gun troop brought down at least one Stuka before they were themselves put out of action. We barely had time to alert everybody within our widely dispersed battalion area. There was no time, however, to move the soft-skinned vehicles, such as the Troop Carrying Vehicles (TCVs), which had been dispersed among the olive groves in the rear of Point 186.

Behind the TCVs were the 25-pounder guns of our supporting battery of 132nd Field Regiment RA. They had time to adapt themselves to an anti-tank role before the first enemy tanks emerged from the smoke of the burning TCVs, almost on to the muzzles of the guns. A short and furious engagement now took place. The gunners firing over open sights at point blank range fought their guns to the last man. Although they suffered heavy casualties, it was the toll they managed to exact on the advancing armour that halted the attack.[27]

Battalion HQ, which was in a strip of wood near the railway station at Tebourba, was attacked and at one point was in danger of being overrun. 'The tanks halted short of the wood and fired into it,' stated the DCM citation in respect of RSM Buck Adams. 'Infantry had succeeded in establishing themselves in houses and trees over the railway line, which overlooked BHQ at very close range.' In the sudden confusion RSM Adams completely ignored all enemy fire and gave orders to everyone to move positions. He quickly restored confidence among the men and succeeded in getting all the wounded out safely.[28]

With only an out-gunned Royal Artillery unit in support, the Surreys took heavy losses in fighting off the attack, yet destroyed eight enemy tanks, and maybe more as the German recovery teams pulled some away in their tactical pull-back. On the Surreys' south-east flank they were adjoined by the US 5th Field Artillery Battalion (FAB), for most of whom, like the Surreys, this was their first battle.

Joe Furaytor of the 5th's A Battery saw his comrades die, and told himself, 'You're a soldier, this is what happens in war. Accept the fact, and accept that it could happen to me too.' Later as Joe and the 5th gunners ran out of shells, they spread out with .50 calibre machine guns, and came into

15

contact with the Surreys. 'We talked to each other and exchanged rations. They had field glasses and as soon as they saw any of the enemy coming in my direction, they'd motion to me and I'd cock my gun ready to fire.'[29]

Tebourba lay astride the only route that German tanks could take through the hills from Tunis to attack Medjez. For the next week the Surreys, together with the Americans, and troops of the Northants and Hampshire Regiments, fought a series of desperate defensive battles, against waves of tanks, mortars and German paratroopers. At Tebourba the dead piled up, and the wounded lay in lines, clinging to life or sinking into death. Yet stretcher-bearers still promised them, 'We'll be in Tunis eating bloody great oranges in a week.'[30]

After the wounded were dragged from the battlefield they were carried by stretcher-bearers, then often slung either side of a mule to get to the first medical aid post. Even then those still alive faced a long tortuous journey to reach hospital. Private John Cooper from the Surreys' fellow Battleaxe battalion, the Lancashire Fusiliers, was wounded in both knees.

> At last we were off-loaded to a Casualty Clearing Station still within shell-fire range and I was amazed to find nurses there. They were superb, for that Clearing Station had all the attributes of a butcher's shop. I was a butcher myself and should know. From there I was taken to a hospital at Souk-el Khemis where two broken legs were diagnosed and both legs put into plaster from thigh to toes. From there we moved to a tented hospital at Bone before finally arriving at the 98th General Hospital in Algiers. I owe a lot also to all those nurses who looked after me on the way down from the Djebels to the base hospital itself. I cannot say enough about them.[31]

Besides the uplift in their spirits from seeing nurses so close to the front, they received another huge benefit in Algiers. Sir Alexander Fleming was resident at the General Hospital, administering his new drug, penicillin, to bring a huge boost to recovery of the wounded.[32]

* * *

In a week of desperate defence in the olive groves around Tebourba, the Surreys' Major Buchanan was awarded the MC, and in the Hampshires Lieutenant Colonel Lee the DSO, and Major Le Patourel the VC.[33] On 3 December a German attack finally captured Point 186, which was crucial to holding Tebourba. In his subsequent report, the Surreys' Intelligence Sergeant, Manning, summed it up:

> With armoured and air support as usual, a German battalion was flung against it and captured it after a morning's hard fighting. From then Tebourba was doomed. Valiantly led, counter-attacks by the

remnants of two other companies failed. Some troops topped the hill but were too weak to hold their gains.[34]

That official report did not do full justice to the desperation of the dwindling number of Surreys to hold on. John Mumford watched one attempt to regain the hill come to naught:

I remember seeing Lieutenant Cecil half way up the hill turning round waving his revolver and calling for his men to follow him, and then he was shot and fell to the ground. What a hero, I shall always remember that Friday afternoon.[35]

Eventually however Panzers cut the road to Medjez, leaving the Hampshires, Surreys and US 5th Field Artillery Battalion nearly surrounded. Tebourba was lost. As dusk fell George Thornton and other survivors followed orders, and began to slip away in twos and threes towards Medjez. 'In the closing darkness a lot of men, including me,' said Thornton, 'were wandering everywhere, there was total confusion.'[36]

The next morning Thornton would watch Stuka dive-bombers hit the inexperienced Guards battalion. And every so often in the chaotic, overnight withdrawal, the Surreys' Major Peter Hill looked back:

We could see many fires and the streaks of tracer ammunition as the enemy tried to shoot up what survivors remained. White Very lights were going up everywhere. We reached a farm at midnight. It was bitterly cold, but most of the men were so tired they just dropped down where they were. All next day we lay up resting and reorganizing. We were reduced to about half the normal strength of the Battalion and had lost most of our transport and a good deal of equipment. We moved back that night to another farm ….

And the next day,

There was a lot of firing on our right flank as the enemy steadily pushed back the American armour. They had heavy losses that day. That night we were withdrawn about fifteen miles to behind Longstop Hill, just outside Medjez. The men marched all through the night and were pretty exhausted on arrival. The next night we were moved again a few miles farther back to a farm owned by the Maire of Medjez. There was a fine orange grove full of ripe fruit, but it didn't last very long, I'm afraid after the Battalion arrived. M le Maire took a poor view of this, and indeed never took kindly to us.[37]

'To hell with the bloody mayor, we were gasping, out on our feet,' said Harry Skilton. 'And we thought, to hell with eating oranges in Tunis.'[38]

17

As well as defending their build-up in and around Tunis, the Germans were also intent on driving the Allies back beyond Medjez. Although by 4 December the superior German armour had defeated the Allies at Tebourba, a week of stubborn resistance by the Surreys, the other battalions of 78th Division and the Americans, had given First Army time to withdraw and consolidate stronger forces at Medjez.[39]

But in just a few weeks of combat since they landed in North Africa, the 1st Surreys had been cut in two. By 5 December when they regrouped in Medjez, the Surreys comprised only twenty-three officers and 350 other ranks. They had paid dearly in fighting the Axis forces to a standstill, losing more than half their original strength of 796.

To add to the Surreys' misery, on 6 December the weather broke. Cyril Ray recorded that it rained for three days and three nights. 'There was no cover for the men and the slit trenches filled with liquid mud.'[40] 'It was cold, the side roads were mud tracks, and the attacks came not across hot desert sands, but from between rock-strewn hills, from behind dense scrub, and out of the dark cork forests.'[41] Allied troops were learning the meaning of warfare in northern Tunisia.

In the confused fighting and retreat from Tebourba, American forces also suffered severe losses. The US 1st Armored Division of 4,000 men was nearly destroyed, and forced into humbling withdrawal. They had begun with 124 tanks, plus similar numbers of howitzers, half-tracks and trucks, of which around 75 per cent were destroyed or lost in the mud. The remaining men and vehicles had to be pulled out of the line.[42]

Though the daring assault by 78th Division to move on Tunis was a gamble that was lost, it had gained time for the Allies, and *The Times* reported:

> The breathing space was not wasted; by the time the inevitable German counter-attack came we were more or less ready for it, and though we lost valuable positions we did not lose Medjez, by far the most valuable of all.[43]

The truth was that the German offensive was forcing the Allies' First Army to fight a desperate withdrawal action.

* * *

Despite the Tebourba setback the Allies regathered in Medjez, and planned another assault on Tunis. Political pressure intensified and the festive season was ignored. The offensive was to resume on the night of 23 December 1942, with a plan to capture Djebel el Ahmera, a mountainous ridge some six miles north of Medjez known as Longstop Hill. It would become the nemesis of the Allies' Tunisian campaign. Until it was seized nothing could move down the valley to attack Tunis.

However, the heavy winter rains had truly arrived. Alan Moorehead described it as:

> Not ordinary rain, but the wild torrential rain of Africa. The ground turned to mud, and it was the mud of that same African extravagance, thick, sticky, and bottomless. The dead were buried in mud and the living were in it up to their knees. Before the astonished eyes of the commanders, tanks went down to their turrets in mud.[44]

At times it was too heavy for even mules to move supplies. The Tunis offensive was cancelled. Even so it was decided that an attack on Longstop Hill must still go ahead.

During the night of 23 December and all of the next day, Christmas Eve, the Coldstream Guards and the US 18th Infantry Division fought in waves to gain Longstop's peak. And like the ebb and flow of the tides, they first gained the summit, lost it, recaptured it, and lost it again. On Christmas Day morning after the second German counter-attack, the Allies withdrew to Medjez with over 500 casualties and another bitter and costly defeat. The Surreys did not know it at the time, but in the New Year they and the Battleaxe Division would be called upon to shed their blood in a second momentous battle for Longstop Hill.

As if mocking the Allies' defeat, the Germans named it *Weinachtshügel*, Christmas Hill. And for them it was a gift to win it back twice, because it blocked any Allied advance in the Medjerda Valley. This failure to take Longstop, combined with the rain and mud, brought the Allied advance on Tunis to a shuddering halt. The disappointment was such that, in London and Washington, rumours were circulating that Eisenhower was to be replaced. The British questioned his competence and lack of experience.

Churchill himself must have been very anxious. At the time, and even years later, Churchill considered his backing for Operation TORCH to be the riskiest decision he made in the Second World War. On 1 October 1942 he had said to his Ministers Eden and Attlee, 'If TORCH fails, then I am done for and must go and hand over to one of you.'[45]

The failure to take Tunis meant that Rommel's Panzerarmee Afrika was likely to join up with von Arnim's growing Fifth Panzer Army. The Allies had to build their strength during the winter. In the Spring they must have sufficient numbers and firepower to overwhelm the combined German armies. If not they would be dragged into a lengthy campaign that might take a year or more to win.

Notes
1. Thornton, Queen's Royal Surreys Association, Newsletter May 2003.
2. Ford, *Battleaxe Division*, pp. 6–7.

3. Veteran's Accounts, Woodhouse, *Memoirs* (unpublished).
4. Ray, *Algiers to Austria*, p. xix.
5. Daniell, op cit., p. 50.
6. Ibid, p. 3.
7. Ibid, pp. 6–7.
8. Ibid, p. 3.
9. Squire and Hill, *Algiers to Tunis*, pp. 11–13.
10. Veterans' Accounts, Mumford.
11. Ibid.
12. Taylor, The Surrey History Centre, Ref ESR/25/TaylorRC/2.
13. Veterans' Accounts, Taylor.
14. Veterans' Accounts, Skilton.
15. Squire and Hill, op cit., pp. 11–13.
16. Queen's Royal Surreys Newsletter, Nov 2002, Major R.C. Taylor.
17. Obituary Sir John Saunders CBE DSO MC, *The Daily Telegraph*, 30 Jul 2002.
18. Squire and Hill, op cit., pp. 11–13.
19. Ray, op cit., p. 6.
20. Cunningham, *A Sailor's Odyssey*, pp. 499–501.
21. Moorehead, *African Trilogy*, p. 490.
22. Squire and Hill, op cit., p. 15.
23. Queen's Royal Surreys Museum, *The Times* (Obituary), 25 Nov 1997.
24. Atkinson, *An Army at Dawn*, pp. 191–2.
25. Moorehead, op cit., p. 502.
26. Ford, op cit., pp. 33–4.
27. Squire and Hill, op cit., pp. 12–13.
28. Ibid, p. 14, and The Surrey History Centre, ESR/25/ADAMAH.
29. Holland, *Together We Stand*, pp. 465–7.
30. Atkinson, op cit., p. 206.
31. Taylor, *Front-Line Nurse*, pp. 100–2.
32. Ibid.
33. Ray, op cit., pp. 18–22.
34. H.C. Manning, The Surrey History Centre, *The Surrey Comet*, 14 Aug 1943.
35. Veterans' Accounts, Mumford.
36. Ford, op cit., p. 47.
37. Squire and Hill, op cit., pp. 20–1.
38. Veterans' Accounts, Skilton.
39. Ford, op cit., p. 49.
40. Ray, op cit., p. 25.
41. Ibid, p. 11.
42. Atkinson, op cit., p. 234.
43. Squire and Hill, op cit., pp. 20–1.
44. Moorehead, op cit., p. 503.
45. Roberts, *Masters and Commanders*, p. 286.

Chapter 2

Tunisian Winter Stalemate: Rain, Mud, Bullets and Blood

The lead scout froze. In the hazy moonlight he had seen a glimmer of the hill's barbed-wire perimeter. Behind him the other five soldiers in the patrol and their leader, Lieutenant John Woodhouse, had also stopped dead. Besides expecting German defenders to open up on any discernible movement, Woodhouse knew, like the other men, that they were now almost certainly into a minefield.

Woodhouse's mind raced. He had been with 1st Surreys in the Tunisian front lines for only a week. It was the first time he had been in charge of a platoon in a combat zone, and now he was in command of his first patrol. He remembered someone saying to him that against soldiers as good as the Germans the only way to find out if they were still there was usually to go on until challenged or shot at.

> I decided that leadership demanded that I went on myself alone, pistol in hand. If the Germans were still there I hoped they would challenge before shooting. I had taught myself some military German phrases which might be useful such as 'Don't shoot'. I stayed motionless for some time, observing the hill from outside a gap in the wire. All was silence.
>
> I walked slowly forward, heart in my mouth, pistol in hand, finger on trigger. Suddenly I was aware of a German soldier, not five metres from me. My finger tightened and fired before I had aimed.

He threw himself to the ground, expecting a fusillade of German machine-gun fire. Nothing, once again there was silence. What now, it must be a trap, he thought. His patrol was some fifty metres back, hidden by the night, waiting and listening. He too listened. It seemed an eternity. Warily he got to his feet. In a stooping shuffle, his pistol held out in front again, he edged forward.

> I realised the German soldier was a corpse propped up to look alive. About forty German Paratroopers lay dead all round the hill. One

21

with a cigar still firmly clamped in his mouth. Two dead German officers were laid out in the back of a small trench. Both had been booby trapped to catch anyone of us unwary. Corpses whole and in bloody pieces, British and German, were lying everywhere. Although I had never seen a dead person before, and avoided looking too long at them, I was not sad or upset.

My shot had been heard by my platoon, who told me later they thought it was the end of me, in just seven days with them. Sure now that the Germans had gone I fired the Very cartridge light to signal this to the battalion.[1]

In the last week of February 1943, the hill known as Fort McGregor, lost by the Surreys only one day earlier, was theirs again.

* * *

In early 1943 the fighting in northern Tunisia spread across the hills and mountains, which stretched from the north west of Medjez to its southeast. Some said the Battle of Tebourba in December 1942, although smaller in scale, had been reminiscent of Dunkirk, another humiliating defeat and a chaotic retreat. According to Captain 'Toby' Taylor:

After the battle the Germans claimed there were more than 1,000 British prisoners or dead. It was probably quite an accurate figure. We in the battalion had lost very heavily in men, vehicles and equipment. For example B Company was now two officers and forty-two men, whereas before the battle it had been four officers and about 110 men.[2]

During December 1942, after giving ground at Tebourba, the 1st Surreys and the whole British First Army had retreated back down the Medjerda Valley to Medjez el Bab. The Surreys' survivors moved back to the hills west of Medjez, regrouped to recover as best they could, and took in reinforcements and supplies. They dug in on the escarpment a little to the north of the village of Oued Zarga, some on the high ground around the village of Toukabeur, guarding the western flank of Medjez. Following the failure to take the outlying Longstop Hill on Christmas Day, the final days of December witnessed the Allies in a disorganized, sometimes panicky withdrawal.

The onset of heavy winter rains before Christmas led to the calling off of any further attempt to drive for Tunis in the near future. The rain turned many roads into quagmires, making them impassable for wheeled transport. The result was that the Medjez salient became surrounded on all sides by Axis forces. Eisenhower, the commander-in-chief of Operation TORCH, was depressed by the setbacks and, it is now known, openly critical of his own failings. A stalemate set in, as both sides tested each other's lines while rebuilding, and accelerating the replacement of casualties.[3]

*   *   *

The losses of 1st Surreys, like other battalions, were made up from a variety of sources. One of the new men already known to the Surreys, was Lieutenant John 'Jock' Woodhouse of the 5th Battalion the Dorset Regiment, and the 43rd Wessex Division. John Woodhouse was the son of Colonel Charles W. Woodhouse, CO of the Dorset Regiment, and Stella, daughter of Lieutenant Colonel Fairlie of the South African National Mounted Police. At Malvern School, despite being in his own words, 'shy and small for my age', he had been an enthusiastic recruit to the Officer Training Corps. On leaving Malvern he had enlisted as a private in the Dorset Regiment in March 1941 at age eighteen, and after selection to an Officer Cadet Training Unit was commissioned as a second lieutenant in June 1942.[4]

In August 1942 he and four other officers from the 5th Dorsets had been sent to Scotland to umpire the war game Exercise DRYSHOD of the 78th Battleaxe Division, when he had been attached to 1st Surreys as an observer. It would not be long before Woodhouse joined them in action.

Then in late 1942, when many junior officers were to be sent from 43rd Division to replace casualties in 78th Division, then fighting in Tunisia, with five others, including my friend Dick Watkins from 5th Dorsets, I volunteered to join the Surreys. Christmas at home was followed by departure, leaving my mother at King's Cross Station. She had kept cheerful through lunch, but at the moment of departure my suitcase burst open. It was old and badly packed. She helped me cram the contents back in, which caused her to burst into tears. As she turned away to her taxi, she would have been only too aware that it might be the last time she would ever see me.

There was snow on the ground, and Watkins and I were both impatient to be on our way. I was aged just twenty, and to me armed with a copy of Tolstoy's *War and Peace*, it was a great adventure into an unknowable future. By 6 January we were on board the liner *Empress of Bermuda* departing Liverpool.

We landed unscathed in Algiers on 20 January 1943. At first we were based in a tented camp three or four miles east of the city. There were plentiful tangerines, eggs, oranges, dates, and I sent several fruit parcels home, though some were rotten by the time they got back.

We five Dorset officers visited Algiers several times for meals and bars, where the popular song of the day was 'Alouette'. I made a will leaving everything to Dad, apart from £100 to my cousin Con

23

Forwood, and £50 to Walter Hodges who served in the Dorsets' ranks with me in 1941. By 8 February I was moving by very slow train, via stops at two transit camps, towards Tunisia.[5]

*   *   *

In early January 1943 the 1st Surreys had moved farther north and west to Sidi N'sir, through the valley known as Hunt's Gap on the Beja to Mateur railway line. The Germans were pushing southwards to break through to Beja, so as to cut the Allies' main supply route to Medjez. It was also the pass the Allies would eventually have to take, for Mateur was a strategic approach to the major port of Bizerte.

The Surreys' infantry companies spread out into widely dispersed positions, took on new men, and blooded them in tough patrolling engagements, slogging through the winter rain and mud. By being able to use local airfields the Luftwaffe had air superiority, which meant that the Surreys could only patrol at night. Captain Toby Taylor recalled this time.

It was here that we received our first reinforcements after Tebourba – B Company being down to two officers and forty-two men. And it was here that the two German Messerschmitts, affectionately known as 'Gert' and 'Daisy', used to swan up and down at tree-top height, shooting up our transport, for there was no sign of the RAF around in those days.[6]

Most days they spent in cold, wet and hastily-dug trenches. The winter temperatures could drop to freezing, and snow in the high hills was not uncommon. In visits to the front lines around Sedjenane and Mateur, Alan Moorehead saw first-hand that unless the troops on patrol could find a farmhouse, a peasant's hut or cave, they could die of exposure as 'This perishing cold, this all invading mud and this lack of hot food could exhaust and kill a man as thoroughly as bullets.'[7]

'The battalion had not been under cover since it left the convoy on 7 November,' said Captain Taylor, 'so the discomfort was acute. At that time no-one realised that the Rifle Companies would not see the inside of a house till April.'[8]

One of the most apt descriptions of what it was like, for an infantry soldier living, fighting and dying in Tunisia's mountains, was by the American war correspondent Ernie Pyle:

There are none of the little things that make life normal back home. There are no chairs, lights, floors, or tables. There isn't any place to set anything, or any store to buy things. There are no newspapers, milk, beds, sheets, radiators, beer, ice cream, or hot water. A man just sort of exists ... The velvet is all gone from living.[9]

24

Through long-range and aggressive patrolling the Surreys fought to block the Germans in a maze of hills and valleys. According to Moorehead, 'Every foot of the front was complicated and dangerous, landmines all over the place, snipers perched in the most unlikely spots, shells and mortars dropping out of nowhere. No prisoners were taken in that terrible skirmishing through the rocks.'[10]

General von Arnim, commander of the Fifth Panzer Army and all Axis forces in Tunisia, repeatedly sent in his troops and tanks to break through First Army. The Axis were desperate to prevent a link up of the Allies' First Army with Montgomery's Eighth Army, who were pursuing Rommel's Panzerarmee Afrika back towards Tunis.

* * *

While the Surreys struggled in the north just to maintain their positions, and both sides built up their forces, farther south where conditions were drier the stalemate was about to break apart.

Although the Allies continued to pour troops, guns and supplies into Tunisia over Christmas 1942 and into the New Year, there was some disarray and indecision at the highest levels in London and Washington. In January Churchill and Roosevelt met in Casablanca, appointed General Alexander to command all Allied land forces in North Africa (18 Army Group) and deputy to Eisenhower, and reaffirmed their resolve to win the Tunisian campaign.

There was a mixture of optimism and belief that it was only a matter of time before they would defeat the Axis forces by pinning them between Montgomery's Eighth Army and the Anglo-American forces of Operation TORCH. However, no-one could foretell how long it would take, or at what cost. The fear was of a war of attrition that could drag out for a year or more. The invasions contemplated by the Allies for Italy and north-west Europe rested upon first defeating the Axis powers in North Africa.

Whilst the Allied commands planned and reorganized during January their fear threatened to become a nightmare. For with their long, controlled retreat across Libya and then into southern Tunisia behind them, Rommel's Panzerarmee Afrika had already begun to combine with General von Arnim's forces in the north. After establishing his forces in the Mareth Line to fend off the Eighth Army, Rommel was intent on preventing the Americans from advancing from the Atlas Mountains in the south-west and cutting off his army from von Arnim's Fifth Panzer Army.

On 8 February Rommel met with von Arnim and Field Marshal Kesselring, who was in command of all Axis forces in the Mediterranean, and convinced them that the best strategy was a drive to the west to destroy the main Allied supply bases, at Tebessa in Algeria, and Le Kef further north-west inside Tunisia. Kesselring wanted to push the Allies back into Algeria, but Rommel and von Arnim agreed between them that it could only be a limited action. Rommel wanted time to focus on defence of the Mareth Line against Eighth Army.

At Sidi Bou Zid on the evening of 13/14 February the 10th and 21st Panzer Divisions launched Operation FRÜHLINGSWIND (Spring Wind). It was a surprise night attack through the rocky terrain of the Faid Pass, previously thought to be unsuitable for tanks.[11] In two days, 14 and 15 February, they surrounded then inflicted a crushing defeat on the US 2nd Armored Division, which lost 100 tanks, eighty-eight half tracks and artillery, and some 1,600 casualties.[12]

Unbeknown to the Panzer crews they narrowly missed capturing the Allies' commander-in-chief by just a few hours. Amazingly, Eisenhower awarded medals near the battle area on 13 February.[13] As he departed Sidi Bou Zid at dawn on 14 February, heading back to his Algiers HQ, he could not have known the scale of the disaster overtaking US forces behind him. Around lunchtime that day, fifty-five miles north of Tebessa, Eisenhower even found time to stop at the site of the ancient Roman city of Timgad.[14] While the commander-in-chief and his party walked the ruined streets and colonnades, his inexperienced American troops were beginning to be slaughtered in a major defeat. Yet worse was soon to come at another ancient site. From Sidi Bou Zid the 21st Panzers surged on and soon took Sbeitla.

*   *   *

Today as you drive into Sbeitla one of the first sights close to the road is Diocletian's Arch dating from AD 290. Sbeitla, originally the Roman city of Sufetula, was founded under the Emperor Vespasian around AD 69–79, when land was given to veterans of the 3rd Legion Augusta as reward for subduing the local Berbers.

As I walked towards the forum and its three temples of Jupiter, Juno and Minerva, just as perhaps Eisenhower had done at nearby Timgad, I saw in places remains of the under-street lead piping for water and sewerage, olive presses and public fountains. So much is left yet so much has gone, and it is not surprising to learn that Sufetula became Tunisia's largest city in the second and third centuries AD.

Yet despite the collapse of Roman rule to the Vandals, Sufetula survived to be a prosperous city under the subsequent Byzantine Emperors. In AD 646 Bishop Gregory was so confident in its wealth he declared Sufetula independent, but the very next year he was killed by Arab followers of Mohammed who then occupied the city.

You feel that the ancient city has seen many conquering armies, like the waves of the sea rolling in and out. When the ebb and flow of the German and Allied forces had ceased, the rich golden stone of Diocletian's Arch still remained and, as now at dusk, must have slowly turned to a near crimson red.

* * *

On 20 February 1943, after driving US forces into flight from Sbeitla, the 10th Panzer Division then drove the Americans back some twenty-four miles west of Kasserine town itself and gained control of the Kasserine Pass. Over the next three days on mountainous roads threading through the western dorsal towards Tebessa and Le Kef, the German Panzers with superior guns and tactics blasted their way forward through poorly prepared American and British positions. By the close of 22 February at a height of 3,300 feet they were close to taking Thala, and only forty miles from Le Kef.

Despite American and British troops fiercely contesting the approach to Thala, Allied command expected Rommel to launch the final attack on the morning of 23 February, and there was little confidence that it could be resisted. Then there would be nothing to stop the Panzers devouring the flat terrain all the way to Le Kef. However, despite Kesselring flying to the front to urge them on, Rommel's advice to pull back was accepted.

The Panzer columns had thinned themselves out in three separate thrusts. They lacked the strength to stretch out further without hope of reinforcements of men and supplies, whereas the Allies' reserves were rapidly building. Rommel was wary of leaving himself vulnerable to an Eighth Army attack to his rear, and could not have known that on the previous evening the US artillery were down to their last few shells. On the morning of 23 February the Panzers turned around before first light, and set off back to Gafsa and the Mareth Line.

* * *

Gafsa had previously been occupied by the US II Corps but fortunately was evacuated just before being taken by Rommel's Kasserine offensive. I found on my visit to today's Gafsa that it is the centre of a profitable phosphate industry, and not surprisingly does not get many tourists. If you do stop in Gafsa, originally the Roman city of Capsa, for longer than the usual coffee break, you can still swim in the two well-preserved Roman thermal pools, view its museum's mosaics, visit its thirteenth century Kasbah, and shop in a small, picturesque medina. From nearby archeological excavations of stone tools and craftwork, it gave its name to a species of homo sapiens, Capsian Man, a forerunner of the indigenous Berbers and perhaps the most advanced at that time in North Africa. It came under Roman rule in 106 BC when the Roman General Marius defeated the Numidian King Jugurtha and then developed into a prosperous colony under the Emperor Trajan.

Roman and Byzantine influence evidently became so entrenched that despite its conquest in AD 668 by the Muslim invaders, 500 years later it was claimed that many of its citizens still spoke in Latin. Since the time of Capsian Man, Gafsa's peoples have absorbed and melded into the conquering waves of Berbers, Phoenicians, Carthaginians, Romans, Byzantines, Arabs, Ottomans and French. Gafsa is so accustomed to invaders and occupation forces, that changing hands between Allied and Axis armies three times in a few months in 1943 must count as hardly a blip in its history.

* * *

Although the Germans withdrew from Kasserine back to Gafsa their Operation FRÜHLINGSWIND had inflicted a series of major battle defeats on the Americans, who lost more than 6,000 men dead or wounded, and another 3,000 taken prisoner out of 30,000. 'We have found that it is best to forget about those friends, not to talk about them. They don't even exist,' said US Sergeant Sam Allen in a letter home.[15] These losses became ignominiously known as 'Kasserine'. In ten days they had been driven back some eighty-five miles, often in panicky retreat, farther than their subsequent defeat at the Battle of the Bulge, two years later in Belgium. The awful slaughter was a brutal lesson in modern war for the inexperienced US forces.

Despite many brave Allied attempts to halt the Panzers of Fifth Army and the Panzerarmee Afrika, the Germans suffered fewer than 1,000 casualties, and only 201 dead.[16] The Allies were lucky to narrowly avoid a strategic defeat, and their main supply depots at Tebessa and Le Kef remained intact. Nevertheless there was to be no respite elsewhere.

* * *

Just three days after Rommel's victories at Kasserine, the next blow against the Allies came in the north, where the 1st Surreys had relocated to the south east of Medjez. They held a front of some seven miles across the Goubellat plain, including two dominating rocky hills some 1,000 yards ahead of the front lines, Djebel Djaffa and Fort McGregor, which Captain Toby Taylor later recalled:

> Of course in no way did Fort McGregor resemble a fort, just a simple hill, scrub covered, with two small quarries on its sides. In those days when D Company defended it, it was however fortified, being completely surrounded by a very strong triple dannert barbed wire fence, knife rests, and a comprehensive minefield.[17]

On the 19 February Lieutenant John Woodhouse joined the 1st Surreys in the Goubellat front lines.

I was put in command of 10 Platoon, B Company, which was under the command of Captain Toby Taylor. The fronts here were exceptionally far apart, with the Germans two or three miles distant across the Goubellat plain. Our position was in the low hills on the edge of the plain. I had a deep slit trench to myself in the middle of the platoon area.

I looked younger than my twenty years and could have passed for seventeen. The men in the platoon, mostly in their early twenties, considered themselves veteran soldiers after two months action. When I made the mistake of asking the platoon sergeant if we could do some training in our positions it was greeted with barely concealed contempt. In the evening I could just overhear my arrival being discussed by the soldiers. I was intended to hear as we both knew. The remarks were on the lines of, 'F— school kids being sent to us now!' It made me bite my lip, and made me determined to put on a good show.[18]

After just two days in the front lines, on 21 February Woodhouse found some time to write home.[19]

My dear Dad,
I am with the Battalion at last. I am OC 10 Platoon, who seem quite a good lot. At the moment it is raining heavily, which means sticky mud and rather unpleasant. I am in a trench about five feet deep with a two-man tent over the top, which keeps it dry, and I can stand up in it. I have a shelf cut in the clay, and a petrol light in an old tin box. That is all for now. I still expect to see you all again this year?
Your loving son, Jock.

Lieutenant Woodhouse wrote to each of his parents separately and frequently, and like most of the troops ached to receive mail from home. On 24 February he wrote to his mother:

My dear Mum,
We had some mail today dated as late as 26 and 29 January, but none for me which is a disappointment. I have twenty-five sheets of paper left; it seems that there is none for miles around. We are dependent on the NAAFI supplies, which are quite excessive in the way of blanco, but short of envelopes and paper! You would be shocked I suppose to hear that I have had my clothes on for six days, and will have them on another four before taking them off! I have washed my feet only yesterday though. You are going to have a terrible job curing me after

the war. Well that is all for now, perhaps I shall become more civilized when we are in Tunis!

Lots of love to all, from Jock.'

*　*　*

On 25 February Lieutenant Woodhouse and the rest of 1st Surreys forgot all about mail from home. General von Arnim launched Operation OCHSENKOPF (Ox Head), to regain control of the Medjez salient. One of its thrusts was to drive the Surreys back from Fort McGregor. Throughout the night of 25/26 February, paratroopers of the Herman Göring Division launched attack after attack, both artillery and ground assaults, against the Surreys.

In front of our B Company there was a small rocky pimple of a hill, sticking up in the plains thirty metres high. The whole of D Company were dug in and wired in on this hill. It was at least 1,000 metres in front of us, too far for effective fire support. The topology and deployments meant that D Company, led by Major Brooke Fox, was isolated on Fort McGregor.

Before dawn we watched as the darkness was streaked with flashes of tracer bullets between D Company, and the assaulting Germans, who had completely encircled the hill. Explosions rent the air as they used explosives to blast holes in the barb wire.

As the darkness paled, the Germans, having been beaten back several times with scores of men killed, made a final assault and successfully reached the top. We had a grandstand view of the bloody fight.[20]

Lieutenant Kindon, a platoon commander in D Company, who was wounded and taken prisoner, described one of the attacks:

A second attack started after a heavier bombardment. This was a much stronger assault. No. 16 Platoon was wiped out and the enemy gained a foothold in 18 Platoon's positions and in my own platoon area. The battle was at its height, intense, bloody and desperate. We fell back to our rear weapon pits and fought on from there.

The enemy pressure now eased off but about ten minutes afterwards, without any pre-bombardment or warning, the paratroopers mounted their third and final attack. I heard our medium machine gun cease firing and almost at once saw a solid wave of paratroopers coming in directly at the manned weapon pits, but there was no stopping this overwhelming attack.

At the same time I could see more enemy coming over the hill from the area of Company HQ, down on top of us, and then for me it was all

30

over. One minute I was in the fight and then – nothing. I came to and found I had some minor wounds and realised that I had been knocked out. I was dragged to my feet by the Germans and led away with five or six other soldiers, through the old Company HQ area, and then away from the hill.

There were bodies everywhere, D Company had gone down fighting, and most of our men lay strewn around, it was a tragic sight. As we passed what was left of the outer wire, the enemy dead increased in number. On the approaches to the hill lay many more German dead.

Lieutenants Kindon and Rook were both wounded and captured with a few others who were still standing. Amongst the dead were D Company CO Major John Brooke Fox, and his second in command Captain Lindsay.[21]

For a time Captain Taylor had been in touch with Major Brook-Fox on the field telephone:

As long as I could talk to John, I knew they were holding their own. After an hour or so he told me his Captain Lindsay had been killed, but he was sure he could hold on. Eventually John's telephone was cut by the explosions and he was out of touch with me and battalion HQ. The noise of battle faded away into almost silence, and the CO, Lieutenant Colonel Bill Wilberforce, agreed with me that the hill was lost.

About a week later, John's wife Angela sent him a parcel. Colonel Wilberforce, knowing that John was my best friend, sent his batman, Wilson, over to me thinking I should have it. It contained a long letter and news about their small son, some pipe tobacco and new underclothes etc. All very sad.[22]

Although the Surreys with other Battleaxe units regained Djebel Djaffa, an attempt to recapture Fort McGregor, when numerous men were quickly lost, was called off. Next, because Fort McGregor's strategic position in the Medjez salient meant that it had to be won back, with a total disregard for any Surreys who might be still surviving there, a massive artillery barrage was opened up at the hill's summit. This was followed by probing counterattacks.

Two Surreys' stretcher-bearers, Sergeant John Davies and Private R. Moore, were awarded the MM and DCM respectively. When Moore found himself being shot at by a sniper, he returned fire with his Bren gun, which then failed on him. Rather than return to the lines, he managed to repair the Bren and began to stalk the sniper. Moore killed the sniper, and brought back the German's papers as evidence.[23]

'Throughout the day huge blasts from heavy artillery enveloped the hill in black smoke,' observed John Woodhouse. 'Other medium guns and 25-pounders joined in, until as dusk fell all was quiet. I was ordered to take a patrol of six men and find out if the Germans were still there.'

Following the bombardment and Woodhouse's night reconnaissance patrol, which luckily found Fort McGregor abandoned by the Germans, the Surreys reoccupied the hill.

As dawn lit the grim sights I searched the dugouts and trenches. I found three German soldiers unwounded and happy to surrender. They were stood with their back to the quarry wall. My soldiers shouted abuse at them, along with cries of 'shoot the bastards'. The Germans were clearly terrified, but safe while I was in command, and probably safe without me. Two or three wounded Surreys had survived our artillery bombardment but were in a state of shock. Fortunately we had never heard of stress syndrome, so did not suffer from it.

The German paratroopers showed suicidal bravery. The Nazi era inspired young Germans with the will to die which made them the best army in the world. Though they achieved the almost complete destruction of our D Company, who had fought to the end, they could not hold Fort Macgregor themselves. As I stood there, I remembered that I had been attached to D Company in Scotland as umpire only six months before.[24]

The battle and artillery bombardments by both sides for Fort McGregor resulted in the whole hill being 'littered with British and German dead, bodies and parts of bodies, which were twisted together into tumbled heaps'.[25] Later the padre estimated that he himself also buried around sixty unknown soldiers.

At the height of the OCHSENKOPF offensive General Anderson considered withdrawing from Medjez, before Alexander insisted on no retreat. In the end British casualties were heavy, including some 2,500 taken prisoner. Yet some 2,200 Germans were also taken prisoner by the British, and possibly a similar number killed or wounded, losses that were far harder for the Axis to replace than the Allies.

Although First Army had been pushed back some ten to twenty miles, this stubborn defence by the Surreys and other Battleaxe Division troops forced von Arnim to halt his offensive in the north. Similarly, on 6 March in the south near Medenine, Eighth Army threw back a counter-attack by the Panzerarmee. Soon after an ill and exhausted Rommel flew home to Germany to recover. Von Arnim was forced to place all Axis forces onto a defensive footing. With hindsight it seems to have been a tipping point.

*　*　*

In the south, despite the first battlefield success on 19 March at Guettar of General Patton's US II Corps, the Mareth Line still held up Eighth Army. The fortified Mareth Line followed the northern edge of the Oued Zigzaou wadi twenty-eight miles across the narrow coastal plain between the Matmata Hills and the sea. To try and outflank the German defences, Montgomery resorted to his renowned 'left hook', when he sent a 27,000 strong, armoured force onto narrow mountain tracks to the west.

Patrols of Eighth Army's Long Range Desert Group had found that the Tebaga Gap, a valley between the Chott el Fejaj salt lake and the Matmata Hills, was a viable route for armoured columns. By 28 March they had out-flanked the Axis Forces. Together with an Eighth Army direct assault on the Mareth Line, this eventually forced the Panzerarmee and their Italian allies to withdraw towards the next defensive line farther north at Takrouna and Enfidaville.

After the Battle of Mareth the route of the retreating Axis forces and the pursuing Eighth Army snaked northwards through the Sahel along Tunisia's eastern coast and past El Jem, site of the world's third largest Roman amphitheatre. From Tunis past Sousse and towards El Jem, olive tree plantations increasingly dominate the flat landscape either side of the road. Surprisingly it is claimed an olive tree can live more than 1,000 years. Perhaps some trees had been witness to passing Roman legions and in 1943 still stood sentinel in the dust of the armoured columns of first the Panzerarmee Afrika, and then Eighth Army.

*   *   *

In March 1943 the rains began to lessen. Planning and preparations were underway again for the spring offensive to take Tunis. With some days around a maximum of 25–28°C it allowed the bringing forward of more troops and supplies.

Within the influx of fresh troops who landed at Bone in Algeria was the 1st Surreys' sister battalion, 1/6th Surreys in 4th Division. There were also reinforcements for 1st Surreys and one of those was Private Frank Weston: 'From the ship we marched to a tented camp,' recalled Frank, 'and a sergeant looked us over, then asked us if we had brought our Baden Powell Scout books with us!'[26]

Frank Weston was eighteen, a square-shouldered, good-looking recruit from Kingston-upon-Thames. When he had enlisted in November 1941 he was only seventeen and learning his trade as a butcher. On the voyage to Bone, like many of the men, he had played cards continually on the boat deck, and when the destroyers' sirens sounded as they chased U-boats, like the others he had hidden his nerves. 'We would be new to action,' said Frank, 'but once ashore when we saw men being evacuated very sick with malaria, we thought the mosquitos would be more frightening than facing the Germans.'[27]

For one of the new men to reach the 1st Surreys, Frank Oram, it was an unexpected return to North Africa. Frank's father had been an RSM in the 1st Surreys and when the battalion had spent many years overseas Frank had been born in Ismailia, Egypt in 1921. While the 1st Surreys had been based in India in the 1920s and 1930s, Frank had gone to school in Rawalpindi with two other boys, Harry Skilton and Jack Chaffer, whose fathers had been senior NCOs.

He had joined the Army as a boy soldier at sixteen in 1937, and at twenty-two the Surreys now needed him. Frank was a little under six feet tall, with an outgoing personality. He had grey/blue eyes that drew you to him, sandy-coloured hair, and an expression that always seemed ready to smile. Frank had a 'can do' attitude, and could turn his hand to repairing cars, weapons, radios, any kind of equipment. He had left behind a young wife, Winifred. Aware that Frank would soon be shipping out to join the Surreys, they had married quickly in January 1943. Yet like many wartime wives, Winifred had insisted there would be no children until the war was over.[28]

In another battalion, the 5th Grenadier Guards, who landed at Bone in March 1943, was the third of those boyhood friends in India, Jack Chaffer. Jack should have been in one of the East Surrey battalions. His father, Henry Chaffer, had been an RQMS with the Surreys, and Jack had intended to follow him into the regiment. That was until he entered the central London recruiting office. 'A smooth talking recruiting sergeant got at me,' said Jack. 'He was thinking of the five shillings commission fee he could earn for every recruit to a Guards regiment, compared to the one shilling and sixpence for an infantry regiment such as the Surreys.'[29]

Jack was a strapping six feet tall, just right for a Guards regiment, and the sergeant soon had him signing the Grenadiers' papers. On 8 December 1941, the day after the attack on Pearl Harbor, Jack presented himself at the Grenadier Guards' Caterham Barracks. Jack was only seventeen but claimed to be eighteen, and yet another teenager doing the right thing. Also like many other recruits, before he sailed for North Africa and into the unknown, Jack had married the girl he loved, Doll. But for now all that was behind him.[30]

* * *

The additional troops, including the introduction of 1st and 4th Divisions to the British First Army of General Anderson, meant that the Allies were gaining numerical superiority over the Axis. After landing at Algiers on 23 March 1943, 1/6th Surreys were taking part in a 4th Division action as early as 6 April north of Oued Zarga. In the barren hill country that bordered the north-west of the Medjez-Tunis road, the fierce sun and dry terrain of mid-April were a world away from the cold, wet and green of England as Cyril Ray noted:

Spring came to Tunisia or to those patches of it, between the crags and rocks, where spring could come. There were marigolds in clefts on the hills, great-headed marguerites in the valleys, and red poppies thick amidst corn. There were longer periods of sunshine between the rainstorms, and the roads began first to dry and then to become dusty. Strategically, the time had come to strike back, and the season of the year now made it possible.[31]

Deep valleys and rocky hills meant all ammunition and food supplies had to be carried by pack mules so that attacking troops were at a huge disadvantage. The orders for 1/6th Surreys were to move up the valley from Hunt's Gap towards Sidi N'sir, drive the Germans back from their defensive positions in the hills, and so clear the way for the coming major offensive. On 11 and 12 April, while taking the Djebel Grembil peak, they came up against fierce resistance from seasoned German troops, and suffered their first casualties, nine wounded and six dead.

A section of the Surreys' 9 Platoon of A Company led by Corporal Cudlip, got into a hand-to-hand fight in the dark.

The enemy were well dug in on the forward slope up which the section was advancing when short range fire broke out. Corporal Cudlip was wounded in the leg and hip as well as four of his section, but he carried on. When he had used up his Tommy-gun magazine, he used the butt against a German whom he killed, splintering the butt on his head. He then brought his section back under cover. For his gallantry in this action Corporal Cudlip was awarded the Military Medal.[32]

Further progress beyond Grembil was halted by dominating fire from the enemy hidden around them in other rugged hills. Despite more losses, as when eight men were killed when a shell landed in the mouth of their cave, the 1/6th Surreys held their ground until they were relieved on 18 April.

* * *

At the same time as their fellow battalion was entering the fray, the 1st Surreys, having regrouped after their successful but costly resistance at Fort McGregor, returned with the Battleaxe Division to fight in these hill country battles north-west of Medjez, collectively known as the Battle of Oued Zarga. To march on to Tunis the Allies had to build up sufficient forces at and around Medjez and this could only be done after the hills to its north, and most ominously Longstop Hill, had been taken.

35

Around this time Lieutenant John Woodhouse was put in command of the 6-pounder guns of the anti-tank platoon.

I was disappointed to go to the anti-tank platoon whose gun attachments were spread over 6 miles, which I visited through the mud on a motor cycle. But my leadership at Fort Macgregor had brought about a complete change in the opinions of me held by my platoon. Instead of ignoring me the soldiers welcomed me to chat. They considered I had shown that I had 'guts'.

On 12 March my first letter from home arrived since I had left in December. The absence of news from home has a devastating effect on morale, and on the same day I found time to write in reply:

My dear Mum,

Wonderful news about mail. First letter of all from you dated 6 Jan, arrived 11 March.

We are still bogged but the rain is less and less frequent, and by the time this reaches you the ground should be hard. I hope to get a bath soon as it is a month since my last! Of course I am now sitting down to a meal at a table, instead of eating bully and spuds with a spoon out of a tin in the open.

One funny thing about rain which war correspondents do not like mentioning is how awkward going to the latrine is after breakfast on a pouring wet day. Ours is not covered in but we have got a seat which is a refinement not invariably found. When rain drops in sheets however and the ground around is slippery, balancing in a bending position over a hole is both very difficult and dangerous. At the moment I am hoping the rain is going to stop ....

Don't worry I am very well, lots of love to all at Melcombe, from Jock.

The heavy rain storms gradually grew fewer in March and the sun stronger. My acceptance by the senior officers in the battalion was eased by the fact that they knew other officers in the Dorset Regiment that I also knew.

By the 1 April we were resting in an olive grove with a mass of yellow flowers and red poppies. We knew the 78th Division was about to begin an offensive, and the poppies made me think of Flanders and the Great War. I lived in the present; the future of the war and our lives was uncertain, unknowable.[33]

Yet Woodhouse was thinking of the future, and after only a few weeks in the front line was looking forward to the war's end. On 24 March he wrote to his father:

36

When we have finished this war, and that seems to involve a journey to Japan next year, I think I shall have had enough of soldiering abroad to last me for some time.

Though strongly attached to life I am conscious of a high sense of duty and believe in fighting to free Europe from Hitler. I do not hate the Germans but rather respect their army.[34]

Woodhouse may have respected the German Army in a military sense, but he was horrified by the devastation they left in their wake. On 25 March he wrote to his mother:

The last day of rain was 21st, then three days scorching sun temperature about 85F, today is cloudy. Yesterday I rode through a town on the front which is in a terrible state of desolation, thank God the Boche did not reach England in 1940.[35]

* * *

In the early hours of the morning 7 April 1943, and beginning with a deafening artillery barrage across a twelve-mile front, the 1st Surreys were part of 78th Division as it led the offensive for Oued Zarga. The Battle of Oued Zarga lasted ten days and raged across a swathe of rocky hills, which seemingly swallowed up the whole Battleaxe Division. Over a back-breaking, mountainous landscape the 1st Surreys were in the front to drive the Germans back from positions threatening the Beja-Medjez road.

Every hill demanded a combination of climbing and skirmishing, often though minefields, and then finally assaulting the German machine-gun pits and occupied hill top villages with grenades and bayonets. Above all it demanded persistence, continual perseverance at every setback, and the steely resolve to keep going both upward and forward as men went down under the enemy's fire. Even harder to imagine is that companies and platoons did this despite often finding themselves out on their own, isolated and running out of water, food and ammunition.[36]

The 1st Surreys' Major Caffyn, during a lull in the fighting on 6/7 April, went looking for a man missing from his C Company, and found him lying dead 100 yards or so away. Then he was surprised by Germans and taken prisoner. Major Caffyn's recollection was that he thought his Company were too preoccupied in digging trenches to notice him being captured.[37] Private John Mumford however remembers the loss of Major Caffyn in the confusion of combat somewhat differently:

I have very vivid memories of what happened on the 6 and 7 April 1943. On the 6th it was a very pleasant sunny day, and as it was my wife's birthday I remember lying on the grass wondering what she would be doing for her birthday. And I also had thought of what was in store for us as the proposed attack was to take place on the following day.

I think it was midnight when we went over the start line, and Major Caffyn led the company single file along many wadis and valleys for a considerable way before calling a halt. I then heard him tell Captain Heal that he was not quite certain of our position, and that we should wait until the barrage went over at 5.30 to see where it landed.

When the barrage did go over the shells fell on the hill immediately in front of us and Major Caffyn said something like, 'Peter, by God we're dead on target.' Then Hell was let loose, and lasted for the next three or four hours until the middle of the morning, when the battle seemed to end.

The chaps were standing around and dealing with the wounded, and I remember one poor lad, severely wounded in the stomach, and we could not do anything for him, but wait for the medics to come. It was then that I saw Major Caffyn on the brow of the hill walking between two Arabs, one on either side, and I thought he was going on a recce. I was certain that the two persons either side of the Major were wearing Arab dress. It was not until nightfall that we heard that he was missing, and I reported to Battalion HQ what I had seen.[38]

Could it be that the Germans had lain in wait disguised in Arab clothes? Or maybe they were Arabs who were looting the dead and then grabbed Major Caffyn and led him to the Germans? Major Caffyn's account makes no mention of the manner in which he was captured, so it will probably remain a mystery.

As the Surreys advanced across the hills north of Oued Zarga and Medjez, Lieutenant Woodhouse had his six anti-tank guns ready to move.

I heard that B Company had severe losses including my friend Dick Watkins, killed in command of 10 Platoon. One of the other two platoon commanders was killed, and another one wounded. Later that day I was with the CO, Lieutenant Colonel G.S. Wilberforce, and he could see there was clearly no need for the anti-tank platoon. I saw my chance to go back to 10 Platoon and B Company, and with the CO's agreement, raced across the ground to regain 10 Platoon. They had been somewhat shocked by their casualties and I was welcomed back. I made sure I sounded full of confidence and showed my obvious and genuine delight being among them again. On the 8, 9 and 10 April the advance continued north-west into the hills against light opposition, and we took about fifty prisoners.[39]

* * *

At the same time as the Surreys fought in the Oued Zarga mountains in the north, in the flatter south on 7 April the first forward detachments of General Montgomery's Eighth Army made contact with leading patrols of US II Corps. The Allied pincer movement was beginning to close in on the Axis forces. Speed was now critical on all fronts to exploit the encirclement and prevent the enemy from controlling his retreat and withdrawing his forces to Italy.

Nevertheless the problem remained. How and where could the Allies break through to close the trap? In the far north, on the coastal approaches to Bizerte, the Americans were held up at mountain strongpoints such as Green Hill and Bald Hill. In the south the armoured strength of the Eighth Army was neutralized by German defences in the hills around Enfidaville. In the central north in the Medjerda Valley there seemed to have been little change since December. North of Medjez the Germans were immoveable. Like leopards in the branches of a tree they lay in wait on Longstop Hill.

Notes

1. Veterans' Accounts, Woodhouse, *Memoirs* (unpublished).
2. Veterans' Accounts, Taylor, and Imperial War Museum, Department of Documents.
3. d' Este, *Eisenhower*, p. 373.
4. Veterans' Accounts, Woodhouse, *Memoirs* (unpublished).
5. Ibid.
6. Veterans' Accounts, Taylor, and Imperial War Museum, Department of Documents.
7. Moorehead, op cit., pp. 512–13.
8. Veterans' Accounts, Taylor, and Imperial War Museum, Department of Documents.
9. Atkinson, op cit., p. 238.
10. Moorehead, op cit., pp. 512–13.
11. Atkinson, op cit., p. 322.
12. Ibid, pp. 339–56.
13. Eisenhower, *Crusade in Europe*, p. 118.
14. Atkinson, op cit., p. 347.
15. Ibid, p. 479.
16. Ibid, pp. 384–90.
17. Veterans' Accounts, Taylor, and Imperial War Museum, Department of Documents.
18. Veterans' Accounts, Woodhouse, *Memoirs* (unpublished).
19. Ibid.
20. Ibid.
21. Squire and Hill, op cit., pp. 26–7, and Surrey History Centre ESR/2/15/16.
22. Veterans' Accounts, Taylor, and Imperial War Museum, Department of Documents.
23. Ray, op cit., p. 42.
24. Veterans' Accounts, Woodhouse, *Memoirs* (unpublished).
25. Ford, op cit., p. 64.
26. Veterans' Accounts, Weston.
27. Ibid.
28. Veterans' Accounts, Oram.
29. Veterans' Accounts, Chaffer.
30. Ibid.

31. Ray, op cit., p. 43.
32. Ibid, p. 42.
33. Veterans' Accounts, Woodhouse, *Memoirs* (unpublished).
34. Ibid.
35. Ibid.
36. Moorehead, op cit., p. 564.
37. Squire and Hill, op cit., p. 32.
38. Veterans' Accounts, Mumford.
39. Veterans' Accounts, Woodhouse, *Memoirs* (unpublished).

Chapter 3

The Battle of Longstop Hill:
The Door to Tunis Opens

On the night of 13 April, 11 Brigade, including 1st Surreys, assaulted Djebels Tanngoucha, Ang and Mahdouma, which, at over 3,000 feet high, overlooked Medjez and Longstop Hill.[1] Lieutenant John Woodhouse was leading a platoon in the attack on Djebel Mahdouma, a formidable mountain that rose very steeply from the valley floor:

> We were shelled by the Germans on our start line before we got away. However with much shouting we got going behind our own artillery barrage, which lifted forward in 'steps' of 100 metres.
>
> It was essential to keep very close to the barrage, so that there was as little gap as possible in time between shells falling on the German trenches, and our arrival with bayonets fixed. In the lead of my platoon I kept close to our shell bursts until one shell passed over my head. It burst with a flash of red and a concussion wave which stunned me. My head rang like a bell as I lay flat smelling the fumes of the bursts.
>
> Luckily the shrapnel had all gone forward or sideways. Though temporarily deafened, I had to press on as we were near the Germans on the summit, who began firing in our direction. Thinking to distract them I told my 2-inch mortar team to fire smoke to our flank. Not in the text book to fire smoke at night, but it succeeded in drawing the German fire. We staggered up the final slopes and the Germans either ran or surrendered.[2]

Battalion HQ was also hit by German shelling. Harry Skilton recalled that:

> There were some casualties but the worst thing was [that] it stampeded the mules carrying the wireless sets, so we had to rely on runners to keep in touch. Despite the communication problems, A and B Companies got up onto Djebel Ang and Mahdouma. Then they were driven some way back by a German counter-attack, and had to do it all again, to regain the positions.[3]

41

In the assault on Djebel Mahdouma Sergeant Thomas Straight of the Mortar Platoon jumped into a dug-out to be confronted by six Germans. He instantly shot one of them, and at the same time thought he would be blasted by the other five. Remarkably he found himself pointing his rifle at the remaining Germans, who threw down their weapons and surrendered. Straight's action brought him the Military Medal.[4]

At dawn Woodhouse and his platoon prepared for a counter-attack:

Some shelling and small arms fire came at us causing one or two to be wounded. Some of the soldiers were showing signs of nervousness, which can spread quickly from one man to another. I countered this by keeping them busy counting and recounting ammunition, digging in deeper, fixing bayonets etc. I kept walking from section to section showing unconcern at the odd shell or bullets, which I had calculated were not as risky as they sounded. All calmed down and the German counter-attack never came close to us.

The weather had been perfect, sunny and hot by day, cold by night. We stayed in the area of Djebel Ang for several days. We were shelled from time to time which stressed some soldiers' nerves more than ever. And digging trenches was hard going in the rocky hill tops. The platoon was down from twenty-eight to fourteen men, but luckily we got rations for twenty-two, plus Norwegian sardines captured from the enemy.[5]

In gruelling close combat, some of it hand-to-hand with its inevitable casualties, the Surreys took more than 1,000 prisoners. Around this time in a letter to his parents, Woodhouse ignored the battle's ferocity and their mounting losses, and with his usual enthusiasm and confidence described how well they were eating:

Rations are excellent. Breakfast – Sausage, army biscuit, margarine, jam, tea. Lunch – Salmon & biscuit, tea. Evening – Steak and kidney pudding, treacle duff and tea. Daily chocolate bar, rum issue at dawn.[6]

Djebels Tanngoucha, Ang and Mahdouma saw some of the heaviest fighting, and the culmination of the Oued Zarga battles.[7] The Surreys won three Military Crosses and a Military Medal. They and 78th Division's other battalions were well on the way to acquiring a reputation as mountain warfare troops and becoming ever more widely known as the Battleaxe Division. Nevertheless, in the Medjerda Valley north of Medjez, the Allies' nemesis, Longstop Hill, was still in German hands.

* * *

In March 2008 I visited the small farming town of Testour in the Medjerda Valley. Sipping the sweet, black version of a local cappuccino, I sat in

42

Testour's main square, where the orange trees and jasmine shrubs show the town's Andalusian roots. For a period in 1942/43 the town was the HQ of 78th Division, and you would swear it could not have changed since that time.

Testour's main mosque, dating from the seventeenth century, has a minaret built like a Castilian bell tower and, unusually for a minaret, even has a clock face, although the hands rotate anti-clockwise. Close by, El-Andalouse Square shows the influence of those refugee Moors from Spain, who fled to North Africa. Somehow Testour seems to have been untouched by the six months of battles in 1942/43, that had engulfed the Medjerda Valley, and only around ten miles away blasted apart the ancient town of Medjez el Bab.

In the Medjez el Bab War Cemetery, alongside some Surreys' graves, I came across the grave of an unknown Australian soldier. Underneath the insignia of the Australian Imperial Force, it simply states, 'A soldier of the 1939–1945 War, An Australian Regiment, Known Only to God.' As no Australian forces were officially deployed in Tunisia, he may have been seconded to the Surreys or another battalion. Or perhaps he was in Special Forces.

Many Commonwealth troops fought in Tunisia. Those who died in and around Medjez were twenty-three Canadian, ten Australian, nine New Zealanders and sixteen South Africans, in the total of 4,865 dead who are buried or recorded at the Medjez War Cemetery and Memorial. The battles in the vicinity of Medjez, Longstop Hill and the Medjerda Valley have left their marks too in other cemeteries of the area. It is a toll spoken of in the same scale as El Alamein and Cassino.

* * *

After their losses in the Oued Zarga battles, the 1/6th Surreys were re-deployed south-east of Testour to what were thought to be less exposed positions, on the Djebel Djaffa and Fort McGregor hills. The hills commanded the roads from the Medjerda Valley through the Djaffa Pass to Tunis. It had been barely two months since their fellow battalion, the 1st Surreys, had fought at great cost to hold onto Fort McGregor.

Sometimes lightning does strike the same place twice, and on 20 April the 1/6th Surreys' recovery plans were brutally ended by a surprise night attack, led by five battalions of the Hermann Göring and 10th Panzer Divisions. The German infantry rode the Panzers to force their way to within a few hundred yards of 4th Division Headquarters. By dawn on 21 April the Germans were in possession of Djebel Djaffa.

It was said that Field Marshal Kesselring ordered the attack, codenamed Operation FLIEDERBLÜTE (or Lilac Blossom), to coincide with Hitler's birthday. Another bizarre theory passed down was that the name referred to the perfumed hair oil used by German officers. The irony was that the comically named Operation LILAC BLOSSOM became a ferocious battle with heavy losses on both sides.

With the Allied build-up gathering pace for the Tunis offensive, the enemy incursion was a major threat – Djebel Djaffa had to be immediately retaken. On the afternoon of 21 April the 1/6th Surreys began a frontal attack up its steep, rocky slopes. The CO of 1/6th Surreys, Lieutenant Colonel H.A.B. Bruno, 'led C company himself, through intense fire and making what use they could of the scattered scrub for cover, he took them to within twenty yards of the top.'[8] In that uphill assault the Surreys saw sixty-eight of their men go down.

They were so close, but in the end the Surreys had to withdraw under smoke cover, with twenty-six wounded and forty-two dead or missing, including Colonel Bruno. However, it had not been in vain. The Germans had been even more heavily depleted, and thinking the smoke heralded an inevitable final push by the Surreys, they too withdrew from the peak. The Surreys second-in-command, Major R.O.V. Thompson took charge.

Major Thompson had joined 1/6th Surreys from the Royal Sussex Regiment, with whom he had served in France in 1940 and had been badly wounded before being evacuated at Dunkirk. The Surreys again climbed up Djebel Djaffa's slopes the next morning, dreading a hail of enemy fire. It never came, and they took the hill unopposed. As they feared, however, they found the body of Colonel Bruno near the hill's crest and buried him there with their other dead.

By regaining Djebel Djaffa, the Surreys freed Medjez el Bab from any offensive threat from the surrounding hills. The Allies now had more men, more guns, more tanks, and air superiority. Yet the Germans still held the vital passes, inflicting terrible losses as they withstood every Allied attack. In the southern and northern coastal corridors it seemed impossible to concentrate sufficient forces to break through, and the Medjerda Valley was blocked by Longstop Hill. After the Germans had defeated desperate Allied attacks on 25 December 1942, they had built extensive defences across Longstop's sprawling heights. They thought their *Weinachtshügel* (Christmas Hill) to be impregnable.

Lieutenant Woodhouse foresaw that the major offensive to take Longstop Hill, and then Tunis was imminent, and although he could not say so in a letter, on 4 April he had written home:

My dear Mum,
    You may get a gap in my letters of a week or ten days in the near future, don't worry about lack of letters will you? I have said before

that must be expected and is only natural while the war is on here. I shall send you lots of postcards etc when we are in Tunis.

Lots of love to all, from Jock.[9]

*　*　*

General Alexander, now overall commander of all Tunisian ground forces, could see that two enemy strongpoints, Hill 609 in the American northern sector and Longstop Hill in the British sector, still blocked the route for the final offensive of the campaign. Longstop Hill, known locally as Djebel el Ahmera, some six miles north of Medjez, two miles in length and some 800 feet high, had to be taken. It was really a mountainous, hog's back ridge of hidden folds and defiles, abutting and commanding the whole Medjerda Valley. Until it was seized and the Allies' left flank fully secured, nothing could move down the valley to begin the main attack on Tunis.

For the Battleaxe Division, and 1st Surreys, there was no respite. From Oued Zarga they moved down the Medjerda Valley through Medjez towards Longstop Hill. By this time the 1st Surreys, like some other battalions, had lost more than half their original strength across all ranks. Besides those killed, wounded and missing in action, men were also succumbing to the ailments of Africa, notably malaria. The result was that the 1st Surreys' headcount had shrunk to around 200 men. Woodhouse was among those stricken by illness.

> On about the 20 April, we were withdrawn to an assembly area north east of Medjez, in preparation for a major divisional attack on the key point of Longstop Hill. For whatever reason on the 22nd I became subject to dizziness, fainting, and extreme weakness. The doctor looked at me, and said 'sand fly fever'. I was sent by ambulance to the nearest tented hospital.[10]

Despite their depleted numbers, on the night of 21 April the 1st Surreys and 8th Argyll and Sutherland Highlanders went forward again towards Longstop. Before the dawn's light they went to ground near the small cluster of dwellings of Chassart Teffaha, and close to the brooding monolith.

All the next day, in shallow gullies or whatever depressions they could find in the open ground, they lay as still as they could under the burning sun. Somehow they managed to take in some food and drink without attracting enemy fire, but snatches of sleep were near impossible for the next morning's assault was on their minds. All through that day the deadly slopes and ridges of Longstop Hill seemed to beckon them to their fate.

At 8.00pm on 22 April 1943 the Surreys' hands went up to their ears. The artillery fire of 400 guns that would last all night shattered the evening and signalled that the battle for Longstop Hill had begun. At 11.30am the next morning the Surreys and the Argylls got to their feet and began their slow climb.

'It was a warm, spring day,' recounted Cyril Ray, 'flowers were blooming on the slopes. The Argylls advanced to the foot of the hill through a cornfield, and soon the machine guns, mortars and field guns opened up on them.'[11]

The German fire cut down the Argylls, and after their Colonel McNab was killed, Major John McKay Anderson DSO took command and led a frontal attack. He was subsequently awarded the Victoria Cross, the citation for which notes that:

> Over a period of five hours Major Anderson led the attack through intense enemy machine gun and mortar fire. As leading company commander he led the assault on the battalion's first objective, in daylight, over a long expanse of open sloping hillside and most of the time without the effective cover of smoke.
>
> During the assault he personally led attacks on at least three enemy machine gun positions and in every case was the first man into the enemy pits; he also led a successful attack on an enemy position of four mortars, defended by over thirty of the enemy ... he received a leg wound, but in spite of this he carried on and finally captured 'Longstop Hill' with a total force of only four officers and less than forty other ranks.[12]

After the loss of the commanding officers not only of the Argylls but also of the two other support battalions of 11 Brigade, 5th Buffs and 6th Royal West Kents, it was the Surreys' CO Lieutenant Colonel 'Bill' Wilberforce, who commanded the combined force on the final storming and occupation of Longstop's heights.

By the third day 78th Division had occupied around three-quarters of Longstop Hill's highest points and a few war correspondents were allowed access to a few of the forward positions. They came upon some of the surviving Surreys laid up in German trenches, with their weapons trained towards the next slope, and making running repairs to boots and equipment.

But they were not the young heroes portrayed to the home public in cinema newsreels, said Alan Moorehead:

> They were hostile, bitter and contemptuous ... a third of them had been killed in the night ... they had seen too much dirt and filth for that. They hated the war. They knew it. They fought because they were part of a system, part of a team. They wanted to win and get out of it – the sooner the better.[13]

Back in the tent hospital on 23 April, St George's Day, Lieutenant Woodhouse awoke:

After twelve hours sleep in a real bed, I felt I was fully recovered. However the Medical Officer ordered me back by train to Algiers for more treatment. Seeing that argument was useless, when we got to the train I walked away and hitch-hiked my way back to the front by 25 April. I had missed the bloody opening day of 23 April. Among those killed in B Company on the assault on Longstop was my batman, Private Rodwell, who stepped on a mine.[14]

With the summit in the hands of 78th Division, Colonel Wilberforce set about organizing Longstop Hill's defence, against possible counter-attack, and the continuing heavy fire from nearby hills. Wilberforce was just thirty-eight, and had been commissioned in The King's Own Yorkshire Light Infantry. After seeing service in India and holding staff appointments pre-war, he had only taken command of the 1st Surreys in October 1942, immediately prior to their embarkation in Operation TORCH. With a carefree manner and high spirits, he 'walked round all the positions, wearing his soft hat and smoking his pipe', encouraging the troops to hang on to their gains'.[15]

On 25 April Lieutenant Woodhouse rejoined 10 Platoon on Longstop Hill, as they hung on to their positions on the captured summit.

That night we were heavily shelled. We lay in our trenches, tin hats over our faces snatching some sleep in brief lulls, and waking from close bursts. There had been almost no rain since March, and while on Longstop we went all one day without any water. It was sufficiently long enough for tongues to swell.[16]

It was not until 27 April, when the Surreys came out of the line for recovery, that Woodhouse was able to write home again, and hinted at the importance of the Longstop battle.

My dear Mum,
    Just a line to let you know, I left hospital two days ago, and so was only away three days. Been at a famous place since I last wrote, we are advancing as you know, and we shall soon have taken Tunis.
    I shall sleep nearly all today, after I have washed off the layers of dirt. Then we shall reorganize the Company a bit, eat dinner, have tea and supper, drink tea and go to sleep again. Very great.[17]

Some time later Sergeant Gostling of HQ Company wrote to the convalescing Captain Payne: 'After the Djebel Ang business we came in to the worst battle of all – Longstop. It really was terrible, and was all the papers say of it.'[18]

For the British infantry Longstop Hill was perhaps the pivotal battle of the Tunisian campaign. For surviving Surreys' veterans such as Frank Weston and John Mumford, when speaking of Tunisia the name Longstop Hill remains the first thing they say, burned still into their minds. John tells of the foreboding beforehand, and relishing a second ration of rum the night before the assault. Both remember the many mates they lost.[19]

* * *

Despite the enormous losses suffered from the enemy's withering fire, the taking of Longstop Hill set the scene for the Allies' final assault on Tunis. Eisenhower acknowledged that 'the battles for its possession from the beginning to the end of the African campaign, probably cost more lives than did the fighting for any other spot in Tunisia'.[20]

With Longstop Hill finally in Allied hands, General Alexander immediately accelerated the flow of additional troops and materiel, to increase the Allied pressure along the whole length of the 130-mile front line. The German generals knew a major offensive was coming, but not whether it would be Eighth Army from the south-east, First Army in the centre, or the Americans in the north-west.

Alexander and Eisenhower held to the strategic view of Medjez el Bab from the time of Hannibal: it was the door to Tunis. The plan was for a spearhead attack in the centre which 'would go in up the Medjerda Valley, a needle-thrust aimed straight at Tunis', using battle-hardened British battalions from the 4th, 1st and 78th Divisions. Once the infantry battalions had broken the initial German lines, the 6th and 7th Armoured Divisions would hammer through the breach 'from Medjez through Massicault and St Cyprien to Tunis'.[21]

* * *

Yet in the last week of April bitter battles continued all along the front lines. One of the fiercest was at Djebel Bou Aoukaz, a 700-foot-high ridge formation, four miles farther north from Longstop Hill in the Medjerda Valley towards Bizerte. After the fall of Longstop, three Guards' battalions spent a week in a battle for Djebel Bou's ridges and spurs.

Both sides mounted an incessant artillery and machine-gun duel, so that day upon day, night after night the troops hung on in their slit trenches, and the dead had to wait. There with the 5th Grenadiers was Jack Chaffer, only a few miles from the 1st Surreys, the regiment and battalion he had meant to join. He recalled that:

The corn in the 'Bou', as we called it, was up to six feet high in places from recent heavy rain, so a rifle and helmet were needed to mark the dead for the stretcher bearers. We could not see each other, so we had to shout to keep in touch. Some comic said the empty helmets were growing faster than the corn.[22]

In that one week the 5th Grenadiers took almost 300 casualties, whilst 1st Irish Guards were cut down to only eighty men. In the ten days to 30 April First Army lost 252 tanks and an estimated 900 dead out of 3,500 casualties. And Tunis still lay ahead untouched.[23]

*   *   *

After Longstop's capture both the 1st and 1/6th Surreys moved to the south-west of Medjez near Peter's Corner and John Woodhouse recalled that:

> By 4 May we were on the flat fields just north of the Medjez to Tunis main road, and once again up against the Herman Göring Division. On 5 May we learned that the final offensive to take Tunis was about to begin. Squadrons of twin-engined bombers roared overhead. Sitting in the tall wheat fields, I had a feeling that I would be killed in it. My letter to my father ended 'Thinking always of England, and at last realise what a great country it is'.[24]

On 6 May the 1/6th Surreys were a lead battalion as the 4th Division infantry began the advance into Tunis. Lieutenant Colonel R.O.V. Thompson was now in command and, with his unflappable style and calm confidence, he continued to give the inspiring leadership enjoyed by 1/6th under their late Colonel Bruno. By 8.00am they had cleared a path through German positions and their minefields, taken their objectives of Montarnaud and Frendj, and dug in. Then the armoured divisions burst through to take Massicault before nightfall.

On 7 May the Allied armour rolled into Tunis, taking Axis forces by surprise. Many enemy troops emerged from bars and restaurants, with stunned stares, and surrendered without a fight. Lead patrols of 1st Surreys were some of the first infantry to penetrate the town. On the same day the Surreys' CO, Lieutenant Colonel Wilberforce, received news that he had been awarded the DSO for his leadership at Longstop Hill. A few hours later he was dead, hit in his staff car by shrapnel from one of the last enemy shells of the Tunis campaign.

Three days earlier on 4 May, with a hint of his yearning for peace, Colonel Wilberforce had written to his former adjutant, Captain H.F. Payne, who was in hospital badly wounded in the leg from the Oued Zarga battles:

> Dear Payne,
> We lost a lot of officers at Ang and Longstop. You will probably have heard Hicks, Hawkins, Birch all killed, Spence missing at Ang, and Giles and McMillan wounded at Longstop.

I hope you will manage to come back, but envy you if you go home, unless it is with a stiff leg. I am sure you know how much you are missed by everyone, but especially by me.[25]

On 8 May, the day after Wilberforce's death, the Surreys advanced in strength with 78th Division and it became a victory march into Tunis. The streets were thronged with people deliriously happy. Lieutenant Woodhouse remembered them waving French tricolours, throwing flowers and reaching out with bottles of wine to the victorious troops.

Early on 8 May we climbed on to open lorries and drove in to the suburbs. My platoon let out a great cheer as we crested a hill to see the city spread out below us and the blue sea beyond. We then marched in fighting order through the city. It was soon obvious that there would be no resistance as we were given drinks by cheering crowds. We were proud and excited by our victory.[26]

That same day he wrote home:

My dear Mum,
Victory in Tunis! You will have just heard on the wireless that the first infantry troops into Tunis were of the 78th Division.
The city fell yesterday 7th and today at 13.00 we marched in and rode part of the way in trucks and Bren carriers. We were cheered almost the whole way, and given drinks and flowers. At one place my truck was mobbed by people and couldn't move. After a hard fight it was a great moment to march down green treed avenues, and through fine broad streets.
I can hardly think at all, and am in quite a daze. Only a few hours ago we were patrolling!
Enough for now, love to all,
Lots of love, from Jock.[27]

* * *

The Allied generals established their HQ in the Tunis seafront suburbs of Sidi Bou Said and La Marsa. In 1858 the Bey of Tunis had compensated the British Government for losses incurred by his corrupt treasurer by gifting his palace at La Marsa to Queen Victoria for use by her ambassadors. In 1943 General Alexander quickly reoccupied the La Marsa palace, recently vacated by German commanders, and made it his headquarters 'the most handsome mess the British Army ever had in Africa'.[28]

Like probably every visitor to Tunis, I quickly found my way to the outlying clifftop village of Sidi Bou Said. It was a cool early March day and, luckily for me, it was keeping the usual tourists in small numbers. As you walk up Sidi Bou Said's narrow main street its white houses and shops, with their doorways, window frames and balustrades in various shades of blue, seem to merge with the sky. Here and there strands of mauve bougainvillea blossom, and down alleyways the sea beckons you.

Despite the tourist trade and souvenir shops, the village exudes a calm perhaps inherited from its founder Sidi Bou Said, a twelfth-century Sufi holy man. Over the years both Muslim and Jewish refugees fleeing from what we now term ethnic cleansing in Alhambra and Spain's Andalusia painted the houses blue and white. Now the colours are government law. It is ironic to think that out of their pain and homesickness came such beauty and peace, sustained to the present day.

*   *   *

After entering Tunis on 8 May 1943 the 1st Surreys, under their new CO, Lieutenant Colonel H.B.L. Smith, based themselves just a few miles from Sidi Bou Said and La Marsa, for a week, at Tunis' port, la Goulette. Some of the Surreys must have wrestled with their own pain and homesickness, while they helped in the clearing of the wreckage from the port's bombardment, and rounded up more Axis prisoners, as Lieutenant Woodhouse remembered.

At la Goulette we even stayed a few days in seaside villas. About 11 May we moved to another suburb, and the driver of the German CinC, General von Arnim, surrendered to my platoon. He was a regular soldier of six years, spoke fair English and had an Iron Cross for taking prisoner six English soldiers in France in 1940. We did not hate the German soldiers, for we knew and understood their lives, the mirror of our own. They had treated our prisoners fairly, as we heard when some had been released.[29]

La Goulette, its seafood restaurants now popular with tourists, is close to the ancient site of Carthage of which only a few ruins remain after the city's destruction by Rome in the Third Punic War. As you now walk around the original Carthage site on Byrsa Hill little evidence remains of the Carthaginians. Even though the Romans rebuilt Carthage so that it became the third largest city, and its Antonine Baths the largest public baths, of the Roman Empire, the Carthaginians are still remembered. In the suburbs close to the Antonine Baths there are reminders, street names such as 'Rue Hannibal' and 'Rue de Phoenicians'.

In May and June 1943 in those same suburbs Lieutenant Woodhouse was briefly involved in civil affairs matters.

I was handed the problem of Jewish property that had been handed over to the Arabs. The Jews now asked us to make the Arabs return it. I spoke enough French to handle it, and I wrote in a letter to my father on 13 May, 'Although I feel sorry for the Jews as the Germans treated them like swine, they now they think they are 'Top Dog'. The French police are mostly pro-Arab.'[30]

* * *

So here in Carthage, originally Hannibal's homeland and then a Roman colony, in May 1943 was another turn in the tide of history. The Allies' defeat of Axis forces in North Africa came with the capture of 250,000 enemy prisoners. With a surprising honesty Goebbels in Berlin likened it to the Nazis' defeat at Stalingrad.[31] For many of the Allied troops it would be the start of a journey like Hannibal's, across the Mediterranean to the European mainland, and through Sicily and Italy to the Alps.

For the 1st Surreys and their Battleaxe Division comrades, the Tunis Victory March and celebrations were a far cry from the earlier resistance of the Vichy French in Morocco, Algeria and Tunis. When, on 14 October 1942 at Greenock on the Clyde, thirty-five officers and 761 other ranks of the 1st Surreys had embarked on Operation TORCH many had never before been under fire. By the end of the Tunisian campaign, they had churned through losses of 681 men killed, wounded or missing in action. The 1/6th Surreys had lost 236 men. Yet the two battalions had carried out their orders and honoured all who had fallen in the past six months. They had captured Tunis.

For many of the troops who had survived the Tunisian battles, feelings of exhilaration and relief to be alive must have turned to a sense of loss and grief for their comrades who had been lost, and perhaps anger at the casualties and the inevitable mistakes made as Lieutenant Woodhouse testified.

I was now in a period of disillusion with the army and in particular with my battalion. In a letter of the 10th of June to my father, I wrote: 'My dear Dad, The army is out as a career. I can name officers who proved incapable of leading men, were opposed to taking actions ... these miserable 'do nothings'.

I was most happy when with my platoon. I considered applying to join the Army Air Corps but withdrew. I was allowed to wear the Dorset regiment or forage cap all the time. I, like others, was intensely proud of being a 'Dorset', and so of course were East Surrey regiment officers proud of their regiment. The regimental system is a source of strength to the army, but had its downside when one was posted to a different regiment.

I found the ceremonial functions irksome, and I was no doubt a 'difficult' young twenty-year-old, probably over confident after a successful three months in action as a platoon commander. Yet a friend of my father, the CO of 105th Light AA Regiment in Tunisia, wrote to him after meeting my CO, Lieutenant Colonel Harry Smith, on the 24 July. 'Woodhouse is a real acquisition to the regiment. He is doing exceptionally well and is one of their best platoon commanders ... I think he is a young man who is definitely going to 'get on' in the service.'[32]

*　*　*

In the words of General Anderson the 1st Surreys had been in combat with the enemy without a break since November 1942 'in extremely fierce hand-to-hand fights including much night work over cruelly difficult ground'. He went on to write in a despatch, 'The 78th Division deserves the highest praise for as tough and prolonged a bit of fighting as has ever been undertaken by the British soldier.'[33]

The Surreys, many barely out of their teens from London suburbs and county towns, had learned to fight for the mountains as well as their fellow Scottish Highlanders. Perhaps even more important after the ignominy and losses at Dunkirk, and the devastation of the Blitz on London that many had endured, they now knew that they could drive the Germans back.[34]

The Tunisian campaign was Eisenhower's first combat triumph as Commander-in-Chief, and his springboard for leading the Allies into Europe. The Tunisian victory confirmed Churchill's quotes after Alamein, and on the commencement of Operation TORCH, that it was 'perhaps the end of the beginning'[35] and that the tide had turned. Yet, in spite of the euphoria, for the Surreys and the Allied armies it also meant that there was to be no turning back. Even worse ordeals were to come.

*　*　*

While the Allied armies struggled for every inch of ground in Tunisia, not surprisingly the planning for the next offensive, the invasion of Sicily, or Operation HUSKY, had to go ahead. It was poorly co-ordinated and riddled with disagreements. Although the strategic decision was taken in January 1943 by Churchill and Roosevelt at the Casablanca Conference, the Allies' military commanders such as General Montgomery were openly critical of the planning.

Worse still, the Germans fully expected that the Allies would next attempt an invasion of Sicily, only 100 miles (160 kilometres) from Tunisia, and were preparing accordingly. Unbeknown to the battlefield commanders this problem had been foreseen for some time.

In the summer of 1942 in the midst of the planning and preparations for Operation TORCH, a small inter-services security committee had begun to look ahead to what might follow. The Allies were under increasing pressure from Russia to open a second front against the Third Reich in

Europe. Once victory was achieved in North Africa the obvious next step would be Sicily. The problem was that this would be obvious to the Germans too.

The Germans must be deceived into believing that Allied forces from North Africa would next invade Europe at somewhere other than Sicily. An idea was conceived whereby German intelligence would be provided with a dead body carrying false, secret documents. The dead body with the uniform and rank of a senior staff officer, carrying supposedly secret documents, would be dumped at sea close to Huelva on the Spanish coast.

It seemed feasible that the officer would be thought to have died in an air crash at sea while en route to Algiers. The Spanish authorities, although neutral, favoured the Third Reich and could be expected to make the papers available to German agents. The documents would be created to convince German intelligence that an invasion would take place somewhere other than Sicily, such as Sardinia and Greece.

Although medical advice supported the feasibility of the plan, finding a suitable dead body of an acceptable age proved to be the first of many practical difficulties. After time-consuming enquiries, the body of a deceased man in his early thirties, who had died of pneumonia arising from exposure, was obtained and medical opinion sought on its suitability. It was thought that, as the body would be kept in cold storage, and encased in dry ice leading up to the time of release into the sea, its subsequent decomposition would seem to be from drowning, and then from being in the sea.[36]

In the face of some initial opposition, and debate at the highest levels, the plan codenamed Operation MINCEMEAT was eventually approved by Churchill with Eisenhower's endorsement on 15 April.[37] A letter was written by the Vice-Chief of the Imperial General Staff, Sir Archibald Nye, to General Alexander in Tunis, to be carried on the body to give it the touch of authenticity. The dead body, in the guise of a senior officer, would also carry two similar fake letters from the Commander-in-Chief, Lord Louis Mountbatten, one of which would be addressed to General Eisenhower.[38]

Much now depended upon a dead man.

Notes

1. Squire and Hill, op cit., pp. 32–3.
2. Veterans' Accounts, Woodhouse, *Memoirs* (unpublished)
3. Veterans' Accounts and Recollections, Skilton.
4. Squire and Hill, op cit., pp. 32–3
5. Veterans' Accounts, Woodhouse, *Memoirs* (unpublished).
6. Ibid.
7. Cyril Ray, op cit., p. 47.
8. Daniell, op cit., p. 169.
9. Veterans' Accounts, Woodhouse, *Memoirs* (unpublished).
10. Ibid.

11. Cyril Ray, op cit., p. 49.
12. Ibid, pp. 49–50.
13. Moorehead, op cit., p. 590.
14. Veterans' Accounts, Woodhouse, *Memoirs* (unpublished).
15. Daniell, op cit., pp. 170–1.
16. Veterans' Accounts, Woodhouse, *Memoirs* (unpublished).
17. Ibid.
18. Surrey History Centre ESR/25/PAYN/6–8.
19. Veterans' Accounts, Weston and Mumford.
20. Eisenhower, *'Crusade in Europe'*, p. 172.
21. Moorehead, op cit., p. 593.
22. Veterans' Accounts, Chaffer.
23. Atkinson, op cit., pp. 498–9.
24. Veterans' Accounts, Woodhouse, *Memoirs* (unpublished).
25. Surrey History Centre ESR/25/PAYN/7.
26. Veterans' Accounts, Woodhouse, *Memoirs* (unpublished).
27. Ibid.
28. Tomkinson, *Tunisia*, p. 57.
29. Veterans' Accounts, Woodhouse, *Memoirs* (unpublished).
30. Ibid.
31. Atkinson, op cit., p. 537.
32. Veterans' Accounts, Woodhouse, *Memoirs* (unpublished).
33. Daniell, op cit., p. 167.
34. Ray, op cit., p. 55.
35. Atkinson, op cit., p. 159.
36. Montagu, *The Man Who Never Was*, pp. 15–37.
37. McIntyre, *Operation Mincemeat*, pp. 127–8.
38. Montagu, op cit., pp. 38–50.

Chapter 4

Sicily's 'Dawn Coast': Helped by the Man the Surreys Never Knew

Because it was known that the Germans already had some convincing intelligence of the Allies' planning for an invasion of Sicily, the challenge was how to make them think that such planning was all a misinformation ploy. Could they be made to think that the preparations were merely cover for another invasion location? The concocted letter sent to General Alexander used the real codename for the invasion of Sicily, Operation HUSKY, as the codename (or cover) for a planned invasion of Greece. The code name BRIMSTONE was used for a fictitious invasion of Sardinia. In essence, the letter was composed so as to convince the Germans that the Allies' real plans to invade Sicily were merely an exercise in deception.

Still it was one thing to possess a suitable dead body to carry the letter but quite another to create a persona for it, a believable person and identity. Because the intelligence staff handling Operation MINCEMEAT had good contacts in the Admiralty, the first decision made was that the body should be an officer in the Royal Marines. This would enable him to travel in battledress, and avoid custom tailoring. In the event, the physical task of clothing a frozen dead body still presented a major challenge, not least placing boots on rigid, unbending feet.

But what should be the man's name and personal background? Following research of the Royal Marines' records, the name Major Martin was selected because there were several officers of the same name and rank. Once his death was reported in the UK, such a common name would create some doubt in the reader over who had actually died. Major Martin's false ID card was stamped as a replacement for a lost card, and given some artificial wear and tear by rubbing and bending.

It was also reasoned that German intelligence experts would ask themselves 'Who is Major Martin?' and look for evidence of his personal life. Fabricated private letters, personal papers, theatre ticket stubs, and other items were prepared and placed on Major Martin.

Major Martin's body was scheduled to be slid into the sea off Huelva on the evening of 29/30 April. The theatre tickets had been bought for

22 April. So if Major Martin's body was recovered by the Spanish authorities around 1 or 2 May, this would support the impression that the body had been in the sea decomposing for some four to six days. But would the body be washed ashore as planned?[1]

On 18/19 April 1943 Major Martin's body was transported in a metal canister, packed with dry ice, by road to Greenock on the Clyde in Scotland. There, at Holy Loch, the canister was loaded aboard the submarine HMS *Seraph* under the command of Lieutenant Jewell, the only one of the crew to know of its contents.

At 4.30am on 30 April, HMS *Seraph* surfaced under cover of darkness and undetected just 1,600 yards from the mouth of the Huelva River. Once the canister was brought up on deck, Lieutenant Jewell dismissed all crew members apart from his four officers. Only then did he brief them on the canister's contents, Major Martin, and the plan to drop his body overboard. Once Major Martin was extracted from the canister, the officers attached a life-jacket, and paid their respects with a short burial service.

It was low tide as Major Martin was lowered into the water. To add to the effect of the imminent tide change, Lieutenant Jewell also used the submarine's screws to direct their backwash to give the body a further push towards land. Now it was up to Major Martin to play his part and carry out the mission.

The first news that Major Martin had made landfall in Spain came on 3 May in a signal from the British Naval Attaché in Madrid. He had received notification that, on 30 April, a Spanish fishing boat had recovered the body of a British naval officer in the sea close to Huelva. Surprisingly, the Spanish authorities had given Major Martin a military burial as early as the very next day. The Admiralty sent instructions to their naval attaché as if Major Martin was a genuine officer, and impressed upon him that all personal effects and important papers that Major Martin was carrying must be quickly retrieved from the Spanish authorities but without giving the impression that his documents were unduly vital.

The Spanish authorities indicated to the British naval attaché that some documents found in Major Martin's possession had been passed through the normal 'naval channels' in Madrid. British Intelligence inferred that this would mean that the documents would have been shown to, and likely copied by, German intelligence in Madrid. Then, on 13 May, the British Naval Attaché received all Major Martin's effects, including his briefcase and its documents still in sealed envelopes, and had them immediately sent on to London. It appeared that German intelligence was playing the game, and covering its tracks.

As soon as Major Martin's effects arrived in London, scientific tests began on the documents. On first appearance, despite the immersion in sea water, the seals on the envelopes seemed to be untouched and intact.

However, in due course the tests showed that the letters had been removed from the envelopes, without breaking the seals, and then replaced. It was clear that Spanish and German intelligence had seen the letters.

To maintain the deception it was critical that normal protocols must be continued. On 4 June Major Martin was reported as 'Killed' in *The Times* casualty list. A wreath and tombstone were arranged for Major Martin's grave in Huelva, and a photograph taken for his family. The British naval attaché thanked the Spanish authorities for their co-operation.

Had a dead man, Major Martin, and his fictitious documents, fooled the Germans into thinking Sicily was only a decoy invasion site? Only a few people at the Allies' highest levels knew of the deception, and hoped for an affirmative answer to that question.[2]

* * *

When the Tunisian fighting ended on 8 May, the 1st Surreys spent time at Hammamet on the east coast of the Cap Bon peninsula, then farther south at Sousse, where you can now drive past countless developments of tourist resorts clinging to the beaches. But in 1943 their recovery time for training and re-equipping was to be a snatched prelude.

It was during this time that Lieutenant Woodhouse heard of the death of his friend, Watkins, with whom he had joined the Surreys from the Dorsetshire Regiment. For once when he wrote home on 6 June, there was a crack in his usual upbeat tone:

> My dear Dad,
>   Watkins' death was a blow, the more so because it was the first time I had lost a friend through action. It is extraordinary how so many are killed almost at once, while others go on and on.
>   Your loving son, Jock.[3]

The Surreys were inspected at Sousse by Montgomery, who told them that they and the 78th Battleaxe Division were to join his Eighth Army. He did not state their mission, but on 10 July it was a secret no longer. The Allies had invaded Sicily and the Surreys would soon join them. The Allies' invasion fleet landed on Sicily's 'dawn coast of Europe'. That is the description given by D.H. Lawrence of Sicily's east coast during his stay before the war in Taormina, a favourite resort of celebrities and the literary set.

Operation HUSKY comprised more than 3,000 ships, carrying a combined force of around 160,000 men, three times the size of Operation TORCH. At the time it was almost certainly the largest ever invasion fleet ever assembled anywhere. In the early hours of the night of 9/10 July, the US Seventh Army and the British Eighth Army began to land on the south-eastern corner of Sicily.[4]

At the same time as the amphibious assault, British 1st Airborne Division soldiers in 134 gliders approached the Ponte Grande bridge, a little south of Syracuse. The bridge was crucial for the early capture of the east coast port. Weather, navigational errors, and friendly fire scattered or brought down a majority of gliders, so that only eighty-seven airborne soldiers reached the bridge.

Fortunately, the Eighth Army's infantry landings farther south on the Gulf of Noto, on the eastern side of the Pachino Peninsula, were more successful. Lead units were able to quickly reinforce the airborne troops and take the Ponte Grande bridge, but more than 600 casualties meant it had been a costly win. Then the coastal towns of Cassibile and Syracuse were quickly captured.

*   *   *

Driving south from Catania to Syracuse in May 2008 I passed the fruit plantations, olives, oranges and vineyards of the Catania Plain, and some of the lush, native vegetation. A vast variety of plants have prospered in Sicily, prickly pear, palms, oleander, bougainvillea, and many, like papyrus, brought from Africa by birds, Arab traders, invaders and migrants.

From a high rocky peninsula the old town of Syracuse, on the adjoining island of Ortygia, looks out onto the Ionian Sea. Ortygia, bridged across a canal, retains much of its Baroque architecture, enticing alleyways, and a reflected light from the sea that on a clear day is reminiscent of Venice. The sea breeze from the south can be dry, no doubt from the influence of North Africa.

The Greeks first settled in Sicily in Naxos and Taormina in 734 BC, and then about 200 years later in Syracuse. Arguably the greatest legacy of Syracuse to civilization was from the work of Archimedes in the sciences and engineering. Others would say it is the gift of drama, and its Greek theatre, where a summer programme is still performed. Today in the Syracuse Greek theatre, built in the fifth century BC, you can sit back on a balmy, early summer evening, and enjoy plays by Aeschylus and other Greek dramatists that were re-commenced in 1918.

*   *   *

In July 1943 the Syracuse theatre productions must have been cancelled as Eighth Army poured past, intent upon imposing their own re-enactment of a Greek tragedy on the Germans farther north. The coastal route that they had to take was a road mined or demolished at every turn of the rugged eastern seaboard north to their goal of Messina. Montgomery must have wished for the engineering genius of Archimedes.

By 12 July the British XXX Corps had advanced north of Syracuse and taken Augusta. West of the Pachino Peninsula, in the Gulf of Gela, the US Seventh Army's landings encountered more difficult seas and stiffer resistance. In an uncanny parallel with Eighth Army, an airborne operation turned into self-inflicted carnage. The 504th Parachute Infantry Regiment troopers suffered 410 casualties, in possibly the worst 'friendly fire' disaster of the war.[5] The Allies were ashore, but how soon and how strong would be the German counter-attack? Had Major Martin played his part?

In the days following the landings, the lack of a cohesive plan to co-ordinate the advances of British Eighth Army and US Seventh Army came to a head as early as 13 July when Alexander met separately with Generals Patton and Montgomery. The two armies were breaking out from their beachheads and converging on Route 124, the only road north to Vizzini, and thence north-east to Enna and Leonforte where the Axis forces were entrenched around Mount Etna. Alexander ordered the US 45th Infantry Division to move back to Gela's beaches so that XXX Corps of Eighth Army could move inland from the coastal plain.

Feeling that he was being put in a secondary role to protect the left flank of Eighth Army, so that Montgomery could be first into Messina, Patton took a most liberal interpretation of Alexander's orders and sent Seventh Army into a headlong rush across Sicily to the north-west coast. He was not going to miss out on some glory and meant to capture Sicily's capital, Palermo. Maybe from there the US Seventh Army could advance along the north coast road to Messina. Yet it meant the Allies were splitting their strength.

On their penetration north of Syracuse, Eighth Army at first met only thin Italian defences, then within a few days they ran into German forces south of Catania. Perhaps Eighth Army's most serious setback was the failure, on 13/14 July, of gliderborne troops to capture and hold the Primosole Bridge. Out of a 1,900 strong force, only 200 landed near the bridge and were confronted by the German 3rd Parachute Regiment who had dropped onto the bridge two days earlier.[6]

The ferocious Battle of Primosole Bridge raged over four days. As the bridge changed hands several times in attack and counter-attack, the dead of both sides piled up and had to be left to rot. When the bridge was finally in Eighth Army's possession on 17 July and secured for crossing, the Germans had made use of the time to establish a defensive line along the Simeto River. By 18 July a toll of around 4,000 casualties and some 700 dead had brought Eighth Army's advance on Catania to a standstill.[7]

Nevertheless, on the north-west coast of Sicily the Germans were coming under increasing pressure from the Americans who had quickly taken Palermo and were commencing an advance eastwards towards Messina. In contrast, the planned offensive drive by Eighth Army, using the narrow coastal route through Catania, and then between Mount Etna and the sea to Messina, confronted a daunting bottleneck.

* * *

Mount Etna is Europe's largest active volcano, and at a height of nearly 11,000 feet it dominates Sicily's east coast. When I drove north at sunset in May 2010 on the *autostrada* from Catania to Taormina, as the sun sank behind Mount Etna's mass, the mountain's silhouette towered along the darkening, western sky line. In that twilight period its shape could be imagined as a brooding, gargantuan sphinx.

The Italian writer Leonardia Sciascia likened Mount Etna to a huge purring cat, which can suddenly lash out in an unpredictable eruption. One of its most recent was in 2002, which destroyed ski resort facilities and a cable car and threatened the village of Nicolosi. In 1943 Montgomery's Eighth Army battled to drive through the narrow coastal strip between Mount Etna and the sea. It was as if the volcano was waiting to pounce, just like the Germans, ready to spit fire and molten lava into their path.

It had become clear that the Germans meant to hold the important port of Catania and the north-east coast in strength as part of a defensive line stretching westwards through the mountains to the important road junctions of Enna and Leonforte, and from there north to San Stefano on Sicily's north coast.

The Germans had effectively blocked the east coast route to Messina. So, as he had done in Tunisia, Montgomery reverted to his alternative tactic of a left hook offensive, this time through the mountains to the north-west of Catania, to assault Centuripe, Adrano and Randazzo. He aimed to split the final defensive line of the Germans around Etna and force them to retreat both on the north and east coasts to Messina.

However, when so many units were depleted and in need of rest the question was who in Eighth Army could carry out the left hook? Despite Montgomery conceding to Patton that the Americans' advance on the north coast should be the main thrust on Messina, Eighth Army needed some fresh troops to drive through the mountains and relieve the pressure on US forces.

Montgomery had hoped that the 78th Division, his most experienced mountain warfare troops, recently proven in the Atlas Mountains in Tunisia, could be kept in reserve and rested for the campaign to come on the rugged Italian mainland. But it was not to be. On 20 July Montgomery called in the Battleaxe Division. After a pitching voyage below decks in LCI landing craft, commonly known as sardine cans, and seasickness that seemed to spare no one, the 1st Surreys landed on 25 July at Cassibile to the south of Syracuse.

61

From Cassibile the Surreys drove by truck up to Palagonia, then from there on foot over tough terrain, in all a journey of some forty miles, to the foot of Monte Scalpello. In the heat of high summer the dust, mixed with the ever-present sulphur fumes from Mount Etna, choked men's throats. Sicily's searing heat, and the dust-covered bodies of the dead of both sides lying unburied on the rocky ground, were to become a soldier's common impression of Sicily.[8]

'I could not help but think back longingly to the freshness of the sparkling Mediterranean,' said the Surreys' Frank Weston.[9] During the recuperation at Hammamet in Tunisia, and the uneventful voyage across to Sicily, Frank had pushed away the nightmare of Longstop Hill. Now the horrors of that battle were back.

The forbidding task given to the 78th Division was to advance over the hills west of the Catania Plain, cross the Dittaino River, take Catenanuova, next throw themselves at the fortress and mountaintop town of Centuripe, then on to assault Adrano, Bronte and, finally, Randazzo, so bisecting the German lines. On the night of 29 July a brigade from the 1st Canadian Division, supported by the 5th Northamptons, crossed the shallow summer stream of the Dittaino River for the attack on Catenanuova. Despite Luftwaffe strikes in the morning that destroyed the Northamptons' supplies and transport and inflicted significant casualties, enemy ground forces were overcome. By sunset on 30 July the Canadians had taken Catenanuova.

'Between Catenanuova and Etna,' wrote Cyril Ray, 'the earth heaves itself into a tumult of ridges and hills, each seeming higher and steeper than the last, separated from each other by rocky gorges.'[10] Into this terrain at midnight on 30 July the Surreys took over 78th Division's lead to drive on towards Centuripe, which blocked the route to Adrano.

Lieutenant Woodhouse remembered how it was nearly a disaster before they even began:

> We attacked north of Catenanuova, as usual at night. And in night attacks it was usual to march to the start line with white tape, so platoons would start together in line. Our artillery fired by mistake on this line, causing a lot of confusion but surprisingly, and luckily, few casualties.[11]

As they moved off, caught under this intense 'friendly' fire, their Major Hill recalled that they could 'do nothing except lie down in the open where we were. It was fifteen minutes before the barrage lifted – about the longest quarter of an hour I have ever spent'.[12]

Exploiting the Canadians' gains, the Surreys with the 2nd Lancashire Fusiliers, made their way into the hills around the right flank, and beyond the rear of Catenanouva. Stubborn machine gunners and snipers were taken out before the Surreys gained their high ground objective two miles to the north of the town.

However, as the Surreys had clambered up one side of a ridge, German paratroopers had simultaneously climbed the other in what seemed at the time like a suicide attack. Lieutenant Woodhouse recalled the clash that followed:

My leading section came face to face with German paras through a cactus hedge. One German surrendered while the rest ran back. We fired at them but in the dark we missed. As it began to grow light we advanced up the hill, and quickly came under heavy machine-gun fire. Sergeant Hawkins was shot through the head next to me.

And soon more heavy firing from our own Vickers machine guns passed just over our heads, bringing showers of twigs and olives down on us. When they stopped and all was silent over on the German positions, I walked slowly forward alone although well covered by my platoon. The German paras had gone.[13]

The confused firefight was heightened by the arrival into the mêlée of a disoriented contingent of the 5th Royal West Kents. However, the chaos of the engagement brought a piece of good luck. The Surreys captured a German officer who carried plans for the order of battle for Centuripe's defences.

The plans showed that the mountain fortress was to be defended by the Herman Göring Division and the 3rd Fallschirmjäger (Parachute) Regiment. The Germans meant to defend north-east Sicily and Messina as long as they could. If Montgomery knew of Major Martin, and the mis-information he carried on false Allied plans, he must have doubted that the Germans had fallen for the elaborate deception ploy.

*   *   *

The captured plans were a huge bonus for Centuripe was a mountain stronghold 'standing high on a razor-backed hill above a wild countryside of ragged peaks and narrow defiles', wrote Daniell, and resembled a medieval fortress.[14] At over 2,000 feet it straddled the highest part of a sharp ridge whose only approach was a twisting road. The Germans had brought a nightmare to the road's every bend, laid mines, blown craters, triggered landslides, destroyed every bridge and, from the town, stared down their gun sights. They meant Centuripe to be an impregnable centre-piece in their Sicilian defensive line.

It was approached by a narrow corkscrew road that ran for a couple of miles along the flank of one of the precipitous ridges jutting out from the main mountain mass. Every yard of this road was commanded from the steep slopes above; the drop below would bring death and destruction to men, mules and vehicles.[15]

In May 2008 I stood next to the ancient, six-sided shrine on Centuripe's highest point, and gazed down the 360-degree views of the surrounding valleys. It felt as if nothing could move without you seeing it. The Romans had thought that Centuripe's inhabitants, like themselves, were descended from the Trojans. They recognized its commanding position, and made it *civitates liberae*, a free city. More recently, in his fight for Italian unification in 1862, Garibaldi called it *il balcone della Sicilia* (the balcony over Sicily), for its commanding views to Catania and Mount Etna.

While 78th Division prepared to assail the heights of Centuripe, a few miles to the north-west the Americans were locked in battle for Troina, originally an Arab-Norman stronghold, and at more than 3,600 feet the highest town in Sicily. Despite Centuripe's daunting position, there could be no let-up, no time for outflanking. To ease the pressures on US Seventh Army to the north, and on Eighth Army to the east, the German line had to be broken.

At first Lieutenant Woodhouse was an observer of an attack by fellow battalions of the Battleaxe Division:

> From a 'grandstand' position in the hills I watched the advance, in the early daylight of 1 August, by the 38 Irish Brigade to capture Centuripe. When our artillery shells burst on the enemy held hills, the Irish, in scattered lines and blobs, pressed on across the valley below and in front of us.[16]

Later that day in the evening the Surreys commenced their assault, once again to battle for the sky. Their orders were to take a hilltop cemetery, or rather a German strongpoint set amongst a myriad of tall, marble tombs, overlooking Centuripe across a steep ravine. It was warm and dark as the Surreys began their two-mile climb.

'From our time in Tunisia's mountains we had become used to going up hillsides,' said Harry Skilton. 'We traversed whenever we could, and just took one small step after another, hoping the Germans did not hear us.'[17]

It was during this advance that Lieutenant Woodhouse had an unsettling experience.

> We climbed up a cobbled mule track winding up the side of a steep hill. Each side of the track was stone terraced, and in many places impassable for two heavy loaded infantrymen at night. Then A Company's assault failed, and a gaggle of troops, perhaps fifty or more, came stampeding back down the track in sheer panic.
>
> The panic in the air was almost tangible. I can remember feeling how contagious was their fear, and just getting a grip on myself in

time. I felt an urge to join them in the crowd, which I quickly suppressed by my sense of duty, and called 'Hold fast 10 Platoon'. It was the only time I witnessed panic, and it was a shocking experience. These troops were stopped lower down the track and quickly recovered.[18]

When the Surreys gained the top of the ridge they were able to engage the German troops dug in behind the tombs' cover. A heavy firefight ensued but the Surreys' small arms and mortars had little effect on the cemetery's stone tombs. The Germans covered every possible approach to the hill's crest with machine guns on fixed lines, so that the Surreys were now pinned down and their attack was stalled. Through all the next day, the Surreys and four other battalions edged forward to hang onto their gains. 'We hung on below Centuripe all day on 2 August,' said Woodhouse. 'This was the only day I remember when we got no food.'[19]

As well as no rations, there was no water or ammunition getting through. The German machine gunners and snipers, using their flares to light up the night sky like New Year's Eve, gave no respite and pounced on any movement. On the rocky hillsides, with only small bushes or cacti giving the pretence of cover, the casualties were increasing rapidly.

The five battalions were now in a miserable position, spread across open ravines and ridges, and facing elimination by the Germans' long-range fire in a battle of attrition. The near stalemate convinced Divisional command to pull back the Surreys, and some other lead troops, a little way in order to launch the full strength of Divisional artillery onto the cemetery and Centuripe town. The battle was at a tipping point. The forward troops, hungry, thirsty and running short of ammunition, could not stay where they were.

But although the Surreys and their fellow battalions were suffering after forty-eight hours of continual combat in the open, the Germans, who had been engaged with the Battleaxe Division with no break for more than four days, must have been even more tired and also running out of supplies. The Division's commander, General Evelegh, decided to make a daring and risky, surprise onslaught to topple Göring's paratroopers.

Leaving only one remaining battalion in reserve, Evelegh brought in the three fresh battalions of 38 Irish Brigade, 1st Royal Irish Fusiliers, 6th Royal Inniskilling Fusiliers and 2nd London Irish Rifles. By committing seven of his nine battalions, and by launching assaults on the town simultaneously from different directions, Evelegh gambled that the massed attack would shock, confuse and over-run the German defenders. It was like placing all your chips on one spin of the roulette wheel.

Two companies of the 6th Inniskillings assaulted the town straight up the cliffs, which surprised the German defenders and made inroads by dusk on 2 August. Shortly the Royal Irish and Inniskilling Fusiliers stormed into the fortress from the south and east, and the London Irish from the west. Throughout the night with a continual feed of reinforcements, they fought their way through the narrow winding streets. By dawn on 3 August the ferocity and skill of the Battleaxe infantry had taken its toll. The German defenders, stunned and confused by all-out attack on a number of fronts by 78th Division, had been pushed out into retreat, and Centuripe was taken.

On entering Centuripe town the troops came face to face with the horrific damage which the Battleaxe Division's attack had inflicted on its inhabitants, and even their dead, as Private Hector Smyth saw.

The enemy had used the large cemetery on the crest of the hill as a stronghold and the artillery barrage had opened many tombs and mausoleums. Skeletons of long dead villagers lay strewn about. In one coffin I saw a skeleton draped with a few black rags which had once probably been a peasant buried in his Sunday suit. All afternoon a sad, steady procession of villagers carrying wooden boxes, makeshift coffins, containing the bodies of their kinsfolk killed during the fighting, wended its way to the cemetery.[20]

On 4 August Lieutenant Woodhouse wrote to his father:

My dear Dad,
Italy '43? Yes we shall do it! Musso is bust, and the whole Axis is busting now all right.
You will know today I am here, as this crack mountain Division the 78th are again front pages. The news fiends are drinking up the strong black headlines as this new year of victories goes on.
The walls of the local towns are covered in Mussolini slogans, looking very ridiculous now! Sicilians are ... refugees, wounded, and half starving inhabitants of shelled towns, nearly all their men prisoners or missing, they seem quite satisfied with our occupation.
Ever your loving son, Jock.[21]

The citizens of Centuripe no doubt would have taken a somewhat different view of the battle for their town.

It had been a classic infantry attack, acknowledged by a grateful General Montgomery as a wonderful feat. The Surreys and the other battalions of the Battleaxe Division were firmly cementing their name as the Eighth Army's elite mountain warfare troops. The taking of Centuripe, the first battle honour of the Surreys' Italian campaign, was a trigger that finally forced a German decision.

Two days after the conquest of Centuripe, a fifth American assault took Troina. General von Senger was forced to order Axis forces to retreat north of Mount Etna to Messina, and from there to begin an ordered withdrawal across the Straits of Messina to the Italian mainland. Nevertheless, everyone knew it was not yet over; the Germans would re-group at every next hill town.

* * *

On my visit to Sicily I took a train journey around Mount Etna, from Adrano to Randazzo aboard the Circumetna Railway, and gazed upon a startling variety of passing landscape. At around 4,000 feet the Circumetna seems to be in places very close to the snow line. The train winds around through terrain that varies from orchards, to vineyards, to bare volcanic rock, to woodland, to sheep and cattle pasture, to native bush land, and all in a haphazard mingling.

Wild flowers flourish here and there within the lava rubble. Some cultivated land and small farmhouses reach up as if challenging the volcano's snowline. Near Bronte, perhaps on farmland once gifted to Nelson by the King of Naples and Sicily in recognition of his help against Napoleon's invading army, you see sheep and cattle on lush grazing land. Nelson had evacuated the King, his family and court followers in flight from Naples to Palermo, where he stayed for a short while. Yet just as Nelson's stay was brief, Montgomery and Allied Forces in 1943 would be gone from Sicily in a matter of weeks. The drums of war as always were impatient.

* * *

Once Centuripe fell, the Surreys and other battalions rested for a couple of days while the Irish Brigade pressed on towards Adrano eight miles to the north. Against the well-drilled, retreating Germans, the Irish battalions fought costly actions to cross the Salso and Simeto Rivers. Many German units, entrenched in caves and stone houses overlooking the river, fought to the last man. A little before midnight on 5 August the Surreys again took over the lead of 11 Brigade, passing through the Irish and their bridgehead across the Simeto River.

The Surreys' first contacts with Adrano encountered mines, shelling, machine-gun fire and infantry attacks that destroyed three armoured cars, as the desperate German defenders tried to slow the Allies' advance.[22]

Woodhouse recalled his company beginning the assault once again at first light:

It was very hot and dry when at dawn on 7 August my B Company, behind the heavy artillery barrage and air strikes, advanced through orange groves uphill to the town of Adrano, which lay on the road encircling Mt Etna.

As I stumbled up the rocky ground I wondered when the Germans would open fire, feeling tense, nervous and super alert. At the edge of the town it gradually became clear that, when our artillery shelling had indicated a major attack, they had pulled out.[23]

The Germans melted away, and by evening the Surreys were in pursuit five miles along the road to Bronte and, in Woodhouse's words:

From Adrano we advanced along the Etna encircling road towards Bronte, companies and battalions taking the lead in turn. Off the road the ground was mostly lava, baking hot in the August sun. The Germans left small rearguards with machine guns and mortars forcing us to deploy and scramble higher up the flanks of Etna. My platoon escaped casualties only by good luck.[24]

On the road to Bronte, Harry Skilton recalled that they were bombarded for the first time by the Germans' *Nebelwerfer*:

We dived for cover but there was none. I pushed my whole body as flat as I could, wishing the ground would swallow me. I thought if the next salvo was closer it would finish me. And my last letter to Jessie had been weeks ago in Tunisia. The Nebelwerfer was a multi-barrelled mortar, and because of the sound its shells were known as 'screaming minnies'. We were ordered to dig in somehow, and hang on for our artillery support. Through the night and next morning we held on, while being fired on from the hills either side of us.[25]

Yet finding somewhere to dig in for cover in Sicily's mountains was far from easy. 'Much of the ground,' said Frank Weston, 'was rock-hard lava from Etna's past eruptions, which cut through our boots.'[26]

On 8 August the Surreys and the 2nd Lancashire Fusiliers drove the Germans from the surrounding rocky slopes, and the 5th Northamptons went through the centre. Bronte was captured. Another nine miles of fighting culminated in the Surreys being first into Randazzo where, shortly afterwards, US forces also arrived.

At Adrano and Bronte Lieutenant Woodhouse saw the horror of war for civilians:

A population, with hardly any men between eighteen and forty, suffered death and injury from bombing and shelling. Mutilated corpses lay in the rubbish while the women screamed. We gave what little food and medical aid we had to spare. Mostly we switched off our emotions or sympathy, not from callous disregard, but from the necessity of fighting the war and the impossible enormity of civilian suffering. We continued the advance as far as Randazzo, suffering further casualties from 'S' mines in the ruins.[27]

Randazzo suffered from a combined onslaught of the Allies' air strikes and artillery bombardment, as well as German demolition explosives.

According to Cyril Ray:

It was a town – it had once held a population of more than 10,000 – with not a house intact. 'You could not tell what kind of town Randazzo had been', reported one correspondent. Every street was blocked by craters and by the rubble of houses that had been simply spilled into it. The Division had seen no devastation quite like it, though they were to see a lot more like it in Italy.[28]

Lieutenant Woodhouse wrote to his parents on 11 August:

My dear Mum,

I am on a hill with crowds of refugees sheltering nearby, they are half starved and ridden with disease. We have fed them out of stuff left over from our rations … it brings home the true horror of war ….

The devastation is absolutely staggering, the Luftwaffe is or was a child's toy compared with the Allied Air Forces out here alone.

My dear Dad,

The Germans are putting up tremendous resistance nothing 'ersatz' about that …. It seems to be a rearguard action but the Germans have their old skill and guts. What they are lacking is guns, tanks and the Luftwaffe. I should like to see an ordinary line regiment of the German Army out here. It is all H. Göring paratroops etc.

Ever your loving son, Jock.[29]

With the fall of Randazzo the Axis forces were now clearly divided to the north and east of Mount Etna and in danger of being cut off and surrounded. They were outnumbered by the Allies on land, sea and air. Leaving detachments to fight delaying battles on the north and east coasts, the Germans withdrew across the Messina Straits back to Italy. They had lost the battles for Sicily but, by 17 August, their typically professional retreat allowed them to extricate the greater part of their forces, guns and equipment onto the Italian peninsula.

*   *   *

After the capture of Messina the Surreys set up camp at the north coast fishing village of Gioisa Marea, where they rested and swam in the warm Tyrrhenian Sea. Most of those left in the depleted ranks of the original complement that sailed from the Clyde had recovered from at least one wound in the Tunisian and Sicilian campaigns. They wondered whether they would survive the next one.

On 5 September Lieutenant Woodhouse wrote home:

My dear Dad,

As you said the last battle was fought by small units, and advances followed the general lines of the roads, Etna of course being an impassable gap in the front. What is so amazing is that country so mountainous has proved so easy to take, even though the tank is almost completely prohibited from operating.

Artillery and aircraft are I suppose the reason why we can do it. Twenty-five years ago Sicily would surely have been impregnable.

Ever your loving son, Jock.[30]

It was here that Woodhouse learned of a decision that would change his life:

The CO, Colonel Harry Smith, told me that 78th Division HQ had ordered the Battalion to form a 'Battle Patrol'. This would consist of a lieutenant, sergeant, corporal, lance corporal, and twelve privates, sixteen men in all. The object was to raise the standard of patrolling. Colonel Smith had selected me to lead it, and the call for volunteers was quickly answered.

All of the patrol were armed with a heavy Thompson submachine gun, known as a 'Tommy gun', except for me. I chose the lighter and simpler German 'Schmeisser' machine pistol. I was of course delighted, not least because the battle patrol was given its own separate billets with me.

Then the Italian surrender was announced during a battalion concert party on 7 September. I remember being very disappointed at first that the prospect of leading my 'battle patrol' into action in Italy seemed to have slipped away. Everyone else appeared delighted, thinking that the war in Italy was over. Within two days it became obvious the Germans had other ideas![31]

* * *

As he was following Eighth Army up Sicily's Ionian coast midway between Catania and Messina, Alan Moorehead, the war correspondent, came upon Taormina, the jewel of Sicily, and wrote, 'It was hot. There was a clear leaping brilliance in the sea, and at midday everything had turned into strident colour, red rocks, green vineyards, a blaring cobalt blue in the sky and then all the bright colours of the tumbledown houses along the shore.'[32]

In 2010 from the heights of Taormina's ancient Greek Theatre, which still sits perched near the summit of Mount Taurus, I looked north and south onto the single coast road to Messina. The road clings precariously on to

Mount Etna's slopes and close to the Ionian Sea. Looking down on the road from Taormina there is a three-dimensional perspective and visual impact far beyond what any map or aerial photograph can give. Had they had the benefit of such a view Eighth Army's planners would surely never have contemplated an attempt to drive through the German defences on such a narrow coastal corridor.

With the Germans gone Montgomery established his HQ in one of Taormina's villas, and hosted a lunch for General Eisenhower, who had flown in from La Marsa in Tunisia. As they sat on the terrace gazing past the bougainvillea to the Ionian Sea and mainland Italy, perhaps they mused that they owed much to Major Martin, 'the man who never was'. But perhaps even they did not know how much, for it was not until long after the war's end that examinations of the archives of German Intelligence disclosed that substantial German forces had been moved away from Sicily to Greece. In retrospect, it does seem probable that Major Martin, the man they never knew, may have saved many lives of the Surreys and other Allied troops, and even averted a disastrous defeat for the Allied invasion.

From his villa's clifftop terrace Montgomery must have watched the sun rise over the dark coastline of Italy, and gazed at its first rays shimmering on the Ionian Sea. While the only sound may have been the cooing of waking doves, perhaps he wondered at the history that preceded him.

Over more than 2,000 years Sicily has absorbed successive waves of invaders and foreign dynasties, Greeks, Carthaginians, Romans, Arabs, Normans, Spanish, Prussians and Austrians. Even Nelson in the Napoleonic Wars had made a brief visit. Following the retreat of the Axis forces, it was the Americans and British in the latest occupation. It was, however, only a stepping stone. On 3 September the first troops of Eighth Army crossed from Messina to Reggio. The campaign for mainland Italy was beginning.

Notes

1. Montagu, op cit., pp. 51–85.
2. Ibid, pp. 78–108.
3. Veterans' Accounts, Woodhouse, *Memoirs* (unpublished).
4. Atkinson, op cit., p. 33.
5. Ibid, p. 90.
6. Carver, *The War in Italy 1943–1945*, p. 34.
7. Atkinson, op cit., p. 127.
8. Daniell, op cit., pp. 180–1.
9. Veterans' Accounts, Weston.
10. Ray, op cit., p. 63.
11. Veterans' Accounts, Woodhouse, *Memoirs* (unpublished).
12. Ford, op cit., pp. 84–5.
13. Veterans' Accounts, Woodhouse, *Memoirs* (unpublished).

14. Daniell, op cit., pp. 181–2.
15. Ray, op cit., p. 63.
16. Veterans' Accounts, Woodhouse, *Memoirs* (unpublished).
17. Veterans' Accounts, Skilton.
18. Veterans' Accounts, Woodhouse, *Memoirs* (unpublished).
19. Ibid.
20. Squire and Hill, op cit., p. 8.
21. Veterans' Accounts, Woodhouse, *Memoirs* (unpublished).
22. Daniell, op cit., pp. 183–4.
23. Veterans' Accounts, Woodhouse, *Memoirs* (unpublished).
24. Ibid.
25. Veterans' Accounts, Skilton.
26. Veterans' Accounts, Weston.
27. Veterans' Accounts, Woodhouse, *Memoirs* (unpublished).
28. Ray, op cit., p. 76.
29. Veterans' Accounts, Woodhouse, *Memoirs* (unpublished).
30. Ibid.
31. Ibid.
32. Moorehead, *Eclipse*, p. 11.

Chapter 5

A Bloodless Coup in Italy: But not at Salerno, Termoli or Larino

Helped by the Major Martin deception and the related decoy plans, the Allied landings in Sicily on 10 July had been exploited quickly. It was a surprise which sent shock waves through the Axis powers. On a hot humid Sunday in Rome, 25 July 1943, Mussolini, Italy's dictator or *Duce*, sat at his desk in the imposing hall known as Sala del Mappamondo, in the Renaissance Palazzo di Venezia. His visitor was Shinrokuro Hidaka, the Japanese ambassador.

A bead of sweat oozed from Mussolini's receding hairline as he implored Hidaka to lobby Hitler in support of his request for more guns and supplies to resist the Allies, who were winning the Sicily campaign. Like everyone else he knew that the invasion of the Italian mainland would be next.

The previous evening Mussolini had endured hours of criticism from his Grand Council, the puppet body of the Italian Fascist regime, who had called for him to hand over power to the King and the military. Later that afternoon, when he made a routine visit to King Victor Emmanuel at his Villa Savoia, Mussolini must have forgotten the Council's censure.

He walked into that meeting with Italy's nominal head of state with a hubris that came from more than twenty years as Italy's dictator. In only twenty minutes King Victor Emmanuel told him that he was finished, that Marshal Badoglio was taking over as head of the government, and then led Mussolini outside to be arrested by the military police waiting for that purpose. It was perhaps the quickest bloodless coup of all time. The collapse of the Italian Fascist regime was welcomed by the Allies, but ironically it would lead to a stiffening of the Germans' resolve to fight for mainland Italy.[1]

* * *

By mid-August the Germans had withdrawn from Sicily across the narrow Straits of Messina to mainland Italy. Taking all their remaining vehicles, guns, tanks and equipment with them, they avoided a bitter fight to the end. Coming so soon after the deposing of Mussolini, it may have left some Allied generals with a perception that the Germans had run away demoralized. Some thought that Rome could be taken by Christmas. Such daydreams would soon be brought back to a brutal reality.

On 3 September 1943 the first Allied invasion of mainland Europe proper began. General Montgomery's Eighth Army in Operation BAY-TOWN was the first to go, landing uncontested at Reggio di Calabria on the toe of Italy. The main attack would come a few days later. In a decision taken hastily after Mussolini's fall, General Mark Clark's Anglo-American Fifth Army would land thirty miles south of Naples near Salerno.

After occupying Reggio with no opposition, the 5th Division and 1st Canadian Division of Eighth Army's XIII Corps began to tackle Calabria's medieval roads and mountainous cart tracks. Ahead of them stretched the demolished sections of roads and hidden mines left by the retreating 29th Panzer Grenadier Division. All must be overcome before they could reach their first objective eighty miles away, the isthmus at Catanzaro.

On 9 September the Allied fleet carrying Fifth Army in Operation AVALANCHE sailed past the Amalfi Coast to its north and approached the Bay of Salerno. The Allies were taking a great risk. An initial force of only 55,000 men heading for Salerno compared unfavourably with the 160,000 in the Sicily landings.

The night before the Salerno landings, 8 September 1943, Eisenhower announced on radio the surrender by the new Italian Government led by Badoglio and the King. Hitler was furious at losing his major ally, and fearful that similar revolts could spread to other Axis countries, such as Hungary and Rumania. The Italians moved Mussolini from place to place, such as the islands of Ponza and La Maddalena, to keep his whereabouts secret. They feared that the Germans might attempt to rescue him and re-instate him as Italy's dictator. Meanwhile, for the Allied troops sailing through the night towards the Salerno beaches, news of Italy's surrender lulled some into a feeling that the invasion would be a walkover.

On the beaches south-east of Salerno the British X Corps of Lieutenant General Richard McCreery went ashore to the left of the River Sele with the aim of heading quickly up the road to Naples and Rome. On the River Sele's southern side the American VI Corps of Major General Dawley made landfall on the beaches directly beneath Paestum, founded by the Greeks in the sixth century BC. Some at the time hoped that one of Paestum's three remaining Doric temples, the Temple of Neptune, god of the sea, would bring the good fortune always necessary for a successful amphibious landing.

Field Marshal Kesselring believed the Allies had to land where they had air cover, and close to the port of Naples, making the beaches south of

Salerno the most likely place. The 16th Panzer Division had been ordered to dig in on the coastal plain, hemmed in by mountains either side of the River Sele, to defend the whole Gulf of Salerno. After escaping from Stalingrad with only 4,000 men, General Rudolf Sieckenius had rebuilt the Division to 17,000, and it was claimed to be the best equipped in Italy.

At first only small beachheads were gained against 16th Panzer, before Clark's Fifth Army came under ferocious counter-attack on 12 September from the Germans' Tenth Army under General Heinrich von Vietinghoff. Although Hitler had approved a strategy of gradual retreat to the Gustav Line south of Rome, Vietinghoff was under orders to first try and throw the Allies back. Defying more than 6,000 sorties flown by Allied aircraft from North Africa airfields and aircraft carriers, the Germans successfully brought in troops through the surrounding mountains from Naples and Calabria.

The British 46th and 56th Divisions, near Battipaglia and at Salerno beach itself, took the initial brunt of an attack by XIV Panzer Corps. In just the first two days Fifth Army suffered over 1,000 casualties. The strength of the German counter-attacks rocked the Allied troops, who had to fight desperately to get a little way inland. Vietinghoff sent his Panzers in a concentrated surge down the valley of the River Sele to exploit the boundary between the British X Corps and the US VI Corps. Such was the overall compression across the Allied salient from the German onslaught that Clark feared that the US VI Corps would be overrun.

On 11 September, however, when news came of the Salerno landings and the Allies' desperate fight to hold its fragile bridgehead, Montgomery ordered the 5th Division to speed north up the west coast to provide support. They reached Scalea on 14 September, having covered 150 miles in ten days. It seemed very slow to onlookers from afar. On the ground it was, as usual, quite different to staring at a map in HQ. As well as primitive winding roads, blown-up bridges and buried mines, the convoys had to overcome surprise ambushes by the elusive German rearguards.[2]

At Salerno on 12 September General Clark had moved his HQ ashore. However, such was the strength of the German counter-attack that just the next day, 13 September, Clark was preparing to evacuate and re-embark with his HQ staff. The Allies' Fifth Army was on the verge of panic and being thrown back into the sea.

Eisenhower had reported to London and Washington, 'I feel that AVALANCHE will be a matter of touch and go for the next few days.'[3] On Churchill's orders, General Alexander, commander of Allied Armies in Italy, sailed into Salerno Bay on the night of 14/15 September. Before dawn he was aboard the USS *Biscayne* listening to a briefing by Vice Admiral Kent Hewitt and his staff on withdrawal plans ordered by Clark. Alexander vetoed them, 'Oh no! We can't have anything like that.'[4] He and Hewitt then had breakfast with Clark in a tent on the beach. A subsequent private meeting between Alexander and Clark in the American General's personal trailer ended with new orders for Fifth Army to hold the bridgehead at all costs.

Norman Lewis of the British Field Security Service, but deployed with some US forces, told how:

> Chaos and confusion broke out on all sides. The story was that there had been a breakthrough by the 16th Panzer Division, which struck suddenly in our direction down the Battipaglia road, with the clear intention of reaching the sea at Paestum, wiping out the Fifth Army HQ, and cutting the beachhead in half. Rumours began to come in thick and fast, the most damaging one being that General Mark Clark was preparing to abandon the beachhead and had asked the Navy to plan for Fifth Army to be re-embarked.
>
> Outright panic now started, and spread among the American troops left behind. In the belief that our position had been infiltrated by German infantry they began to shoot each other, and there were blood-chilling screams from men hit by the bullets.[5]

Lewis recalled that in the panic such was the confusion and fear that American troops were instructed by some officers to club any German prisoners to death with their rifle butts. He also

> saw an ugly sight – a British officer interrogating an Italian civilian and repeatedly hitting him about the head with a chair, treatment which the Italian, his face a mask of blood, suffered with stoicism. At the end of the interrogation ... the officer called in a private and asked him ... 'Would you like to take this man away, and shoot him?' The private's reply was to spit on his hands, and say, 'I don't mind if I do sir.'[6]

A retreat from Salerno was too horrendous for the Allies to contemplate. Naval staff plainly stated that the troops could not be re-embarked. The landing craft had not been designed for embarking troops from beaches and any attempt to do so would result in a killing ground. It would isolate Montgomery's Eighth Army in Calabria and put them at serious risk of being driven back to Reggio. Stalin's demand for a second front in Europe would not be met and the planning for OVERLORD, the Normandy invasion, would be deferred. As Alexander had insisted, Fifth Army just had to prevail.

A naval bombardment by every ship, notably by the battleships HMS *Warspite* and HMS *Valiant* and the cruisers USS *Philadelphia* and USS *Boise*, was mounted. Waves of bombing sorties by B-17s, carrier-borne aircraft and supporting Spitfires of the Desert Air Force from Sicily were thrown at the German counter-attacks to avert disaster. The Luftwaffe fought back too, sinking the cruiser USS *Savannah* and crippling HMS *Warspite* with the first use of air-launched radio-controlled missiles.

Before Alexander had met with Clark on Paestum beach in the early morning of 15 September, he had approved the release of the 82nd US Airborne Division from Army Group Reserve to support the beachhead. On the night of 13/14 September, paratroopers of the 82nd had dropped into the American sector. Simultaneous with Alexander's arrival, the British 7th Armoured Division began landing to strengthen X Corps. Within these reinforcements from X Corps' reserve of infantry were some troops of the 1/6th East Surrey Battalion, who were drafted for their sister regiment the Queen's Royals (West Surrey). These were the first East Surrey troops to land and see action on the Italian mainland, although Jack Chaffer, the 'would-be' Surrey, was there with the 5th Grenadiers. Such was the crisis in the battle, even AA gunners within the reinforcements were converted to infantry as soon as they got ashore.

The combined effect of pouring in the reinforcements, the naval shelling, continual aerial bombardment, and the growing threat of Eighth Army support from the south forced the German Tenth Army on 17 September to pull back north to the Viktor Line. This line ran along the River Volturno north of Naples in the west and the River Biferno to the east which the Germans planned to hold until at least 15 October to give time for the Gustav Line south of Rome to be built before winter.

Allied casualties had grown to around 9,000 against the Germans' 3,500, but the Salerno bridgehead had survived.[7] The landings were secured but as the Royal Navy's Admiral Cunningham said, 'The assault had come very near to failure, and for a time the situation was precarious.'[8] It was an early sign of the bitter struggle for Italy that lay ahead.

*   *   *

While Eighth Army had diverted some forces to help at Salerno, their main body was expanding its offensive eastwards. Because of the Italian surrender, the British 1st Airborne Division were able to land by ship on 9 September, unopposed near the top of the instep of Italy's heel at Taranto. Despite their divisional commander being killed in their first contact with German forces on 11 September, 1st Airborne quickly secured the local airfield.

To exploit this early gain, a small force was quickly put together drawn from 1st Airborne, 56th Reconnaissance Regiment, The Royals, the 25-pounders of 17th Field Regiment, and some Sherman tanks of 3rd County of London Yeomanry. They pushed on up the Adriatic Coast to take Brindisi and Bari, and rushed towards the Foggia airfields. Despite firefights with residual units of the German 1st Parachute Division, by 27 September A Squadron The Royals and B Squadron 56 Recce were able to seize the airfields and clear out their German counterparts. Able to take heavy bombers, the Foggia airfields were seen as the highest priority for the Allied air forces. Washington and London rated them of immense strategic value, as they would allow the Allies' bombers to mount strikes on industry and infrastructure targets in northern Italy and southern Germany.

At the same time the movement of German troops into northern Italy was being accelerated, which only strengthened Field Marshal Kesselring's determination to fight and hold the Allies south of Rome. The Germans disarmed the Italian armed forces and requisitioned manpower and all necessary supplies by force.[9] The Italian capitulation had reinforced Hitler's resolve to rescue Mussolini and restore him as head of a Fascist government in Italy. Needing to counter the impression that the Axis was collapsing and show that he was still in control, Hitler sent General Kurt Student, commander of XI Parachute Corps, and an SS detachment under a Captain Skorzeny, to find and rescue Mussolini.

Following the German withdrawal from Salerno, and oblivious to Hitler's dilemma over the deposed Mussolini, Eighth Army quickened its advance through Taranto, which it was using as a base for moving up the Adriatic Coast. Between 19 and 29 September most of the 78th Division landed at Taranto with the 1st Surreys landing on the 23rd.

Lieutenant Woodhouse obviously found time to go shopping in the vicinity, and wrote home on 26 September:

My dear Mum,
    The towns out here have more in the shops than English ones have had for three years, silk stockings, hair cutting scissors, handkerchiefs by the box full. Very busy, and as the Germans look like going back 200–300 miles, will continue to be busy. I shall probably have champagne on my birthday.
    Lots of love to all from Italy, Jock.[10]

With the collaboration of the new Italian regime the Surreys then boarded a train north-bound to the port of Bari. The speed with which they were moving north seemed all too easy.

At the numerous unannounced stops along the track, many men could not resist jumping off to grab bunches of grapes from the wayside vineyards. After the footslogging of Tunisia and Sicily it was luxury, yet a luxury that would soon be forgotten. The German strategy was to gradually retreat up the Italian peninsula, by way of pre-prepared lines of defence, usually aligned with one of the many rivers or mountain ranges. They would choose when and where to make a stand to force the Allies to pay a high price for every advance.

At Bari, once they were in possession of motor transport, the Surreys in their 11 Brigade set off north again, towards their first objective, some

150 miles away on the Adriatic coast, Termoli. They were accompanied by 4 Armoured Brigade and 56 Recce, the reconnaissance regiment of 78th Division. Termoli's early capture by the Battleaxe Division was intended to provide cover for the seaborne landing of the Division's other two brigades, 36 and 38 (Irish). Although the plan was to occupy Termoli before the Germans could consolidate their line of defence, early winter rain was threatening to slow things down.

German troops were withdrawing in a coordinated, tactical manner to major defensive positions on the Viktor line along the Biferno River. It was also the route of one of the few east-west roads. The Battleaxe Division was tasked with crossing the Biferno and taking Termoli, which was the lynchpin to the eastern side of the Viktor Line. Its capture would outflank the Germans and force them to withdraw again to their next line of defence.

Engagements were unpredictable but continual, as the German rear-guards chose their places to fight, some supported by Luftwaffe air strikes. Mile after mile every road to the north had been cratered or demolished in chosen places by the retreating Germans. Every road crossed rivers too numerous to count. In the four miles between Serracapriola and Campo-marino on the road to Termoli every bridge had been blown up.

The devastated roads and frequent firefights meant that the Surreys were back to footslogging to deal with every obstacle and German ambush. 'I marched twenty-one miles on my twenty-first birthday, 29 September,' said Lieutenant Woodhouse. 'I was told to report to the CO that evening, where to my agreeable surprise the CO congratulated me "on coming of age" with a whisky!' Somehow the CO had found out his real age and that he had advanced it a year in order to enlist in March 1941.[11]

On 30 September Woodhouse had time to write once more:

My dear Mum,

I am near enough to my birthday to be still quite conscious of it. Foggia was captured that day too, so it was well marked. Now Naples appears to be almost ours and I think ... the Russians are hammering the life out of Germany so we shall be home before long!

The Germans aren't putting up much of a fight out here. I thought of you all at home ... and look forward to a really good time next year. I am very well and enjoying life. Italy is not a bad country at all. I will buy silk stockings for you and send them when I can, anyway you can have them when I come home.

All for now, Lots of love, from Jock.[12]

Even allowing for Woodhouse's natural optimism, the victories in Tunisia, Sicily, and the fast-paced advance from Taranto, had created some degree of euphoria.

It was to be short-lived. On 2 October leading troops of 78th Division were within a few miles of the Biferno River, a little to the south of the port of Termoli. Meanwhile the Surreys, with orders sending them up again into the hills, left the main force at Serracapriola. They began a fifteen-plus-mile climb to take Larino, a Molise hill town at a height of 1,119 feet in the foothills of the Monti dei Frontani, part of the Abruzzo mountain range, to secure the Division's western flank.

* * *

The Abruzzo and Molise Region stretches across the wild central hinterland of southern Italy, from north of L'Aquila around 100 miles north to south to the Biferno River valley. The Parco Nazionale d'Abruzzo, which was until the late-nineteenth century a royal hunting reserve, is one of Europe's finest nature and wildlife parks. Close to L'Aquila, the Abruzzo's snow-capped mountain ridge of Gran Sasso d'Italia holds Italy's highest mountain south of the Alps, Como Grande at 9,554 feet. Midway up Gran Sasso d'Italia is the Campo Imperatore, a flat plain that is home to wild horses and sheep in summer and ski resorts in winter.

In August 1943 a Gran Sasso resort was host to Mussolini's detention. When the SS Captain Skorzeny began to pursue Mussolini's trail, the new Italian regime transferred their former leader from house custody on the island of La Maddalena to the Gran Sasso's Hotel Imperatore. The King and Marshal Badoglio had plans to hand him over to the Allies and thought the hotel's remoteness offered greater security.

Three weeks before the battle for Termoli, the Germans launched a daring commando raid to capture Mussolini. A force of 120 paratroopers and SS commandos, led by Captain Skorzeny, landed in gliders next to the Gran Sasso's Hotel Imperatore. Mussolini's stunned Italian guards offered no resistance. Skorzeny grabbed Mussolini, shoved him into a small single-engined plane, and flew him back to their Luftwaffe base near Rome.

Two days later Mussolini flew to Rastenburg, the Wolf's Lair in East Prussia, to meet Hitler. By the end of September the ex-dictator was re-installed as *Duce*, head of an Italian puppet government in northern Italy based at Salo on Lake Garda. Hitler's message was clear – the Axis pact was still in place, and every inch of Italy would be defended. Battles like Salerno and Termoli were just the beginning.[13]

* * *

'We'd heard of Mussolini's arrest,' said Harry Skilton, 'but whether he was rescued or not, it meant nothing to us. We were climbing into the hills towards Larino, through rain, mud, destroyed bridges, and lost vehicles blown up by mines.'[14]

Sergeant Manning of the Surreys' HQ Intelligence recalled that:

The road before us had been mined and several bridges were demolished. Beginning our fourteen miles advance at six o'clock in the
morning we reached Ururi at three in the afternoon after a skirmish
with the enemy rearguard. On the way we lost a Bren carrier and an
anti-tank gun blown up on the mined road.[15]

The Surreys' Battle Patrol, led by Lieutenant Woodhouse, probed carefully
into the village of Ururi. As usual the fear was booby traps, mines, and
hidden German rearguards waiting in ambush. After some stealthy reconnaissance and contact with a few of Ururi's locals, it appeared the village
had been vacated very recently by the Germans. Woodhouse was surprised to find that they had left the telephones in working order so that
friendly villagers called their friends in Larino for information on the
Germans' whereabouts.[16]

Manning wrote that as they approached the fringe of the village:

Leading Bren carriers had the experience of entering one end of the
village almost as the last Germans left the other. The narrow village
street was crowded with inhabitants, who turned out to cheer and
stare at the first British troops they had ever seen. Two companies
pressed on through the village, hard on the heels of the retreating
enemy.[17]

To the west of Ururi, the hill town of Larino straddles the main east-west
road to Naples, about fifteen miles south-west of Termoli. It is said that
nearby in 217 BC the Roman General Fabian won a minor engagement
against Hannibal. Near to Piazza San Lorenzo, you can clearly see the
ruins of its Roman amphitheatre. It was built in the first century AD, and
could hold up to 12,000. Larino's cathedral, dating from the tenth century
AD and restored many times since then, is considered one of the finest
examples of Gothic architecture in Italy. Today Larino's population is
7,157, yet in 1656 it was virtually wiped out when 9,625 of some 10,000
citizens died of the plague. As the Surreys closed in on the German positions in October 1943, those Larino citizens remaining in their homes must
have wondered whether they might meet a similar fate.

The Surreys' orders seemed straightforward enough. They were to block
any German reinforcements coming from the west.

On 3 October Lieutenant Woodhouse led the Battle Patrol off at dawn
ahead of the battalion in the direction of Larino, with orders to find out
where the Germans were.

Fatally I was also told – 'Be careful, you may meet Canadians who are
somewhere on our left flank.' By 12.00 we had covered fifteen miles

and were near Larino. It was a country of low rolling hills, occasional farm houses, and olive groves. I halted the Battle Patrol in a small deserted house on a slight hill, posting a single sentry to observe a possible approach along a small stream. The sentry reported sighting a single man approaching along the stream. I looked and saw he was wearing a khaki drill shirt, similar to ours and the Canadians.

While his men took cover in the house, Woodhouse stepped outside and, through his binoculars, watched the man's approach. Something about the figure seemed suspicious.

The soldier in khaki drill stopped and while he did so we suddenly saw a platoon or more of German soldiers running through an olive grove with obvious intentions of getting behind us. Instantly I shouted 'Run for it!', and did so myself. This made for disaster, as I did not wait to see if the Battle Patrol followed. Only the Patrol Sergeant Bunting escaped with me.

In the race to put some distance between themselves and the German troops, Woodhouse became separated from Bunting. After finally reaching the cover of some trees, Woodhouse stopped. Why had his men not heeded his shouted orders and followed him? The enormity of what had happened hit him.

Hearing no sound of pursuit, after a mile or so, and having lost Sergeant Bunting, I slowly returned to the scene of the disaster, hoping against hope to find some of my soldiers. All was silent. They must have stayed where they were. Surrounded by the Germans and seeing no choice but death or surrender they must have chosen the latter.

I headed back to rejoin the battalion and report the loss of all of my patrol. This considerable catastrophe gets no mention in the regimental history! Various lessons became ingrained in my military character as a result. Take all possible precautions for all possible eventualities. Make sure there is always an emergency rendezvous known to every man. Never become over confident.[18]

This disastrous incident was reported somewhat differently in *The Surrey Comet* of 12 August 1944, presumably from official sources. It described the patrol being split into two parties and men becoming casualties or taken prisoner after firefights with the Germans.[19]

Lieutenant Woodhouse was correct to describe it as a catastrophe. Besides Woodhouse himself, the Battle Patrol comprised Sergeant Bunting, a corporal, a lance corporal and twelve men. Fifteen men had been lost, fifteen of the battalion's best and most experienced men. It speaks much for Woodhouse that, as the Battle Patrol leader, he was able to get over this, recognize his misjudgement and learn from it. Later that morning the Surreys' A and B Companies, forewarned by news of the loss of the Battle Patrol, climbed up towards the Larino ridge.

* * *

While the Surreys began the fight for Larino, the 2nd Lancashire Fusiliers headed north-east towards Termoli and waded across the Biferno River. Also on 3 October, at 2.00am 1 Special Service [Commando] Brigade, made up of 3 (Army) Commando and 40 (Royal Marine), and the Special Raiding Squadron, landed north of the Biferno's mouth close to Termoli's port. By 8.00am this force, under the command of 78th Division, had secured the harbour, penetrated the town and, in places, pushed out beyond its perimeter, seeking to make contact with the Lancashire Fusiliers. They were followed up in the evening of 3/4 October by another sea landing of 36 Brigade, who bulldozed shallow fords to drive vehicles across the Biferno.

Termoli now has a population of around 30,000. It lies on a slim promontory on the north side of the Biferno River. When you walk the old town you are drawn to its most prominent feature, Termoli Castle built in the eleventh century by the Norman King Robert I, then restored by Frederick II in the thirteenth century. The town retains its old walls, a twelfth-century cathedral, quaint streets and houses, many rebuilt and painted in a range of pastel shades. As you wander through the maze of narrow streets, there is always a glimpse of the sea, in summer a vivid blue against the ochre of an arch or a building's corner. To the north Termoli's fine beaches and resorts are often thronged with holiday-makers.

In October 1943 it was to be no holiday for the Battleaxe Division. On 3 October it began to rain. For eighteen hours it rained, bogging down the Division's supply vehicles.[20] The landings by the Special Service Brigade had forced a small German garrison force, *Kampfgruppe* Rau, to withdraw from the port and the town's approaches. However, some accounts have it that in and around Termoli there were also a few units of the 1st Parachute, 29th Panzer Grenadier and 26th Panzer Divisions, and that by nightfall on 3 October some Panzers had probed into parts of Termoli town, and in places were pressing to within a few hundred yards of the commandos' bridgehead. Hopes of an early occupation of Termoli in the face of low-level resistance were beginning to fade.

* * *

Allied intelligence also knew that the 16th Panzer Division was on the move towards Termoli. As soon as Kesselring had heard of the Allies' attack on Termoli he ordered 16th Panzer to move from the Volturno on the western side of Italy, to counter-attack the 78th Division from the north and west of Termoli.

A long range reconnaissance patrol in the mountains on Eighth Army's left flank, a unit known as Popski's Private Army (PPA), was camped in some woods near Castel Vetera at a height of around 2,000 feet in Val Fortore. Lieutenant Colonel Vladimir Peniakoff ('Popski') had founded the unit in North Africa and it was similar in role to the Long Range Desert Group or the present-day SAS. With their campsite and jeeps in amongst the trees and hidden from the road by a cluster of large boulders, they had settled down to a midday meal. When they heard the rumble of approaching tanks, they quickly doused their fire, then watched from cover. Peniakoff and his men waited, hardly daring a whisper to each other.

> There was nothing else we could do. Our fortress had no back door and we were trapped. Two German scout cars showed on the road and pushed on towards Castel Vetera. Ten minutes later they returned, stopping opposite our level patch of woods; one remained while the other drove down. Meanwhile the tanks had stopped out of sight; half an hour later we heard them grinding up. Time dragged on; a first tank came into view and was waved off the road into the wood by the men in the scout car; others followed clanking, to be dispersed to cover under the trees. By nightfall we had a squadron leaguered, somewhat uphill from our position, between us and the road. Just after dark more tanks arrived and these leaguered below us.[21]

Peniakoff was able to identify them as two squadrons of 16th Panzer. For the rest of the afternoon and evening Peniakoff and his men lay still and quiet, guns at the ready, expecting at any moment a German patrol to walk around the boulders that shielded them. But in that time Peniakoff came up with a daring plan to allow themselves to escape. Around 1.00am they crept as close as possible to each group of tanks, laid explosives with long fuses, then retraced their steps. Under cover of the detonations they drove their jeeps onto the road and escaped. In the ensuing confusion the Panzer squadrons even fired on each other. Later Peniakoff was able to radio in to the RAF the map references of the Panzers' position and, from not too far away, watched the air strikes go in. Peniakoff however was not able to verify that the two Panzer squadrons, which were only thirty to forty miles from Larino and Termoli, had been hit.

On 4 October the 8th Argylls and 6th Royal West Kents advanced north some five miles from Termoli along the coast road, Highway 16, aiming to capture the village of San Giacomo. A patrol of 56 Recce, probing north along the coast towards Pescara, captured a motorcyclist of 16th Panzer. It was the first firm and alarming evidence that forward units of 16th Panzer were in such close vicinity, and within striking distance of Termoli. The Argylls and 56 Recce withdrew to the brickworks near a road junction with the east-west Highway 17, and on their left the Lancashire Fusiliers and West Kents also dug in. Only four infantry battalions, two Commandos and some Special Forces were across the Biferno River. The infantry were on their own, cut off on the north side of the river. All that day and through the night of 4/5 October the four infantry battalions fought to hold on.

Despite rain, air strikes and the Surreys' battle at Larino, which were hindering the movement of German reinforcements, Montgomery was taking an uncharacteristic gamble to capture Termoli and break the Viktor Line. He had only part of the under-prepared 78th Division in position across the Biferno River. So although the counter-attack by 16th Panzer was not a total surprise, when it came in force, despite a slow build-up by the Germans, its strength and ferocity was a shock.

A torrid unequal battle, tanks versus exposed infantry, had commenced for Termoli. Devoid of armoured support, lacking anti-tank artillery and any reinforcements, the 78th Division infantry was being systematically killed, and pushed back all around the Termoli perimeter. A bulldozed ford over the Biferno did enable six Sherman tanks to cross, before it became a morass from the rain and flooding river. It achieved little as four of the Shermans were quickly destroyed by the Germans' superior Mark IV Panzers.[22]

During 5 October the Germans forced the defensive lines back to within a half mile of the town. The dead piled up and field surgeons called for more help. At one point two surgeons had operated on thirty wounded, and faced a line of eighty more stretcher cases.[23] Up against an armoured division, the Battleaxe infantry, whose experience had been gained in mountain warfare in Tunisia and Sicily, was facing annihilation or ignominious retreat.

*   *   *

When Lieutenant Woodhouse returned alone, and reported the total loss of the Battle Patrol in the early morning of 3 October, the Surreys knew what was in front of them. Major Roger Andrews led A Company and Major Peter Hill B Company in an assault on the ridge in front of Larino.

One of the platoons was led by a much-respected New Zealand officer, Lieutenant J.F. 'Chips' Louis, renowned for his toughness and aggressive patrolling. One of Louis' platoon, Private Lawrence Fish, recounted what happened:

With our platoons and sections in open order we advanced up the slope as daylight emerged. My platoon under Lieutenant Louis approached its objective, a farmhouse on the crest of the feature, when

85

we were suddenly engaged by machine-gun fire, and we rushed the building to find the Germans had left. We cleared the farmhouse, checked the immediate area and fanned out along the ridge, but we were not able to make any further progress for several days.[24]

The two companies' attack took over a number of German positions on the ridge before they had to dig in. Since German troops still occupied some higher ground on the ridge itself the two companies were exposed and stuck in a precarious position. Supplies could only be brought up at night, and the men had to scavenge. Corporal Busty Capon knew they were there to stay for some time, and quickly shot some escaped turkeys. Then he saw the pigs.

He killed and dressed one, hanging it in a fig tree to cure. It seemed however that the carcass was visible to the Germans, and we were subjected to showers of mortar fire whenever the carcass was approached. After dusk it was taken down and the cooking process commenced. Later that evening everybody got a mess-tin full of pork for supper which was very welcome, apart from the pieces of shrapnel with which it had been liberally peppered.[25]

The infantry were always hungry. Living off the land was essential to supplement a lack of rations, to sustain men's strength and will to keep fighting, and just to survive. 'We saw shooting wild or farm animals, chickens, goats, sheep, and even one time an ox,' said Frank Weston, 'as inevitable and necessary plunder of war for us to get by. I was often called on to use my butchering trade.'[26]

While the Surreys' A and B Companies were stuck on the forward ridge, the rest of the battalion was also spread out in exposed positions and under continuous shelling and mortaring. Sergeant Manning reported: 'When HQ transport at the head of the remainder of the battalion, itself came under machine gun and anti-tank gun fire as it moved along the narrow, white ribbon of road, we had to perform a rapid turnabout.'[27]

The Surreys' dispersed deployment made them very vulnerable to any concentrated attack. For the Surreys' CO, Lieutenant Colonel H.B.L. 'Harry' Smith, the lack of knowledge of the Germans' intentions must have been a gnawing concern. Surprisingly, he turned once again to Lieutenant Woodhouse.

On 5 October, perhaps to shake me out of depression, the CO ordered me to lead a daylight patrol of a section of the carrier platoon on foot, to see if a ridge in front of us was occupied. Advancing well spread out, we quickly came under fire and had to run back, speeded on our way by the familiar 'crack' of bullets just missing. Two men were hit but survived. This ended daylight patrols.

Woodhouse's opportunity to lead a patrol again, and obtain up-to-date re-connaissance information, was well timed. The same day the commander of XIII Corps, Lieutenant General Dempsey, paid the Surreys a visit.[28]

Dempsey met with the Surreys' CO, Lieutenant Colonel Smith, and forbade any attempt to attack the German positions so as to avoid any more risk of losing what was held. He impressed upon the Surreys that the Larino ridge had to be held at all cost. 'By containing the enemy at Larino, the Battalion is making a valuable contribution to the battle for Termoli, which is hanging dangerously in the balance.'[29] For Dempsey knew that the planned reinforcements of the Irish Brigade, supposedly in a convoy sailing towards Termoli, had to land during that night of 5/6 October, if 78th Division was to hold the bridgehead.

As the two officers walked past him, Private Harry Skilton in HQ Company saw the strain in Smith's face, and thought the Surreys' positions were hanging dangerously too.

> The worry was that if the Division's main forces were driven back from Termoli, we would be isolated, stuck out on a limb. And we knew from intelligence reports that some of 16th Panzer was moving in our direction and towards Termoli. If they sent only a few tanks to break through at Larino, without any armour or anti-tank guns of our own, we would be sitting ducks.[30]

If a German attack broke through the Surreys at Larino, it would paralyse 78th Division in its left flank and rear and cut all the overland supply routes from the south. This would isolate the Battleaxe battalions on the north side of the Biferno River, where they would be easily driven back by 16th Panzer and very likely destroyed.

Said Harry Skilton, 'Men continuously went down to constant mortar and sniper fire. We only knew that we had to hang on, for however long it took, and for all we knew it might be to the last man.'[31]

* * *

On the edge of Termoli itself, the Argylls and others made a brave but losing stand at the brickworks site to try and stem the German offensive. Before they were forced to withdraw on 5 October they lost more than 160 casualties. Among the seven officers killed was Major Jack Anderson, who had won a VC and inspired the Argylls and 1st Surreys in their memorable conquest of Longstop Hill in Tunisia. It was a tragic loss, yet a greater disaster now threatened.

To save the troops in the bridgehead across the Biferno, and have any chance of turning back 16th Panzer, the river had to be adequately bridged so that tanks could cross to support the infantry. Major Tom Buchanan, who had been with the Surreys in Tunisia, and was now commanding the

5th Northamptons, described the dilemma. 'Throughout the morning heavy rain fell, and the movement of transport became extremely difficult. The roads were treacherous, and the fields a sea of mud.'[32]

The fresh troops of the Irish Brigade had to come ashore that night into Termoli harbour as planned. Another day without getting tanks across the Biferno, and German Panzers could be rolling into Termoli town. This in turn would prevent any further reinforcements from the sea. Another twenty four hours without the influx of the Irish Brigade could see 78th Division forced back into a bloody retreat south across the Biferno River. It would mean a strategic defeat for Eighth Army and the Allies.

Notes

1. Annussek, *Hitler's Raid to Save Mussolini*, pp. 1–7.
2. Neillands, *8th Army, From the Western Desert to the Alps, 1939–1945*, pp. 276–304.
3. Atkinson, op cit., p. 214.
4. Ibid, p. 231.
5. Lewis, *Naples '44*, pp. 8–10.
6. Ibid, pp. 13–14.
7. Atkinson, op cit., p. 236.
8. Cunningham, *A Sailor's Odyssey*, p. 571.
9. Porch, *Hitler's Mediterranean Gamble*, p. 507.
10. Veterans' Accounts, Woodhouse, *Memoirs*, p. 17.
11. Ibid.
12. Ibid.
13. Annussek, op cit., pp. 1–7.
14. Veterans' Accounts, Skilton.
15. Manning, The Surrey History Centre, *The Surrey Comet*, 12 August 1943.
16. Squire, and Hill, op cit., pp. 14–18, The Queen's Royal Surrey Regiment Museum, March 1992.
17. Manning, op cit.
18. Veterans' Accounts, Woodhouse, *Memoirs*, p. 17.
19. The Surrey History Centre, ESR/25/PAYN/8.
20. Ray, op cit., p. 86.
21. Peniakoff, *Private Army*, pp. 386–9.
22. Ray, op cit., p. 88.
23. Ford, op cit., p. 125.
24. Squire and Hill, op cit., p. 18, The Queen's Royal Surrey Regiment Museum, March 1992.
25. Ibid.
26. Veterans' Accounts, Weston.
27. Manning, op cit.
28. Veterans' Accounts, Woodhouse, *Memoirs* p. 17.
29. Daniell, op cit., p. 188.
30. Veterans' Accounts, Skilton.
31. Ibid.
32. The Surrey History Centre, Buchanan, op cit.

Chapter 6

Across the Trigno and Sangro Rivers: To the Winter Line

On 5 October the battle for Termoli teetered at a tipping point. Despite the persistent rain, a Bailey bridge over the Biferno River was finally completed during the afternoon and some tanks began moving across. Together with support from the 5th Buffs and some strikes by fighters from the Desert Air Force, the tanks pushed out to link up with the 2nd Lancashire Fusiliers. But there was no additional support for the Surreys at Larino.

As night fell the critical reinforcements of the Irish Brigade began coming ashore into Termoli, though not as they had anticipated into a secure bridgehead. The three battalions, the 6th Royal Inniskilling Fusiliers, the 1st Royal Irish Fusiliers and the 2nd London Irish Rifles were thrown into desperate street fighting, heavy shelling and a burning town under siege. Major B.H. Westcott, commander of H Company, London Irish Rifles received a traumatic welcome he never forgot.

Under fire, and in the dark and chaos of Termoli's congested, narrow streets, the Irish Rifles and Major Westcott struggled to find their designated assembly point. Westcott's orders were to lead H Company to the town's northern edge and gain positions in a cemetery and some nearby high ground. A dawn attack by Stuka dive-bombers only made things worse.

In time they got away, dealt with minor resistance en route, and soon came upon the cemetery. Westcott turned his back to the graveyard, and began to direct deployment of his men. Suddenly his body was twisted half-around, like a puppet, and hit the ground. From about twenty-five yards distance, a German sniper hiding in the cemetery had shot him in the back. Westcott's first thought was that someone with a wrecking hammer had pole-axed him.

> The bullet entered my left shoulder and then into my chest, deflating my left lung. It then hit my rib-cage, four ribs broken, ricocheted off my ribs and exited from the middle of my back about a quarter-inch

from my spine. The date of my wounding was 6 October 1943, which was Val's birthday – so for all the wrong reasons I am one of the few husbands who never forgets his wife's birthday![1]

That date, 6 October, was to be decisive for everyone, for the Irish Brigade was the Battleaxe Division's last card. The attack by 16th Panzer came to a climax with support from Panzergrenadiers, who broke through the lines in a number of places. In a desperate and chaotic battle to hold them back, the Lancashire Fusiliers and the Argylls resorted to bayonet charges. Behind the lines the 138th Field Regiment Royal Artillery kept up their fire on the Panzers, eventually bringing down their range to a record low of only 750 yards.

Yet the new troops of the Irish Brigade were feeding through to the front lines and began to make a difference. Approaching midday the Irish battalions' counter-attacks, with the support of artillery and some eighty Canadian tanks, were forcing the Panzers to pull back. By 13.00 hours they had recaptured the brickworks and its nearby road junction. On the extreme western flank by 17.00 hours the Inniskillings gained San Giacomo and a little later the London Irish had gone north along the coast road and reached across the River Sinacre.

Next day 16th Panzer were in full withdrawal to the north. The insertion of the Irish Brigade's fresh troops had turned the battle at the eleventh hour. By this time at Larino the Surreys' casualties had risen to seventy-one, including Captain P.H.G. Smith killed. Yet they still held those same positions on the Larino ridge. The stubborn fight by 78th Division for Termoli over nearly a week, and not least the Surreys' blocking of the south-west flank at Larino, had made the victory possible. Two Surreys' stretcher bearers, Corporal Stanley Kemp and Private Frederick Ramsey, were awarded the Military Medal for bringing in the wounded under fire.

On 8 October the Germans also withdrew from Larino and the Surreys went in to receive a joyous welcome from the townsfolk.

In contrast the Surreys' Lieutenant Woodhouse was still feeling dejected. Only a few days since he had lost all fourteen men of his Battle Patrol, he wrote to his father:

My dear Dad,
It is a long time since I last wrote and I feel it may be some time before I write again. It has been a week of continual heavy showers, usually at night. In this depressing weather further depression came upon me as my old command is no more just now. This was a tremendous blow to me, and I had a further unpleasant show two days later ..., so I am now back reading and writing ....
Ever your loving son, Jock.[2]

With the fall of Termoli and the Viktor Line broken, the gamble had paid off, and so enabled Eighth Army to consolidate on a latitude parallel with Rome. The Battleaxe Division had come through again, but they had been lucky. To their north lay a country of river upon river, and an enemy who had withdrawn with his forces intact. Could they still be in Rome by Christmas?

*   *   *

The Sangro River is born in the wild mountains of Italy's premier national park, the Parco Nazionale d' Abruzzo, from where it cleaves a broad valley down to the Adriatic Sea. Around a third of the territory of the central and eastern regions of Abruzzo and Molise is taken up by the Maiella, Gran Sasso and Abruzzo National Parks.

In the spring a visitor to the Abruzzo National Park sees the most diverse of the three parks, ablaze with the colour of more than 1,000 species of trees and wildflowers. If you are lucky you may catch sight of the few remaining Marsican bears and Apennine wolves. Much more numerous are the roe deer, red deer, wild boar and Apennine chamois. Around two thirds of the parks are heavily wooded, a haven for more than 300 bird species, and there are still some golden eagles.

The Abruzzo's Apennine mountains reach up to the 9,560 feet of the Corne Grande in the Gran Sasso massif. Home to Europe's southernmost glacier, Il Calderone, the mountains are said to sometimes have more snow than the Alps and feed many rivers, such as the Biferno, the Trigno and the Sangro, which flow down to some 120 miles of Adriatic coastline. About thirty miles from the coast the Sangro River now enters the man-made Lake Bomba, which is a magnet for summer watersports or for many to sit and watch the crimson sunsets. Perhaps most important, Lake Bomba's post-war damming has prevented the regular flooding in the Sangro valley's coastal region.

Over recent years the Abruzzo has been one of the fastest growing regions in southern Italy, with rapid increases in industrialization and tourism. In the autumn and winter of 1943 the Abruzzo's wilderness areas were much more untamed. While the forests' leaves turned red, the rivers ran amok.

*   *   *

On the Biferno River at Termoli, and at Larino, Eighth Army had only narrowly avoided a catastrophic disaster. In the first real battle in their advance from Reggio they had risked throwing forward only the 78th Battleaxe Division, with a commando brigade and some armour, and came up against the first of the Germans' pre-prepared defensive lines. Just as they had been on their own in the Western Desert of North Africa

91

until Operation TORCH, on Italy's Adriatic coast Eighth Army were now masters of their own destiny.

The spine of the Apennines separated them from General Clark's Fifth Army on the west coast. There were very few east-west roads, and in any case these became near impassable in the rain, mud, ice and snow of winter. From here on the Germans would stand and fight on every one of the innumerable rivers and lateral dorsals which led down to the Mediterranean and Adriatic coastlines. All the way to the Alps the terrain was perfect for defenders.[3]

Although German forces had withdrawn northwards to the Trigno River, for two weeks Montgomery insisted on building up reinforcements, matériel and transport and would not allow any major advance. The fragmented approach of the offensive at Termoli that had led nearly to a defeat was not to be repeated. It was obvious that the Germans would be entrenched and waiting, like crocodiles, on the north side of the Trigno River, some fifteen miles up the coast.

The forward patrols pushing out from Termoli continually came up against fierce ambushes and traps laid by the German rearguards, who often sent patrols forward with one or two tanks. Sergeant Manning described the German operations:

> About eight to twelve infantry would work through the crops rather like a pack of hounds, supported by a tank which remained in hull down position at about 100 to 150 yards distance. As soon as the German infantry came under fire, the tank would open up with long bursts of MG [machine-gun] fire, while the infantry withdrew.
>
> On two occasions the enemy attacked with fighting patrols of fifty to eighty infantry, working through an orchard and covered by as many as three to five tanks. These attacks both took place just after first light. One tank worked ahead of the infantry, while the remainder lay back.
>
> On encountering opposition, or a locality thought to be occupied, the tanks fired bursts of MG at random, presumably to draw fire and thus discover our positions. When no fire replied, they immediately sheered off at a distance. Owing to bad light it was impossible for our anti-tank guns to fire a shot. A concentration of forward artillery was then brought down on them, which caused them to immediately withdraw.[4]

Harry Skilton was in a Surreys' platoon, when it was attacked by three tanks:

> Two Mk IV tanks, first from hulldown position, opened fire on us with machine guns from a range of 400 yards. Still firing, they then came

within about 200 yards from us. Then the third tank came in between the two others, more or less right up to our positions where we were dug in, and directed a spray from a flame-thrower at us.

We were firing both machine guns and Brens at the German tanks, but it did not seem to have any effect. One of our mortar men managed to get off a PIAT anti-tank round, but then he was burned by the flame-thrower. Not sure if he hit a tank, but it must have been enough, because they withdrew, and we did not have to leave our trenches.[5]

On 19/20 October came Eighth Army's most northerly penetration, when the London Irish Rifles assaulted a high ridge and the town of Petacciato. After its capture they looked down into the Trigno valley. The Trigno River was only three miles away.[6] Around the same time, after moving on from Larino north along the coast road, the 1st Surreys established the right flank of 78th Division on the estuary mouth of the Trigno.

* * *

Shortly before they reached the Trigno, on 16 October, the 1st Surreys' CO, Lieutenant Colonel H.B.L. Smith, formed a new Battle Patrol. Despite the catastrophic loss of fourteen men under his command at Larino, and his consequent despondency, Lieutenant Woodhouse was made its leader. He remembered that:

Understandably there was hardly a rush to volunteer! As the division slogged its way across river defence lines, we went out always at night, as a series of recce and fighting patrols. We tended to operate in patrols of four men, linking two four-men patrols when more recce was required. Training, as well as practice, made us more effective than patrols made up by the rifle companies, where patrols differed in their composition from night to night.

All the 78th Division battalions' battle patrols were given authority to wear the 78th Divisional sign – a yellow battle axe on a black background – over the left breast pocket. All other soldiers wore the divisional signs on the upper sleeves of battledress uniform. This distinction of the Battle Patrol made us proud to be members of what we considered to be an 'elite' group.[7]

While Lieutenant Woodhouse saw his Battle Patrol as an elite group, the Surreys' Captain Toby Taylor viewed them from a somewhat different perspective: 'The Battle Patrol was now a permanent part of the Battalion. It consisted of all the roughs and toughs – the men who in peacetime did not make particularly good soldiers, but in these conditions were invaluable.'[8]

* * *

93

Early on 23 October some infantry units of the Irish Brigade and the Lancashire Fusiliers waded across the Trigno's upper reaches. The river was wide but not much more than ankle deep.[9] They picked their way through the heavily-mined valley floor and hurried to dig in near some woods. North of the wooded and undulating plain lay the San Salvo ridge and Vineyard Hill close to the town of Cupello. From this high point between the Trigno and Sangro Rivers, the Germans shelled the probing infantry.[10]

Yet again following their pull back from Termoli to avoid heavy losses, the 16th Panzer Division was occupying that high ground. They were in front of San Salvo and in well-prepared defensive positions. From there the Germans scanned the marshy and heavily-mined valley below, like eagles searching for any movement that would betray their prey.[11]

Soon after those first crossings of the Trigno, on the night of 23 October, two companies from the Surreys waded across the deeper water of the river's estuary. They dug in straddling the railway line within a mile of German troops who held the San Salvo railway station. For the next week patrols struck out every night seeking the enemy's dispositions.[12]

'One of the more bizarre patrols at this time,' said Lieutenant Woodhouse, 'was to a hut behind the German lines to meet a Scots woman with information for us. It was difficult to concentrate, while wondering if it was a trap, and half expecting to be rudely interrupted by the Germans.'[13]

Later Woodhouse would recruit the woman's Italian husband, Dr Guido Fano from the surrendered Italian army, as an interpreter and guide.

Rain became incessant, preventing supplies getting through and hindering the build-up of forces. What supplies could get through also came at night, often by the amphibious DUKW vehicles. During the day the Surreys hunkered down, some in scattered houses or in any cover they could find, to avoid being targeted by the German artillery.[14] The troops were continually freezing cold, and wet from either wading rivers or the constant rain. It was misery, with the continual fear and premonition of the next shell or bullet.

Frank Weston found it painful to think back to those times, 'It was hell, we lived like animals, cold, wet, mud everywhere, our feet, socks and boots always sodden. The Trigno and Sangro battles were the first real hard slog, the first of the big battles in Italy.'[15]

Sergeant Gostling of the Surreys' HQ Company had similar feelings, and wrote another letter to the hospitalized Captain Payne:

My dear Captain Payne,
   We are once again in this wretched and horrible country Italy. The rain hasn't stopped for more than an hour since we have been here, and I really think this is the worst country in the world for rain,

including Manchester! The mud is over a foot deep in places and everything is well under it. I understand that up at the front the Yanks are firing their guns until they have embedded themselves right into the mud, and then they cover them up with earth, or more mud, and go and draw up some new ones.[16]

Cyril Ray, however, observed how the deterioration in the weather came as no surprise to the local inhabitants, who were used to the hard winters.

Before the end of October they were wearing fur caps and great black woollen cloaks. There was snow on the hills by then, grey skies, bitter winds, and drenching rain. Seventy-eighth Division was soon hung with mufflers, greatcoats, and leather jerkins, and the RASC brought up, just in time, new battledress, woollen underclothes, great-coats and gum-boots. There was even a rum ration for some of the luckier night patrols. Before the end of October radiators were being drained at night.[17]

Nevertheless, the weather and the enemy had to be overcome before the full force of winter bore down. On the night of 27/28 October the Irish Brigade launched an attack to take San Salvo. A preceding artillery barrage was countered by German shelling and mortar fire, with fatal precision against the advancing Irish. As they were to begin their climb up the San Salvo ridge, the Royal Irish Fusiliers lost their CO, Lieutenant Colonel Beauchamp Butler, and their two company commanders, all three killed. If that was not bad enough, all of the Fusiliers' platoon commanders were either killed or wounded. The London Irish also lost several officers. Despite digging in, the Irish battalions were forced to withdraw at first light. For a week, while more reinforcements were brought up, Eighth Army had to resort to night patrols and hold on.

Before attempting another offensive, there was a need to confuse the Germans and deceive them as to where the next attack would be. A number of diversionary attacks, and bombardments by artillery, air strikes and naval shelling, were mounted on Vasto and Cupello, the towns north of San Salvo. The naval shelling's objective was to make the Germans think there might be an amphibious attack farther up the coast. Could the deception work? Before dawn on 3 November, 36 Brigade launched 78th Division's main attack on San Salvo.

Even with hindsight no one can say whether the deception tactics were successful, and certainly not at the time. For two days the Battleaxe battalions fought back and forth through San Salvo's streets.[18] At one stage in a frontal attack on San Salvo railway station, the Lancashire Fusiliers became bogged down all day. The 1st Surreys were called forward, and when they began a flanking attack on the station the Germans finally withdrew.

With barely a pause the Surreys and their Lancashire comrades began an overnight march, a further five miles inland to the small town of Cupello. There, before dawn on 4 November, the Surreys' B and C Companies attacked and overran outlying enemy positions. By 10.00am Cupello was occupied.[19] In the midst of the fighting the Surreys' stretcher bearers were again fearless in recovering casualties, this time Privates Frederick Poll and Harold Merritt, who were each awarded the Military Medal.[20]

As the Surreys made camp for the night, and brewed up in Cupello, a most bizarre and amazing coincidence took place. The camp sentries challenged two figures emerging out of the darkness. The two men appeared to be bedraggled civilians, shuffling forward with their hands in the air and shouting excitedly in English. One of the sentries realized suddenly who they were. It was unbelievable.

Lieutenant H. 'Crabbers' Crabtree, the Battalion's Mortar Platoon commander, and Corporal Salmon, both taken prisoner in North Africa, had escaped from a prison camp in Italy. Disguised as Italians, they had walked through the German lines, somehow avoided recapture, and arrived by sheer chance back with the Surreys. It was stranger than fiction, and it must have seemed that fortune was trying to make good those awful losses in Tunisia.[21]

While 78th Division expanded the bridgehead, forcing the German forces back towards Vasto, further upstream the 8th Indian Division made another crossing of the Trigno. Both divisions now concentrated their assaults to take Vasto and other towns and villages. The pressure built so that there was no choice but for 16th Panzer to retreat.[22] But again it was controlled. Just as it was at Termoli, the Surreys would find that the German withdrawal was not all that it seemed.

* * *

In pursuit the northward drive pushed on from the Trigno across innumerable high ridges. Two more rivers were forded, the Sinello and the Osento, both uncontested.[23] On 8 November the Surreys reached the hill town of Paglieta where they looked down into the wide Sangro River valley. It was already a case of déjà vu, but yet again it sickened their stomachs. Both of the main bridges, on the railway line near the coast and on Highway 16 further inland, were destroyed. The last of the German rearguards and demolition parties were in full view, leisurely crossing to the river's north bank to take up their next defensive positions. Without their artillery support the Surreys could only watch, and try not to think of the next battle.[24]

And they could see that a fearful battle loomed. On the Sangro's far side the estuary plain, in some places two miles in width, stretched away to the escarpment that hid the next German defences. Farther back there rose up snow-capped mountains, the real goal of the retreating Germans. The rain fell continually, river levels rose and flooded the valleys, and mud was everywhere. In places the Sangro was around six feet deep and 100 yards wide. The cold bit deeper.[25] As the freezing rain seeped from sodden clothes into the men's bones, so did the real meaning of Kesselring's Winter Line.

'There was snow on the hills, grey skies, bitter winds, drenching rain and winter clothing was already appearing,' recalled Lance Corporal Jim Farrell, a driver with RASC. 'So much for sunny Italy!'[26] Everyone gradually realized the awful truth. As the Germans had planned it, Eighth Army had reached the Winter Line just at the time its name implied.

Although the Allies had a favourable ratio of fourteen divisions to the Germans' nine across the Winter Line, the separation of Fifth and Eighth Armies by the central mountains prevented the concentration needed to gain a decisive breakthrough. The Winter Line was actually a series of lines, or defensive positions, that stretched across Italy at its narrowest width of eighty-five miles, from along the Garigliano River through Cassino in the west, over the central Apennine mountains, and then along the Sangro River to the Adriatic Sea. The Germans' defensive strategy was favoured by the winter weather and terrain, and their ability to draw upon another fourteen divisions north of Rome for reinforcements when needed.[27]

The Winter Line had been built by forced labour in some places up to twenty miles in depth, and in some stretches as here with the Sangro, it only began some way north from the river. The Germans were in possession of concrete pillboxes, machine-gun pits, reinforced farmhouses, and countless miles of barbed wire, hills, mountains and rivers. Field Marshal Kesselring's orders from Hitler were no longer to fight rearguard actions followed by withdrawals but here, at the Winter Line, to bring the Allies to a shuddering halt.

As well as establishing positions at Pagliete, the Surreys, together with the Lancashire Fusiliers, also occupied the village of Torino and put an observation post on Monte Calvo from where they could look down on the Sangro. The approach to the river and its crossing were going to need careful planning. Opposing 78th Division on the other side were the Germans' 65th Infantry Division, and their continual foe, 16th Panzer Division. The other enemies, rain, sleet, icy winds and mud, were becoming ever present. In a different way they sometimes seemed worse. When it deluged in the mountains the river level could quickly change from one to six feet and, as it neared the estuary, flood to 200 yards wide.

Patrols were put across the river every night as there was no cover for daylight operations. German patrols aggressively contested this no man's land, but their main strategy was to wait in their concrete emplacements and bunkers in and around the villages of Mozzagrogna, Fossacésia and Santa Maria, on top of the ridge some two miles away.[28]

Night after night from Paglieta the Surreys' patrols waded across the Sangro River holding on to low-slung ropes. On one night the Surreys' Battle Patrol, led as always by Lieutenant Woodhouse, infiltrated the German-held railway station.

On 14 November I led the Battle Patrol at full strength on an eight-mile patrol through the German front to Piazzano Station. We had the help of an Italian ex-officer of their Alpine troops, Dr Guido Fano, who had joined the battalion as an interpreter.

Over an open field we approached a small cluster of houses, finally coming to a deep ditch between us and the first house. We watched carefully for signs of an outside sentry. We had been ordered to take a prisoner. Then after a time we crossed the ditch and waited just outside the house. A German soldier appeared on a path leading to the house. Without a sound we grabbed him and he stayed silent.

With their adrenalin racing, Woodhouse and his men then pushed their luck even further. There was no noise coming from any of the houses, so maybe the rest of the Germans were asleep. It was too tempting to leave them in such comfort.

Between us we split up some captured German explosive charges, which we carried, placing them on the shuttered windows of the house, and on an armoured vehicle.

They crept away as quietly as they could, hearts in their mouths when someone's foot crunched on a twig. When the explosions shattered the calm of the night they ran, hoping to God they were heading back the way they came.

We made a fast escape with our prisoner keeping up, in spite of wearing his greatcoat. The eight miles back to Paglieta took just over three hours, returning at about 0400 hours with no casualties. Unlike the carefree approach to the disaster at Larino, I now spent many hours in particular in planning and, if possible, rehearsal.[29]

For this raid and similar previous actions Lieutenant Woodhouse received the Military Cross, and Lance Corporal Leonard Wood the Military Medal.

Of course many patrols did not end so well. One night a large patrol of eighty or so of the Royal West Kents led by a Major Denis Forman set out to destroy a German strongpoint known as 'The Red House'.

In complete darkness on a cold November night, they waded the chest-high waters of the Sangro. Despite temperatures only just above freezing, all assembled on the far side. In the initial attack two men were killed and four seriously wounded. Forman split the patrol in two, so that with one group he could withdraw with the wounded. The firefight intensified, with the result that only eighteen men out of the thirty-eight in his group survived.

When reporting on his attempt to bring back his wounded men, Major Forman said:

> Of course, I should have left them. It was a fatal misjudgement – but I just couldn't do it. They had been the ones out in front, they were screaming 'Don't leave us,' they relied on us to get them out .... But if we had buggered off as soon as we had chased the Germans out, we would have lost no more men, come back with several prisoners and done everything we had set out to do.
>
> By trying to save four wounded men, I must have killed twice as many and allowed the attack to end up as a rout.

Major Forman later recounted how the official history described the patrol as a great success, and glossed over the loss. 'But you can't fool the soldiers in the field. From that day on the gully in the escarpment with the Red Farm at its base was known throughout the Division as Forman's Folly.'[30]

Despite the atrocious conditions and losses in the fight to cross the Sangro, on 12 November Lieutenant Woodhouse wrote home in his usual buoyant, matter-of-fact style:

> My dear Dad,
>
> I suppose I have done thirty or more operational jobs since I landed in Africa, and have developed a technique and almost a sixth sense about the business. It is the only part of war that appeals to me as truly an art of war. Strategy is presumably an art to a certain degree, but tactics seem to me to be very stereotyped, and attack and defence is just a matter of will and weapon power.
>
> I have a bed and slept right through the night of 10/11th, first full night for two weeks.
>
> After seeing one or two places in Italy and Sicily, I doubt if air attack can do any more than they are doing to help us win. Close support by medium bombers has devastating results as we saw at Massicault, and to a lesser degree out here and in Sicily.
>
> Ever your loving son, Jock

To his mother Woodhouse describes Paglieta as if it was a holiday resort:

> My dear Mum,
>
> Now I am in a lovely little town, Paglieta, high up over a river, and we are being splendidly looked after. I have a bed with sheets in a

house, and a little dining room where I preside over our own little mess of five men from HQ. I have my old platoon as well as my HQ job to do so life is very full.

But never since we left England have we had a better time, nor have I ever felt so well.

Paglieta is only lightly damaged, and I have my old 10 Platoon billeted with me, a bed with sheets …. In the morning I read the weekly 'Times' up to 25 September …. write, walk around the town, make a plan for a patrol, and read the divisional intelligence summary. We have a drink with local English speaking Italians …

Owing to heavy rain our food couldn't come up for the day of your birthday, but this is what we had:

Breakfast – Fried bread, fried eggs, tomatoes, with chips.

Luncheon – Roast chicken, lamb cutlets, fried potatoes, peas, flapjacks, melon and apple, and vino.

Dinner – Spaghetti and tomato casserole, fried potatoes, bread, fruit, and vino.

Not so bad, so I celebrated your birthday too!

Afternoon walk, sleep, buy eggs and apples. Then visit B Company commander for talk, mostly 'shop' and personalities …

That is the sort of day I have here …. Some nights of course there is work to be done – patrols.

Love to all, Jock.

But his mother would not have missed the veiled significance of his last sentence. Woodhouse himself commented, 'This exceptionally easy time was written with an eye to my mum's morale. All my letters were cheerful and optimistic.'[31]

* * *

While the Surreys were at Paglieta, Montgomery came forward to survey the Sangro and assess the challenge of fighting a way across it. Frank Weston remembered him stopping on the road:

We were trudging along in the mud, cold, wet and thoroughly brassed off. We called out, 'Give us a V, Monty!' The 'Vs' were horrible Egyptian cigarettes that Monty often handed out. Monty obliged and called us over to his truck, he was standing on the back of it. He spoke to us for some time, giving us praise and telling us what a fine job we were doing. Then we trudged on.[32]

Although Montgomery was popular with the troops, they were clearly not fooled by his apparent largesse and confident pep talks.

So what was the result of Monty's reconnaissance? According to a regimental history:

What was seen was a wide river bed of many channels with a steep bank on our side, a plain on the other side about a mile in width and then an escarpment about 150 feet high. Beyond the escarpment there was higher ground still. The approaches to the river were muddy and treacherous and the bridges blown. The river bed itself was about 400 feet across.[33]

Over the escarpment the Germans watched and waited. The plain was heavily mined and the Germans could direct their fire at any movement. The Allies still harboured a vague hope of taking Rome before Christmas, so the Winter Line had to be breached. The goal was Pescara from where Eighth Army could move west to support Fifth Army in an offensive on Rome. Montgomery ordered that the crossing had to be made close to the coast so as to exploit Highway 16.[34]

Despite the difficulties Montgomery expected 78th Division to somehow force the Sangro crossing. As always for river crossings, the efforts of the Royal Engineers were indispensable. One of their Bailey bridges over the Sangro, at 1,126 feet (343 metres), was one of the longest spans ever built in all campaigns.

Sergeant Eric Garner of the Royal Engineers remembered that

the Sangro was a 78th Division battle .... The critical point was to secure and bridge the passage of Route 16, the only road in the region capable of handling a full division. About 1,000 feet of bridge and abutments had been blown, and the whole area was mined and under artillery observation. On 21 November five battalions of 78th Division crossed the river and we got a 140-foot Bailey across the main stream. On the next day 4 Armoured Brigade and 11 Infantry Brigade got over, and then the river rose and the Bailey bridge submerged.[35]

Despite these forces managing to build a fragile bridgehead on the north side, casualties were high, and more armour and troops had to cross. The need for more tanks was critical. It became a nightly dogfight as patrols from both sides fought to eliminate each other, and tried to keep below ground during the day. The Eighth Army troops in the bridgehead had to hang on, and pray for the rain to stop and more reinforcements to somehow join them.

Once again the Surreys were thrown into wading across another river estuary. Late in the day on 24 November, to reinforce the bridgehead, the Surreys struggled through the Sangro's flooding water. Rather than the constant danger of being hit by enemy shelling, on foot, in the dark, and weighed down by their kit, the threat was drowning or even hypothermia

101

in the freezing cold water. Against currents running at seven knots, which on the shorter men were waist to chest height, one man could carry only a day's rations, small arms and a little ammunition.[36] Once ashore on the extreme right of 78th Division and close to the sea, they pushed forward to dig in not far below the Germans' lines on the Fossacésia Ridge.

Re-supplying the infantry battalions on the north side of the Sangro became tortuous to the extreme. Heavy rain for two days caused the river to keep rising and, on the approach routes, vehicles ground to a halt in the mud. Again it was mule trains that brought forward supplies, first to the Sangro's mouth, then transferred to DUKW amphibious craft to make night crossings. On the far bank, where there were no mules, it was the odd jeep and just plain manhandling.[37]

'Our rations could not get through,' said Harry Skilton, 'and we went for maybe a week without even a brew of tea. In our holes in the ground, whether awake or in snatches of kip, we were sodden all the time.'[38]

Lieutenant Woodhouse led several recce patrols up to the German trenches.

> In constant fear of mines from which the battalion suffered many casualties, I nearly always led the short range patrols, since it was impossible to direct the leading scout in the dark. My own eyes and ears were my best protection. Our bridgehead was supplied by amphibious trucks (DUKWs), and we were encouraged by the two destroyers of the Royal Navy, who added their gunfire to the divisional artillery, and medium bombers of the RAF.[39]

* * *

Fresh troops of the Battleaxe Division were gradually brought across the river into the bridgehead on the Surreys' left flank. Yet repeated thrusts at the German lines were thrown back. Then the rain eased and the river level began to fall so that on 27 November more armour was able to begin using the Bailey bridge again. Now the build-up accelerated. A massive bombardment was launched with artillery, air strikes and naval guns off the coast, until, on 29 November, 38 Irish Brigade with tanks in support broke through to take the villages of Santa Maria and Fossacésia. To distract the Germans from the concentrated Irish spearhead, the Surreys simultaneously mounted a diversionary attack.

The momentum then built so that by the end of December's first week the Allies were well established on the north side of the Sangro. Montgomery wrote in his report to London:

> In spite of continuous rain and acres of mud I managed to get a good bridgehead over the Sangro; the trouble was to get my tanks and supporting weapons over, as the river was in flood and low level

102

bridges merely disappeared. I took a good few risks. Twice I was pushed back to the river – once on my right, and once on my left. But we came again and refused to admit it couldn't be done. The troops were quite magnificent, and in the most foul conditions you can ever imagine; the Sangro normally is about eighty feet wide, and it became swollen to 300 feet and rose several feet; the water was icy cold as heavy snow fell in the mountains where the river rises. Many were drowned. Eventually we succeeded.[40]

The Winter Line had been pierced but not broken. The next German fortresses were Orsogna in the mountains, and Ortona on the Adriatic coast. December brought even more rain, the Sangro rose even further, so that by 5 December all bridges were either washed away or under water. The New Zealand Division did manage to cross the next river, the Moro, entered Orsogna, and then had to withdraw because of lack of weapons and ammunition. The Canadians also crossed the Moro, and were drawn into an epic house-to-house battle for Ortona. Montgomery was forced to write:

> I am fighting a hell of a battle here. The right wing of my army on the Adriatic side consists of three Divisions. I am opposed there by three and a half divisions; this combined with the mud, makes it not too easy.

By 10 December rain brought all operations to a halt. A breakthrough to the Pescara River and port began to seem a distant dream. Montgomery's goal, of gaining control of the main east–west road from Pescara through Avezzano to Rome was not going to be attainable. Yet the Allied front line had now edged forward and extended along the northern side of the Sangro River, through the mountains and around Cassino, then along the south bank of the Garigliano River to the west coast.

The truth, however, was that like a spider, Kesselring had drawn the Allies into a web of defensive lines, such as the Sangro, the Gustav, the Bernhardt and the Adolf Hitler Lines, that exploited the mountains and rivers to enmesh both Allied armies. It was where the Germans meant to stand and throw them back. There were to be no more planned withdrawals. The orders from Hitler were to fight the Allies to the death in these positions, and bring their advance to a standstill.[41] Whilst the Allies had fourteen divisions, the Germans had nine with supporting armoured units in the front line, and another fourteen divisions farther back to draw on. The potential threat of a major German counter-attack was always in Allied commanders' minds.

*   *   *

For now, though, in the first week of December, with Eighth Army firmly beyond the Sangro, the Surreys were sent back supposedly for rest and recovery, sixty-five miles south-west to the mountain town of Frosolone. Lieutenant Woodhouse wrote of the B Company billets, in the Frosolone law courts:

> We even had electric light. Then from 10 to 14 December I got some leave in Naples staying at the officers' club. I met a friend of the family and Dorset officer, Brigadier Harold Matthews, the base commander, who took me for a two-hour trip to see Pompei under a smoking Vesuvius. Back at Frosolone on 15 December, the Army Film Unit took photos of my battle patrol handling 'pigeon post', something we never subsequently attempted.[42]

The rest of 78th Division had moved back to the mountain resort and market town of Campobasso, only twelve miles from Frosolone. The Surreys had dreams of leave and visiting the town's bars and cafes. 'That was short-lived,' remembered Frank Weston. 'Six days later we were moved back into the line to take over higher ground in the mountain villages, Forli del Sangro, Castel del Sangro and Acquaviva. Life was hell, snow made things harder, and we were always hungry.'[43]

The Surreys were charged with holding a ten-mile front across bleak and wild country, overlooking the higher reaches of the Sangro, and on their western flank at Acquaviva they were in contact with the extreme right wing of Fifth Army. By late December some twelve inches of snow meant the Battleaxe Division was in another constant struggle, to keep open the east west lines of supply and communication.[44] The struggle to maintain a continual supply of basic rations never brought enough food, and the severe cold heightened men's hunger.

Lieutenant Woodhouse recalled that the Battalion held the hill top village of Capracotta while on the other side of the Sangro's deep valley the Wehrmacht had a few outposts.

> Most of the houses on both sides of the valley had been blown up by the Germans, but small numbers of Italians, mostly women, children and old men, stayed in their ruins. When we were at Capracotta, I bought three sheep for my 10 Platoon at a cost of about 1,000 lira, £2/12/0. I could afford it. While a private's pay was 70p [14 shillings] per week, I was paid 87½p [17/6d] per day.[45]

The cold and constant patrolling in rain and snow was very similar to their previous Christmas spent in the Tunisian mountains. This time some good fortune was to come their way. A few days before 25 December a Surreys' patrol was ordered out with orders to capture some Germans, and perhaps more importantly, to grab any chickens that could be found for the

Christmas dinner. Imagine the patrol's astonishment when they came upon a lost NAAFI supplies unit, who were making camp in the middle of no man's land. Before the NAAFI men and their trucks could make a panicky retreat, the patrol leader was able to purchase 800 tins of turkey meat, presumably at a large discount.

During December, January and into February the conditions were arctic, resulting in some men developing frostbite. Yet they had to keep on with the patrolling. Patrols were dangerous and unpredictable missions at any time, yet they had to be sent out every night to control no man's land and ensure up-to-date intelligence.[46] When the snow was frozen men had to be wary of the crunch of their feet, and ward against automatic weapons freezing up. Because of the vastness of no man's land, in the dark a patrol from either side could easily reach the territory of the forward positions of the other without being confronted.[47]

It was cold, exhausting, and nerve-racking work. Spring seemed a long way off.

Notes

 1. Carver, *The War in Italy 1943–1945*, pp. 86–7.
 2. Veterans' Accounts, Woodhouse, *Memoirs* (unpublished).
 3. Ford, op cit., p. 142.
 4. Surrey History Centre, ESR/25/TAYLORC/1.
 5. Surrey History Centre, ESR/25/TAYLORC/1, and Veterans' Accounts, Skilton.
 6. Ford, op cit., pp. 143–4.
 7. Veterans' Accounts, Woodhouse, *Memoirs* (unpublished).
 8. Taylor/Imperial War Museum, Department of Documents, *Seven Sunrays*, p. 28.
 9. Ray, op cit., p. 94.
10. Ibid, pp. 94–5, and Ford, op cit., p. 146.
11. Ford, op cit., pp. 148–9.
12. Daniell, op cit., p. 188.
13. Veterans' Accounts, Woodhouse, *Memoirs* (unpublished).
14. Squire and Hill, op cit., p. 15.
15. Veterans' Accounts, Weston.
16. Surrey History Centre, ESR/25/PAYN/7.
17. Ray, op cit., pp. 93–4.
18. Ford, op cit., p. 150.
19. Ibid, pp. 153–7.
20. Daniell, op cit., p. 188.
21. Squire and Hill, op cit., p. 15.
22. Ford, op cit., p. 157.
23. Surrey History Centre, ESR/25/PAYN/8.
24. Daniell, op cit., pp. 189–90.
25. Neillands, op cit., pp. 296–7.
26. Ford, op cit., p. 158.
27. Neillands, op cit., pp. 297.
28. Ford, op cit., p. 158.
29. Veterans' Accounts, Woodhouse, *Memoirs* (unpublished).
30. Ford, op cit., p. 163.

31. Veterans' Accounts, Woodhouse, *Memoirs* (unpublished).
32. Veterans' Accounts, Weston.
33. Squire and Hill, op cit., p. 15.
34. Neillands, op cit., p. 299.
35. Ibid.
36. Ray, op cit., p. 100.
37. Daniell, op cit., pp. 190–1.
38. Veterans' Accounts, Skilton.
39. Veterans' Accounts, Woodhouse, *Memoirs* (unpublished).
40. Hamilton, *Monty – The Battles of Field Marshal Bernard Montgomery*, p. 192.
41. Neillands, op cit., p. 299.
42. Veterans' Accounts, Woodhouse, *Memoirs* (unpublished).
43. Squire and Hill, op cit., p. 19, and Veterans' Accounts, Weston.
44. Squire and Hill, op cit., p. 19.
45. Veterans' Accounts, Woodhouse, *Memoirs* (unpublished).
46. Daniell, op cit., pp. 192–6.
47. Ray, op cit., p. 109.

Chapter 7

Snow Line Patrolling

In the first days of January 1944 heavy snow came to the Abruzzo mountains. It found the 1st Surreys entrenched and strung out on the southern side of the upper reaches of the Sangro River. One of the Surreys' companies held the devastated village of San Pietro where only the church was still standing, while another occupied Capracotta, a small winter sports resort perched on a cliff overlooking the Sangro.

'I could ski,' said Lieutenant Woodhouse, 'my first chance since January 1939. The weather was mainly fine with frost at night.' The Battle Patrol was now equipped for winter with string vests, windproof jackets with thick white fleeces, oiled socks and boots with skis.

He wrote home on 4 January – it was a year since he had left:

> My dear Mum,
> A year has passed now since we said au revoir; I feel that this year we shall all be together again.
> New Year's day we had a blizzard! Since then sun and snow and today, a red letter day, 4 Jan 1944 I skied this morning!!!
> Also you will be pleased to hear that I have been given the MC – now do NOT please imagine me doing bayonet charges against Boche, it is just a routine award for the many patrols etc, which I have done.[1]

This was a massive understatement by Woodhouse. The rigours and nerve-racking danger, of continually planning and leading night-time patrols behind enemy lines can only be understood by those who have also done it and survived to recount the experience.

* * *

'A snow line patrol', from the memoirs of Lieutenant John Woodhouse:

> At times the road up to Capracotta had more than fifteen feet of snow over it in several places, when all supplies had to be dragged on sledges for the last twelve miles. In similar mountains on the north side of the river were the Germans. They were reported by the Italians to have a scattered outpost line halfway up them, and a mile from the river. It was the Germans' habit to visit the part-wrecked villages on their own side of the river to get food and anything else they fancied.

Owing to the Germans' destruction and looting of villages and farms, it became clear that we could rely on the local Italians as guides. The thorough destruction of the roads in the valley made an attack of any size most unlikely, and the Germans were content to let sleeping dogs lie. Except that a few shells landed occasionally on the outskirts of the town, Capracotta lived peacefully with its 400 Italians and its British garrison of about 200 men.

On 18 January I was ordered to take a patrol across the valley and capture a prisoner. We needed information on the Germans' strength, and what regiment or other units we were up against. The following is an account of this patrol, typical of many patrols in Italy's mountains, which I recorded not long afterwards.

John Woodhouse transcript:

After dinner in the Battalion HQ quarters below Capracotta, I spread out a map on the table, and addressed the CO, Lieutenant Colonel Harry Smith, and the Intelligence Officer.

'The scheme, Sir, is this. We shall find a crossing place on the river, probably get an 'Eyetie' (local) to do that. Then I plan to push on to the wooded part near the top here. I will collect a specimen [German prisoner] *that night off one of the tracks leading to the Boche outposts, and bring him back over the river before dawn. But depending upon what we find it may take a few nights. I am going to establish a forward base at San Georgio just our side of the river, with a section from D Company if you will Ok it, Sir.'*

The CO nodded. 'Yes, that will be all right. But before you leave San Georgio, I want you to send me the final details of what you are going to do. How many men are you taking with you?'

'The whole lot, Fourteen men, Sir.'

'Right, and Charles, you must arrange some system of signals back to Major Harvey and D Company.' Like my men in the Battle Patrol, everyone knew me as Charles, or Charlie, despite my family nickname of Jock.

'Yes Sir, I am having a wireless at San Georgio, and light signals for artillery concentrations on different spots.'

'Right, well you know what we want, but do be careful Charles, you've got your MC so don't go and do anything rash. However, I suppose your gang of desperadoes will make the night hideous with sudden death, and then we must take the consequences!'

I laughed. 'That's Ok Sir, safety first with me.'

'Tell George [the Quartermaster] *to give you some rum,' said the CO, getting up from the table. 'And you can tell your Battle Patrol they will get some leave after the show is over.'*

* * *

108

The next morning was fine, and the snow a brilliant white. The Battle Patrol had finished their breakfast, and as I walked into the room they were cleaning their Tommy guns. The room was bare except for fourteen neatly folded blankets round the wall.

'Morning all,' I said cheerfully, and stood slightly hesitantly just inside the doorway.

'Any news, Charlie?'

I was waiting for that greeting, using my nickname like we all did in the Battle Patrol group. With a broad grin I walked into the centre of the room.

'We'll be moving soon. We're going up to Capracotta. Nice little job and we'll probably be away several days. Tell you about it when we get there. Meantime get packed up. Be ready to move at 14.00 hours. The road is open to Capracotta, and I've got two 15-cwt trucks to get us up there.

Bunting, I'll have a look at the Tommy guns in half an hour, so get cracking boys.'

I then sat with Sergeant Bunting on top of the piles of blankets, and gave him all the dope, told him of the details of food, ammunition, and clothing to be collected, worn or carried. It was all discussed and agreed between us.

* * *

At 14.00 hours all was ready to go – but not quite all it seemed!

'Varney!' shouted out Bunting.

'Yes?'

'Where's the rum?'

'Isn't it on the truck Sarge?'

'You ought to bloody know, I told you to bring it.'

'It must be in the billet then.'

'Well ***** off and get it.'

Varney returned breathless with the missing jar, amidst a volley of unprintable comments from his comrades on the backs of the two trucks. We set off, farewelled by a few troops from Battalion HQ, who were looking on and exchanging ribald remarks. Before dawn next day we moved with a section of D Company closer to the river Sangro. At 22.45 hours that evening the fourteen-man patrol who were to cross the river stood in silence fully dressed and armed in the little room where the D Company signaller and two stretcher bearers lived.

I spoke quietly.

'You all know just what we are going to do. Jerry is not expecting us, and we are not going to let him suspect that we exist. Not yet! Remember we'll be in his country, so alert all the time. Oh, the CO has promised you leave when we come back, so we'll put on a first class show. All ready? Good, let's go.'

The guide and I set off in the front. The new moon would give us light as far as the river, before it set behind the mountain. After one and a half hours

109

we were all sweating under our heavy loads, as we trekked silently through the snow. Ahead the noise of running water told of the nearby river. I told the guide to wait and, taking two men with me, moved stealthily towards the river.

At the edge twenty yards of swirling water, then dark shadows. The only noise was the water and its rattle over pebbles and stones. After waiting and watching I threw a stone across the river, and heard its fall quite distinct to the river noise.

I whispered to Corporal Gage, 'Follow me Frank, a few yards behind and downstream. If I am swept away you can catch me!' I sent the rest of the patrol back a bit, and told them to cover our crossing.

Into the ice-cold stream I went, up to, then over, my knees. I waded across as fast as I could, the water sometimes waist high. Tense moments, maybe there were Germans waiting, in the shadows – maybe – maybe not? Not! Good! The patrol then crossed and regrouped. On again up a mule track with the Italian guide for half a mile, until the ruined village of Ateleta made a darker mass in the gloom ahead.

The guide went ahead with one soldier while the patrol halted. Ten, then twenty minutes went by. Bodies quickly cooled, wet feet going numb. I moved forward in the darkness a little closer to the village. Then little sounds of movement, men approaching. As the leading man stepped by, I stood up.

'Ok?'

'Oh, Tenente!' he gasped. The men behind him appeared by his side. He was the local interpreter. 'Good morning, you are welcome here, we . . . .'

'Good,' I interrupted, 'can you take me now to a house, clear of the rest of the village, where we can stay? Secondly are there any Germans nearby?'

'No sir, no Germans, never at night in the village. I show you house now.'

It was an imposing house standing alone, separated by 150 yards of rubble from the nearest building still standing. A fire was soon burning inside, and the legs and boots of the soldiers steamed round it. I went outside to join the four men on guard.

'Corporal Gage?' Frank emerged from the shadows. 'Frank, walk round this place with me.' I detected a slight smirk on Frank's face. I had only addressed him as Corporal, because of the locals now with us. It was hard to see much in the starlight, but it was clear that any approach to our house over the rubble would be certain to make noise.

'Put two men on guard. Its 0200 now; one hour on for each pair. Me on with Varney at 5.00 hours. Leave yourself off tonight. Cover the path with one here, and the other by the door. There is no other entrance and all ground floor windows are sheltered.'

When day came, two Italians maintained a watch on the approaches to the ruined village. There were still perhaps twenty civilians existing in Ateleta. Wearing a blue civilian overcoat over my uniform, I walked round the village with our guide/interpreter, learning what I could of the Germans' habits and locations.

At 12.00 hours, after a meal of fried bully beef and eggs, I talked to the men.

'There is a post on the spur east of here about 800 yards away. They can see the village but not this house. The guide thinks there are about ten Germans there. There is an unoccupied village about 500 yards above the post. We will go there and take a look. We should be able to take a prisoner from there, maybe by cutting their telephone lines. No shooting unless we have to, remember the aim of this patrol is to get a prisoner for identification.'

'Who's going, Charlie?' asked Gage.

'Well I want our two newcomers, Smith and Hammond, with us. I'll leave four of your old stagers for a night off here, Cambridge, Scaife, Varney and Godfrey.'

Later Cambridge came up to me. 'Charlie, can I have a word with you, Sir?' He looked determined.

'Yes of course. What is it?'

'Me and Scaife want to come with you. We were first to join you, we feel we got more right to come out than most of the rest.'

'You are too good to keep coming out all the time. I've got to try out the new boys haven't I? Now you'll be in charge here. If the Boche come into the village, you will go to the bridge on the south side and wait for me to come back. Probably about 03.00 hours. On no account start shooting down here. They must not know that we are on this side of the river.'

'Bunting, get the wire cutters, six magazines and two grenades each.'

Every man carried a Tommy gun, while I carried a German Schmeisser machine pistol. We all wore rubber-soled boots, no anklets, but trousers buttoned at the bottom of the legs. Sergeant Bunting wore a black beret, the others woolly hats, while I indulged my liking for the forage cap of the Dorset Regiment. These variations had the practical advantage of making visual identification of the wearer easier in the dark. We stepped silently into the freezing night.

The silence was not quite complete. The fabric of our uniforms whispered as we moved, and from time to time a stone might rattle as it was displaced. We went steadily uphill, but every few hundred yards I halted, when everyone sank to their knees, looked and listened. In the Battle Patrol our hearing became trained to be super-sensitive, so that we could listen and identify the slightest sound.

After one and a half hours the outline of a large barnlike building emerged from the gloom. The Italian guide went forward to the heavy wooden door. A prearranged knock and the door opened slightly. There was brief murmur of voices, and the guide turned with vigorous arm movements for the patrol to come in.

111

There were three men inside. They said the Germans walk through here at different times every evening. I wondered what time they would come through tonight. All the next day we hid in a room on the upper floor.

The Italians were against an ambush close to here. Nearby houses were occupied, and they would be shot by the Germans in reprisal.

So we set up some ambush points farther away. I ordered my men to call on the enemy to surrender before shooting, provided there were no more than two of them. On the second night, which was very cold, we waited in ambush all night on a path between two German posts, but no one came. Then in the daylight our sentry reported two German soldiers walking towards our houses.

They did not appear cautious. Two of my men confronted them at close range with a shout in German of 'Hände hoch!' (Hands up!) One German dropped his rifle in sudden shock and raised both hands. The second leapt away but did not escape being shot through the stomach after running a few yards. We carried the wounded German back to our house and gave him morphine. He was about eighteen and called softly 'muti' (mum) as he died. I felt sad for her and her son. No one else took any notice.

As I watched the wounded prisoner die, for about an hour, I felt a deep sadness at the futility of war. I had seen many men killed and wounded, but this was the first time I had watched one of the enemy die. I have never forgotten him.

The other prisoner was twenty. He said he knew Germany would win the war. A new Luftwaffe was being built, and they would push the Russians back to Moscow in 1944. He was from the 5th Austrian Mountain Division.

On my return to base I was immediately called in to meet the new Eighth Army commander General Sir Oliver Leese, who was on a visit to 1st Surreys with the GOC 78th Division, Major General Keightley. Leese was immaculate in the service dress, I rather less so!'[2]

* * *

In December General Leese had succeeded General Montgomery, who had been recalled to the UK to prepare for the D Day invasion scheduled for June 1944. For such a meeting of senior commanders, in the remote extremities of the Eighth Army front lines, it could only mean one thing. The Surreys and 78th Division would soon be moving on for the next offensive to break the Gustav Line.

Notes
1. Veterans' Accounts, Woodhouse, *Memoirs* (unpublished).
2. Ibid.

Chapter 8

In the Grip of Cassino

Approximately mid-way between Rome and Naples, where Italy's pen-insula is only some eighty-five miles in width, sits the town of Cassino. On Cassino's eastern side, stretching for over sixty miles to the Adriatic Sea are the mountains and valleys of the wild Abruzzo region. At the Abruzzo's western edge is Cassino's monastery hill, the 1,700-feet high peak of Monte Cassino. On its summit, overlooking the five-mile-wide Liri Valley, sits the ancient monastery of St Benedict. Farther west are more mountains ranging across to the Tyrrhenian Sea. In 1944 the only viable north–south road was Highway 6, which ran through the Liri Valley and Cassino town, under the dominant gaze of Monte Cassino.[1]

In mid-February 2006, I caught the 8.05am train from Naples Centrale to Cassino. I wanted to visit the site of the legendary battle, deliberately in winter, to try and gain a glimpse in some sense, however faint, of the horrific conditions that prevailed during the Cassino battles in 1944. As we pulled out of Naples and its suburbs of nondescript apartment blocks, Vesuvius was in full view. It was a cold morning with intermittent sun and rain, and cloud or smoke covered the volcano's peak.

Gradually Naples' urban sprawl gave way to vegetable fields, vineyards and orchards, showing the first buds of spring beginning to open. But then the hills in east to west rib lines closed in, and the cloud and rain increased. At Capua darker clouds hid the mountain peaks, and water lay by the track.

When we reached Teano, which in the past had been a refuge for the Benedictine monks from earlier conflicts, the curved tin roofs of some depot buildings near the station looked like rusty survivors from the Second World War years. After Teano the train crossed deep, wooded ravines. The mountains were higher and steeper, some with peaks pro-truding through wisps of cloud, which hung like the smoke of battle.

Through the next stops at Vairano Caianello, Mignano and Monte Lungo the mountain slopes became sheer, rock faces strewn with boulders. The clouds became grey-black and swirled lower, as if hiding their prey. At Rocca d'Evandro I felt a sensation of passing through ranges of hills and mountains that would never end.

And then we were there, the train pulling into a very ordinary looking Cassino railway station. Stepping onto the platform I immediately noticed a small memorial to the 2nd New Zealand Division, who sacrificed so many men there in battles against German troops. I quickly photographed the plaque, which states: 'In Memory of those New Zealanders, Who gave their Lives, And in Honour of all Who served at Cassino in 1944.'

Walking from the station into driving rain, I headed towards a taxi to take me up to the Monte Cassino Monastery.

'*Scusi, scusi, signore!*' Two Italian railway police cut me off and quickly escorted me back to their office for some questions in halting English, and a phone call to verify my passport. Feeling like a terrorism suspect I answered their questions for a bemused fifteen minutes or so, explaining that I was just a tourist.

I am not sure why they found me suspicious. Maybe it was because of that photo I took on the platform. Maybe suspicion is inbred in Cassino police officers. For those climactic battles for Cassino, were just the most recent of numerous destructions to befall the town's inhabitants, and the Monte Cassino Monastery over the last 2,000 years.

* * *

The mountaintop monastery of Monte Cassino is arguably the most important monastery in western civilization. St Benedict established the monastery as the Roman Empire disintegrated and the Benedictine Order with their scholarship provided a lifeline from the knowledge of the ancient Greeks and Romans. It became a lifeline that made possible the Renaissance.

In AD 480 the man we now know as St Benedict was born the son of a Roman patrician near Spoleto in Perugia. Later in his childhood he lived with his family in Rome but, disillusioned by the corruption and deca-dence of the declining Empire, he moved to Subiaco. There he spent some time as a reclusive hermit, before being asked by some monks to be their leader. He then founded twelve small monasteries but, after surviving a poisoning attempt, he and a few of his supporters fled south into the Abruzzi Mountains.

There around AD 529 St Benedict founded the Monte Cassino monas-tery, reputedly taking over a still active Temple of Apollo, in what was left of the Roman fort of *municipium Casinum*. Part of Benedict's Rule for all monks was the principle of spiritual reading, which included transcribing the great works of Greek and Roman literature. Ever since the Monte Cassino Monastery has been looked upon as a place of holiness, learning and art. Through the Dark Ages this knowledge was spread by the Benedictine and other monastic orders throughout Western Europe.

114

In 577 the Monte Cassino Monastery was destroyed by the Lombards. The monks fled to Rome, where their teachings and ideas so impressed the Papal authorities that in 717 the monastery was rebuilt by Pope Gregory II. Monte Cassino then prospered so well that in 787 Emperor Charlemagne visited the Abbey and granted it vast privileges. But in 883 its second destruction came at the hands of the Saracens.

In the middle of the tenth century its rebuilding began again, culminating in the lavish restoration of the Basilica by Abbot Desiderius. A third tragedy struck in 1349 when an earthquake left only a few walls still standing. Restored yet again the Monastery was then to last until 1944 when, during the four drawn-out battles for Cassino, Allied bombers pounded it into piles of rubble.

But the benefit of hindsight now shows that the Monastery's destruction in 1944 was not quite the tragedy it appeared to be at the time. Some months before the First Battle of Cassino in January 1944, two officers of the Herman Göring Panzer Division, a Captain Becker and Lieutenant Colonel Schlegel, on the orders of General von Senger und Etterlin, had arranged the evacuation of the Monastery library's priceless collection of ancient books, manuscripts and other valuables. General von Senger was commander of the XIV Panzer Corps, an Anglophile, graduate of Oxford University, and lay member of the Benedictine Order. As Allied forces converged on Cassino in January 1944, General von Senger and those two officers foresaw perhaps the greater threat to the treasures of Western faith and philosophy.[2]

* * *

The first battle for Cassino, from 17 January to 11 February 1944, was a natural continuation of Fifth Army's advance up the western coastline of Italy. After four months of battle upon battle, fighting through the countless river valleys and mountains from the foot of Italy and Salerno, both Fifth and Eighth Armies were brought to a standstill, blocked by the Germans' Winter Line. The coastal routes, east and west, were too narrow for a breakthrough, while the Liri Valley and Highway 6 were perfect for a defending army.

The Allies decided to mount another amphibious landing. It would be at the fishing port of Anzio, north of Cassino and only about forty miles from Rome. A few days prior to the Anzio landings in mid-January 1944, General Mark Clark's Fifth Army would make the first attempt to break the Gustav Line, one of a number of defensive positions making up the Winter Line. It would become known as the First Battle for Cassino. The thinking was that, in a double hammer blow, the Allies would trap German forces in the pincer movement of the two offensives, and create a circuit breaker to force them to withdraw.[3]

Clark's plan was for XI US Corps to cross the Rapido River five miles south of Cassino and capture Sant'Angelo before breaking through onto Highway 6 into the Liri Valley. On their left flank the British X Corps would cross the Garigliano River on 17 January before moving up to Highway 6. On the right the French Expeditionary Corps would have commenced climbing on 11 January through the mountains to capture Monte Cassino. This would then allow Fifth Army to drive north on Highway 6 up the Liri Valley, to join up with the Anzio landings planned for 22 January.[4]

On 20 January the 36th Texas Division moved up to cross the Rapido, to the south of Cassino. Mines in the flooded approaches hit them hard, while heavy German artillery destroyed many of their boats and bridges. Only a few companies got across and then were pinned down by the German shelling. On the night of 22 January, with their ammunition running out, those who were still alive swam back across the river. The 36th Texans had lost 1,681 men.

In a second crossing on 24 January the 34th (Red Bull) US Division forded the Rapido to the north of Cassino. In three days of bitter fighting a small bridgehead was gained that enabled a few tanks to cross. Meanwhile on the left, the British X Corps had gained a small bridgehead, more a foothold across the downstream Garigliano, before being held up. On the right to the south-east of Cassino the French took and held Monte Trocchio and Monte Belvedere.

Over the next ten days the US 34th, with the remaining troops of the 36th, captured Monte Maiola and Monte Castellone, and gained positions only 600 yards to the north-west of Monte Cassino. On rocky ground, with the only cover possible from self-made stone sangars, the American troops were raked by German machine guns from overlooking high points. In February's freezing rain the Americans made a final assault to take Cassino and Monastery Hill. Despite losing 80 per cent of their number, it was in vain. Nevertheless, they held onto their gains, Snakeshead Ridge, Mortar and Death Valleys, and gave them names that would haunt the Allies for months to come.[5]

While Fifth Army haemorrhaged in the wintry claws of the Gustav Line at Cassino, the Anzio landings on 22 January came under serious threat of failure from a German counter-attack. At one stage ten German divisions were pitted against only four Allied divisions. Anzio was not going to make the Germans withdraw to the north. A second attempt to break through the Gustav Line at Cassino had to be made immediately.

Some Eighth Army troops, such as the 78th Division, including the 1st Surreys, were ordered to move across from the mountains to bolster Fifth Army, but they would not be ready for the next Cassino battle. The second assault on Cassino was to be led by II New Zealand Corps. On 15 February

116

it was preceded by an air raid of 254 bombers, which blasted Monte Cassino's monastery to little more than rubble.

On the same day as the air raid, the New Zealanders rushed forward along a railway causeway and, despite blown bridges, crossed a canal and the Rapido River. By midnight they had captured Cassino railway station. However, on 18 February, without any tank or anti-tank support, the New Zealanders were driven back, and the second battle for Cassino was called off.[6] All that was left was to consolidate the small but hard-won gains.

Similarly at Anzio, as German Panzers drove deep into the Allies' bridgehead, it had become another killing ground which appeared to be going nowhere.

*　*　*

1st Surreys move into the Cassino Front

Both before and during the second battle for Cassino, Eighth Army had begun to move forces across the Apennines to the west to join up with Fifth Army. It was not going to have an immediate impact. Hindsight suggests that the planners had some doubts that the second attack on Cassino and the Gustav Line could succeed. The Allies' main objective had now become Rome, for which the two armies must combine to break the Gustav Line.

As the battalions of 78th Division crossed the mountains to join forces with Fifth Army they were able to look down upon what was left of Cassino town and its bombed monastery atop Monte Cassino.

Even at a distance and to eyes not unused to destruction, the ruins of Cassino were awe-inspiring. This was indeed a stricken town. Not a single whole building remained, only fragments of walls and heaps of rubble. Those jagged fragments of buildings had a ghostly, slightly obscene quality that is hard to describe; it was like a forest of stalag-mites. Cassino in destruction was different from all the other places.

Away to the left ran the thin streak of the Rapido River, stretched like a steel cord across the entrance to the Liri Valley. The fortifications on its far bank linked up with the mountain range which began behind Cassino, and became higher as it went east till it culminated in the towering peak of Monte Cairo, over 5,000 feet high, and the anchor of the Cassino defence system.

Stark and clear now was the one that was the most important of them all, because it was the key to all the others – Monastery Hill.[7]

By 19 February the 1st Surreys had made their cross-country trek through the mountains in freezing rain, snow and blizzards south-west to

117

Capua near Mignano. For a few days they regrouped in a brief bivouac in two-man tents amongst some olive groves. But by 23 February they were into the front line.

On a miserable winter's day the Surreys drove their vehicles forward, to take over from the New Zealanders on the south bank of the Rapido River. Lieutenant G.L.A. Squire, a platoon commander in A Company, peered into the murk.

> The weather was very foggy and the journey seemed interminable. At times when the fog thinned one could see kilometre stones beside the road, and it was a little disconcerting to see how close we were getting to Cassino town. So it was with some relief when I saw the Brigade Commander roar past my vehicle in his jeep and drive towards the head of the column where he halted.
>
> Orders were soon passed down the column to debus, unload the 3-tonners which, in addition to personnel and weapons, carried blankets rolled in bundles of ten on the basis of one per man, and march back along the road to where guides would meet us.

In the fog the Surreys had gone too far, and if it lifted they would be in full view of the Germans on Monte Cassino. The 3-ton vehicles could not be turned around because of the roadsides being mined, and once the men had set off back down the road at great speed, the drivers had no option but to reverse at maximum revs.

'Fairly soon afterwards the fog lifted,' said Squire, 'and we had our first view of the Monastery perched on its hill, which seemed so close one felt every movement was bound to be seen from there. Luckily for us we were by then under cover.'[8]

It was the Surreys' first lesson at Cassino: only move at night if at all possible. They were now deployed over a three-mile stretch, on the south-eastern bank of the Rapido River opposite the town of Sant'Angelo, held by the Germans on the other bank.

The terrain was well-wooded which, together with sunken lanes and cart tracks, provided ideal ambush locations. Any movement or discernible presence seen in the Germans' binoculars brought down shelling from the surrounding mountains. Day by day, however, particularly at night, concentrations of tanks, vehicles, bridging equipment and assault boats, and dumps of equipment and ammunition, were being assembled, ready for a cross-river offensive. Every night the Surreys' patrols went out, either to keep their German equivalents away from these preparations, or over to the German side of the Rapido to reconnoitre potential landing places and pinpoint the enemy's defensive positions.[9]

On the far side was an intricate network of minefields, belts of wire twenty-feet in depth, mutually supporting strongpoints and considerable numbers of semi-mobile dug-in pillboxes. Behind lay a belt of concrete emplacements and weapons pits.[10]

For a month the Surreys held the river frontage, continually repulsing German raids from the other side. Beyond were the Surreys' next goals, Cassino and the now shattered remains of the Monte Cassino Monastery. It was still held by the Germans as the lynchpin of their Gustav Line, and it still dominated the Allied positions on the south side of the Rapido. Every night around fifty men went out on patrol, often crossing the fast flowing and deep river, to probe the enemy's defences. Lieutenant Woodhouse described the first patrol he did there, while the Surreys were under the command of the New Zealand Division.

I led my men towards the Cassino railway station, which the New Zealanders had gained and then lost only a few days before. The debris of defeat was scattered around, including rubber assault boats from the Americans' failed attempt to cross the river in January. The patrol proved to be uneventful, yet all the time I felt the bombed ruins of Monte Cassino monastery to be like a malevolent eye looking down on us.[11]

* * *

1/6th Surreys climb into the Aurunci Mountains
On 21 February 1944 1/6th Surreys disembarked with 4th Division at Naples. It was almost to the day as their sister battalion, 1st Surreys, had moved up to the Rapido River. From Naples 1/6th Surreys motored north up Highway 7 close to the Tyrrhenian coast, then, short of the Garigliano River, struck north-east and inland. Once across the Garigliano at Skipton Bridge, they began a march with full packs up slippery, precarious mule tracks into the Allies' mountainous Garigliano bridgehead.

There the Surreys and the 4th Division were to relieve 46th Division in positions that ranged from Valle di Sujo, in the south, across the mountains that stretched to Rocca d'Evandro, on the Naples to Cassino railway line. By 24 February the Surreys were climbing into the Aurunci Mountains to the north of Monte Cassino. Not surprisingly, coming from their recent recovery camp in Egypt, they shivered in the severe Abruzzi winter. It seemed like only yesterday that they were cursing the heat and dust of the desert. Now they trudged for ever upwards in snow, ice, rain and mud, and struggled to sleep in the bitter cold nights.[12]

There was no time for acclimatization. The Surreys were stunned at the desolate terrain and how their comrades had fought in such conditions for more than five months since Salerno. How were they going to take over from 46th Division, and sustain this fight?

Daniell described the boulder-strewn wilderness, which was the Surreys' new battleground.

They saw how British and Germans hung on to their bleak positions, overcoming prodigious problems of supply, living in small rock sangars within sight and range of each other. Supplies, which had to include water, were brought from the enormous dump at Skipton Bridge by jeeps, then by mules, and then by Basuto bearers, to supply-heads. For the final stage of the journey each battalion and company sent down men to the supply depots, to back-pack to the front line sangars.

It took from twenty-four to forty-eight hours to get a casualty back to the advanced dressing station, with six men to carry a stretcher over the difficult tracks to the Regimental Aid Post. The casualty was then carried back by native troops who lived in little sangars at 200 yard intervals along the tracks. Every two or three miles there were first-aid posts, where a medical officer could re-dress wounds or give an injection of morphia. There were also little cemeteries.

The men occupied small stone sangars, breast-works sometimes covered in with ground sheets, from which day-time movement was not advised. On many hills British and Germans occupied the reverse slopes of the same feature, sometimes no more than fifty yards apart, with the crest as 'no man's land.'

As a rule units could not observe the enemy on the reverse slope of their own feature, but they could see them on the nearby hills. It was possible, therefore, even though you could not see your own enemy, to warn your neighbours if theirs showed any signs of activity.[13]

When on 1 March the Surreys took up new, exposed positions around Monte Fuga and Monte Ornito, they were closer to Cassino, and eyeball to eyeball with German positions. Any move whatsoever during daylight brought down heavy machine-gun fire and mortar shelling.

Snow lay about among the outcrops of rock and men had to move with the greatest stealth, for one stone dislodged could start a minor avalanche and attract unwelcome attention from the enemy. There had been much fighting when Ornito was captured several weeks before, and one could never be sure whether the figures lying about on the rocks were really dead.[14]

The troops lived under constant fear of being hit by the next salvo of mortar shells from the other side of their hill, a machine-gun burst, or a sniper's bullet. One particularly heavy bout of shelling killed Major J.O. Strode MC, and six other men.

On 10 March B Company was approached by five German stretcher-bearers under a white flag, carrying a casualty. It was a long-dead corpse, with a note attached, 'This English soldier we found in the high point 759.' Was this some kind of ruse? No chances could be taken, and the five Germans were taken prisoner. Later it was learned they were indeed from the medical unit of the German 71st Division.[15]

The same day the Surreys finally got some respite, pulling back into reserve at Valle di Sujo. Five days later that respite was cut short when they moved back into their previous positions near Monte Cassino. There they watched the air raid on Cassino town, and waited for the orders to support the next attack to break through the Gustav Line.[16]

*   *   *

1st Surreys patrol and wait on the Rapido

On the south bank of the Rapido the 1st Surreys and their 78th Battleaxe Division were poised to cross the river, to exploit the strategy for the third Battle for Cassino. The plan first called for 5 New Zealand Brigade to attack Cassino town from the north and then take its nearby Castle Hill. Then, at the end of the day, 5 Indian Brigade would take over to assault Monte Cassino and its monastery. In reserve, 78th Division, including 1st Surreys and a brigade of American tanks, would await the order to exploit the breakthrough. Once again the battle would begin with a massive air raid, this time onto the German positions still dug in amongst the ruins and rubble of Cassino town.[17]

For three weeks continual rain and cloud caused a day-by-day postponement of the air raid and the planned attack. Troops were stuck in exposed positions in the mountains and forward areas, waiting for the go-ahead signal. Each day the phrase 'Bradman will not bat today' meant another postponement. Casualties from the attrition of shelling, machine-gun fire, snipers and exposure to the weather mounted, and morale was fraying. Every night everyone had to be ready, in case the weather cleared, to go the next day.

'In all that rain and continual enemy fire, somehow we always got hot food, tea and good drinking water,' said Harry Skilton. 'How they did it, God knows, but it was said to be because of the 'Cassino Cooker'. Though I never saw it in operation.'[18]

Captain W.A. Smurthwaite, a Medical Officer, also spoke of the Cassino Cooker.

> Somewhere in the history of those times, there should be mention of the tremendous service of two groups of people, who incidentally came into the jurisdiction of the MO, and whose efforts always seem to go unsung. I refer to the Battalion cooks and the operators of the water truck.

Food and water are immediate and enduring necessities after all. Water, if unpurified, can decimate a battalion as quick as any enemy, and to my recollection, this never happened. As for food, the cooks were always up there, serving whatever they could rustle up in spite of weather, hustle, lack of supplies and busted equipment.

The 'Cassino Cooker' was a miracle of simplicity, efficiency and improvisation. It was also about as safe as a truckload of napalm! The equipment was made up of jerricans, a cigarette tin with wire handles, a cork, a darning needle, and a trench about a foot wide and ten feet long. Add a handful of rags, and some petrol and you're in business.[19]

Along the Surreys' river frontage, patrols were sent out every night, each with different objectives. For C Company's No. 15 Platoon their task every night was to act as a human trip-wire, to give warning of any German incursion onto the Rapido's south side. The platoon commander, Lieutenant G.T. Rose, described their routine:

We moved out every night after dark. About 250 yards from the river, we sat out the night in slit trenches, watching and listening. On a moonless night towards the end of the month the left-hand slit of our position was overrun by an enemy patrol, and two men were taken prisoner. It was a bad situation, because we couldn't open fire without endangering our own men, and we could see absolutely nothing – only listen to the fracas.[20]

An important part of the Surreys' patrol work was to lay marker tapes leading to decoy river crossing points, and position boats to fool the Germans. It had to be done on their nightly patrols, but only allow a small amount of tape and boats to be visible, so as to deceive the Germans into thinking such preparations were genuine.[21]

* * *

For the real crossing point over the Rapido, Lieutenant Woodhouse and his Battle Patrol had orders to find a suitable stretch where the battalion could get across and to be able to do so on a moonless night with poor visibility.

Below the German position at Sant'Angelo, but further downstream, I had observed a place where the river left the embankment on the German side by 100 metres. On a very dark night I took a patrol in an American assault boat to this point. It was too dark even to see the water. The river was about twenty metres wide and deep. We pushed silently off and half minute later I saw, dimly, what at first appeared to be another boat shooting past. Whatever I had seen, seconds later I realized that we were being swept downstream very fast. Somehow we

122

got control, and found the far bank clear. The whole Battalion crossing the Rapido was going to be very hard.

The Battle Patrol was being called upon to undertake an increasing number of patrols, not to penetrate behind German lines, but into the heavily contested no man's land.

On 29 February at dawn, I took Private Dickinson and another soldier in a patrol forward of the battalion front lines. We found a barn and crawled in. From one side in a small room we could look down on the flood plain of the Rapido River valley to the German positions close to Sant'Angelo. Sergeant Dickinson was lying beside me, Tommy gun in hand. I was looking through my binoculars. Our third man was watching to our right front two metres away from me. Suddenly from the corner of the barn on our left came a cry in English of 'Hands up!'

There were two German soldiers, one with a pistol, the other with a Schmeisser. I was paralyzed with shock. Dickinson was not in shock. Spinning round and onto his back, he fired a burst, the German fired too, but leapt back behind the barn wall. I decided we should run for cover. Returning with a larger force an hour or so later, we found the Germans had also run, leaving a Lüger pistol, the handgrip shattered by one of Dickinson's bullets. Bloodstains showed the owner's hand must also have been hit.

For once I was shaken by this near miss, and I suspect it must have shown when I reported our ambush to the CO. Sergeant Dickinson was cited for the Military Medal, which was later awarded, but the next day, 1 March, the CO told me he had decided I needed a rest and therefore I was to go to command 16 Platoon in D Company. The Battle Patrol was soon broken up, Sergeant Bunting and the men returning to other companies. I was very disappointed but, in truth, the density of the German front below Cassino gave no scope for the Battle Patrol to penetrate the German positions undetected. The CO of D Company, Major Enoch Harvey, was a popular regular army officer from the Royal Berkshire Regiment. Lieutenant Colonel Smith told Major Harvey that he did not want me sent on patrols for a while.[22]

The letter Woodhouse wrote to his Mum on 1 March showed the passion he had for the work of the Battle Patrol, and his men:

My dear Mum,
You will see I have changed address; I was dismissed from the Battle Patrol with not a word of thanks, and then not even sent to my old company. The Battle Patrol was really a 100% fighting force with a magnificent spirit, and now partly scattered away.

123

However it is an ill wind ... and I suppose you will be glad I have given up the Battle Patrol. I had done so many patrols, it has been a bit of a wrenching.

Your ever loving son, Jock.

Despite his attempt to rationalize the decision, Woodhouse was devastated to lose this command. As always though, he did not let a setback stop him from being ever ready to respond to orders and requests for help.

'On 2 March Major Harvey asked permission from Battalion HQ to send out a patrol that night,' said Woodhouse. 'He knew that I knew the ground in the front and I think he wished to see it for himself, and gave me command of the patrol.'

Harvey and Woodhouse set out with four men of D Company to look for places to bridge the river. Woodhouse, who was supposed to be taking an overdue rest in D Company, should not have been in the group. On what was meant to be a purely reconnaissance mission, it appears that Harvey and Woodhouse were tempting fate.

We set out with Private Vic James as a leading scout, then, following me, Napier, Major Harvey and two other privates – Moody and Hart. We went for 300 metres along a track to a T-junction. James, the lead scout stopped just before reaching the T. I crawled up beside him. 'There are some men there,' he said, 'I heard them'. I waited and listened.

I hardly knew James, who had been in the company just two days. After listening longer than I wished, I decided we must go on and take our chance. We went on one by one to the right of the T junction. We went about 500 metres and then came out of the olive trees and on to the flood plain of the Rapido opposite Sant' Angelo, where I pointed out various features to Harvey. Around midnight we returned towards the T-junction which, because there were mines either side, we had to pass through.

We were going very slowly, mindful still of James' previous warning, even though no enemy action had resulted on our way out. A hundred metres short of the T-junction the Germans fired about a dozen mortar bombs around it. I whispered to Harvey 'There cannot be any enemy there, they would not have fired those bombs if there were'. We resumed our move. As soon as we reached the T-junction, a burst of firing and explosions, I think it was only for a few seconds, blasted us.

Instinctively Woodhouse and the patrol dropped, trying to claw themselves into the ground. Half stunned with dirt in his mouth, Woodhouse regained his senses and began to rise to his knees. A German stuck a gun in his back. This is it, he thought, just as he had told his sister, Ann. Killed in action.

Instead of pulling the trigger, the German shouted a word or two, which made it very clear that they wanted me as a prisoner. The German troops, about six, I guessed, had been in an ambush position no more than three or four metres from the track, when they hit us.

Their fire, or two or three grenades, had taken Harvey, but missed me apart from a small grenade fragment on a leg. Private Moody and another soldier behind us were not caught up in the firing and must have managed to dive into some cover. My Schmeisser was later found by the Battalion with a round jammed in it. But I have no memory of firing, and believe I fell flat when the firing began.[23]

* * *

'Ginger' Moody had been bringing up the rear of the patrol and had thrown himself to the ground before scrambling into some bushes. When the firing ceased all he could hear was a shout or two in German. He could see nothing, then there was silence. After a short while he moved and somehow found his way around the T-junction, and back to the Surreys' lines.

Sergeant Frank Gage, previously a member of the Battle Patrol, came awake in a start, instinctively reaching for his gun. Ginger was shaking him, and gasping, 'We got hit. I think Charlie's bought it!' 'Charlie' was the special nickname in the Battle Patrol for Lieutenant Woodhouse. In a close-knit unit, where rank was subservient to their teamwork and personal bonding, Frank Gage was especially close to Charlie Woodhouse, and, despite its recent disbanding, he always would be.

While there was still some night left, Frank and Ginger, carrying as much ammo and grenades as was practicable, set off back to the site of the ambush. Desperate to find what had happened to their comrades, they moved at a fast pace. Their usual caution was forgotten. Frank tried to put it out of his mind that Charlie could be dead.

They quickly found the dead body of Major Harvey and Ginger went back to get two stretcher-bearers. For two hours Frank searched for Charlie, hoping against hope that he might find him lying wounded somewhere. As he scoured the area his despair mounted, and memories of his friend began to dominate his mind. Always at the end of an operation, Charlie would say to him, 'You made my day, Frank.' As dawn began to lighten the sky, Frank found himself covering the same ground again and again. Finally he turned back towards the Surreys' lines. Charlie was gone.[24]

* * *

While Frank searched in vain, Woodhouse and James were taken at a run by their German captors, back to a boat crossing point over the Rapido at Sant'Angelo.

> Somehow Vic James and I made it until we got to the German positions. At the company HQ in a deep well-furnished dug-out, a tall fair-haired 'Lieutenant' spoke some English. I was seated and given a cigarette while he reported their success to his HQ. He told me how pleased he was to capture us, despite their own mortar firing so close to them.
>
> Major Harvey's wallet was produced with his identity giving him away by his visiting cards and, more seriously, a letter from 11 Brigade HQ to him in 1st East Surrey Regiment. It was strictly against orders to carry any personal details and papers on patrol. I only had eight cigarettes, hanky, pencil and 400 lira in my pockets. Also an escape map which was not found. When the German 'Lieutenant' asked me what regiment I was in, I stayed silent. He laughed and said, 'He's certainly an Englishman!' They were not sure until this night whether there were Americans or British facing them.[25]

Woodhouse agonized over why they had been caught by surprise. Had he erred in his judgement about the T-junction? If he had been leading his Battle Patrol, would they have made better decisions? Had he not given enough credence to James' report of hearing voices?

The end result was that Major Harvey, who had led D Company with distinction throughout Sicily and Italy to this time, was dead, and Woodhouse now a PoW. For the Surreys, losing both Major Harvey and Lieutenant Woodhouse, their experienced and valued Battle Patrol leader, was a devastating loss. They could only console themselves with the thought that the Germans would maybe find Woodhouse to be a handful to keep under lock and key.[26]

* * *

When dawn broke on 15 March some sunlight began to edge through the clouds and mountains which surrounded the Liri Valley and the Cassino battleground. The rain had finally stopped and, later in the morning, the air raid to signal the start of the third battle to break the Gustav Line finally rained down on the German lines.

> At eight o'clock in the morning the first wave of bombers was seen flying high above Cassino. They circled the town, looking to the men below like lazy silver insects, and soon the ground itself seemed to shake with the fury of the bombardment. For over three hours the

machines went over in waves – Fortresses and Liberators, in formations of eighteen and thirty-six.

Over 1,000 aircraft took part; some 500 blasted Cassino with 1,100 tons of metal, while 300 fighter-bombers, with as many fighters as cover, attacked targets immediately nearby. There was no such opposition from either enemy aircraft or flak. No land forces in the war had yet seen such a massed attack on so small a target, and it seemed to those watching that at last we had found the key to success in attack, without the inevitable casualties of an infantry assault.[27]

It proved to be wishful thinking. At midday, as the last bombs fell, the New Zealanders attacked. They immediately ran into German troops who were supposed to be dead. German infantry and paratroopers emerged from the town's ruined buildings and many, it was later discovered, from reinforced cellars, even from deep underground tunnels, to put up an unexpectedly strong defence. Also unanticipated was the extent that the bombed buildings and craters obstructed the bringing up of tanks and artillery to support the infantry. To add to the misery, the rain began again. It flooded craters, ditches and any depression, and the mud was back.

Despite flurries of snow that added to these difficulties and the enemy's fire, by the end of 17 March the Indians were on Castle Hill and the Gurkhas on Hangman's Hill. Yet the plans were in disarray, and it was far from over. At night, and through those underground tunnels, reinforcements of German paratroopers from General Heidrich's 1st Parachute Division further infiltrated Cassino's killing ground. The fighting intensified, particularly around what remained of the Continental Hotel, and became more confused.

In making their gains, the New Zealanders' losses were more than 1,300 and the Indians above 3,000.[28] The Allies rushed forward reinforcements overnight, up to the Indians and Gurkhas on Castle and Hangman's Hills. The revised plan was to launch an assault on the afternoon of Sunday 19 March onto the remaining part of Cassino town and the monastery's ruins on Monte Cassino.

It was as if there had been an intelligence leak of the planned attack. On that very Sunday morning the Germans opened up a massive machine-gun fusillade and mortar bombardment. In its wake German infantry and paratroopers poured down the slopes of Monte Cassino and pre-empted the Allied attack planned for the afternoon. Their clear intent was to re-take the Castle and Hangman's Hills.[29]

* * *

In those first three weeks of March, while the Allies endured the 'on again, off again' suspense of waiting for the rain to ease, and then with a break in the weather, finally launched the third battle for Cassino, Lieutenant Woodhouse found himself subjected to the humiliation of being a PoW.

I was in the hands of 15th Panzer Grenadier Division. On 3 March Private James and I were passed back from a company to battalion HQ, a few hundred metres away. We were given coffee and cigarettes in a dug-out, which was five or six metres deep. The battalion commander spoke English, and told me he had served in the Afrika Korps. He had been wounded in Tunisia in March 1943, so escaping their surrender in May. We were driven back to perhaps a Division HQ, where for the first time I was asked my rank, and the Germans learned that I was an officer.

Formal interrogation took place at 0100 hours on 4 March. I had had very little sleep for two days. The interrogation was polite but threatening, telling me such as 'You only make thing worse for yourself if you don't talk,' 'No one knows you are a prisoner.' The Germans had identified 1st East Surrey Regiment from Major Harvey's 11 Brigade letter. My interrogator was clearly puzzled that our patrol included a major and a lieutenant. They concluded that it was the CO (Harvey) and his Adjutant (me) visiting our Battalion outposts.

I was then held with a Pioneer Corps officer, Jock Crichton, in a house with ten German soldiers. After four days we went to Fiuggi where we joined a group of recaptured PoWs in the 'Grand Hotel'. Dark depression now began to creep over me. I could imagine what was going on in 1st Surreys from hour to hour. There was nothing to do all day, except to think of various ways to escape.

Hunger began to take hold of me. Breakfast was a slice of bread and acorn coffee, lunch a half litre of barley soup, supper a slice of bread and margarine and jam. On 13 March we were moved to 'Cinema City' just south of Rome. We had an unpleasant interrogation on arrival, and witnessed the interrogation of an old Italian peasant and six Russians. This was a shouting bullying performance, and ours followed it. I thought that the dregs of armies always end up at base camp, and the 'Wehrmacht' was no exception.

Early on 15 March we were withdrawn further back through the near empty centre of Rome, which I recognized from my first sight of the Colosseum from the back of a lorry. In the afternoon we reached the prison camp of Laterina near Arezzo. We were kept on starvation rations and could only think, and dream, of little else but food. On the evening of 21 March we were put on a train. Soldiers were sealed in forty-six to a truck, officers twenty-three to a half-wired-off truck, with six German guards in the other half. In the afternoon of 22 March we reached the German frontier in a snowstorm at the Brenner Pass.

Next day we reached our destination, Moosburg near Munich. Some of us fainted on the way from hunger and cold. That night we were issued with a Red Cross food parcel, one between two.[30]

On his way to that PoW camp, Lieutenant Woodhouse wondered if he would survive, and if from no other cause, would he just starve to death?

* * *

At Cassino by the evening of Sunday 19 March the third Allied attempt to take the town and its Monastery was in serious trouble. Likewise, the Anzio bridgehead was stuck in a battle of attrition and had become another static killing ground reminiscent of the First World War. Many men must have wondered if the only way out of these battles without end could only be by death.

The pressure from London and Washington, however, to break out from Anzio and Cassino, was unremitting. The weeks were sliding by and Rome must be taken before the end of May. German divisions must be kept engaged in Italy, ideally destroyed, and prevented from being deployed back to north-west Europe. The Normandy invasion planned for early June must be protected from any counter German build-up. How to do that on the ground at Anzio and Cassino was, of course, much more difficult than looking at maps in Whitehall and the Pentagon. The planning staff of Alexander and Clark had to find some new approach.

Notes
1. Smith and associates, *The Cassino Battles* (Queen's Royal Surreys Association Museum), p. 1.
2. Majdalany, *Monte Cassino, Portrait of a Battle*, p. 6.
3. Smith and associates, op cit., pp. 1–3.
4. Carver, *The War in Italy 1943–1945*, p. 109.
5. Smith and associates, op cit., pp. 2–3.
6. Ibid, pp. 3–4.
7. Ray, op cit., pp. 111–12.
8. Squire and Hill, op cit., p. 26.
9. Surrey History Centre, ESR/25/PAYN/2, Manning.
10. Smith and associates, op cit., p. 11.
11. Veterans Accounts', Woodhouse, *Memoirs* (unpublished).
12. Daniell, op cit., pp. 200–1.
13. Ibid.
14. Ibid, p. 202.
15. Squire and Hill, op cit., p. 34.
16. Daniell, op cit., p. 202.
17. Smith and associates, op cit., p. 15.
18. Veterans' Accounts, Skilton.
19. Squire and Hill, op cit., p. 28.
20. Ibid, p. 27.
21. Smith and associates, op cit., pp. 4–6.

22. Veterans' Accounts, Woodhouse, *Memoirs* (unpublished).
23. Ibid.
24. Veterans' Accounts, Gage.
25. Veterans' Accounts, Woodhouse, *Memoirs* (unpublished).
26. Daniell, op cit., p. 195.
27. Ray, op cit., p. 114.
28. Ibid, p. 116.
29. Smith and associates, op cit., pp. 4–6.
30. Veterans' Accounts, Woodhouse, *Memoirs* (unpublished).

Chapter 9

Anzio Hell for the Grenadiers: And a 'Would Be' Surrey

In the Anzio bridgehead, near the 'Factory', sometime between 22 January and 9 February 1944, the 5th Grenadiers were dug in against a massive German counter-attack.

Jack Chaffer stepped onto an old ammunition box and craned his neck just enough to peer above the rim of his trench. Rivulets of rain streamed down his gas cape, into the ankle-deep, muddy water. Munching on what was left of a stale NAAFI sandwich, his face did not show it but he almost laughed. What was in the sandwich he could not guess; it was tasteless, but at least the rain softened it up.

About twenty yards away a lorry stopped on a mud track. The driver and his mate got out and began unloading bodies, just throwing them into a ditch. Jack carried on chewing the sandwich – he had seen this routine countless times. Then he stopped chewing and swallowed hard. But there was nothing wrong with the sandwich. One of those bodies looked like that corporal he knew, a good friend in the HQ Support Company.

I hauled myself out of the trench and walked over to the ditch, still holding my packet of sandwiches. I looked down into that ditch, and yes, it was him all right. He'd copped it.

I did not feel anything, just turned away and trudged back to the trench, eating the last of my sandwiches. I told the other men in our trench, that he had 'bought it', or 'cashed in his chips', or 'played his last card', or some other slang we used. Anything other than saying he was dead.

Someone said, 'No more favours now in getting extra rations or kit.' Other than that, it did not seem to register, and everyone got on with whatever they were doing, even if it was nothing.

We were continuously dog-tired, too weary to feel anything. At times we seemed to move and operate in a sort of daze, like zombies, as if we were half dead.[1]

* * *

On his return journey in early January 1944 from a conference in Tehran with Stalin and Roosevelt, Churchill stopped in Tunis to meet with Generals Alexander and Eisenhower. In Tehran Stalin had been dismissive of what he saw as slow progress in the Italian campaign, which to him was a diversion. He was impatient for the Allies to launch the Normandy invasion, Operation OVERLORD. If the Germans could not be limited to no more than twelve divisions in northern France, Roosevelt and Churchill were reluctant to press ahead. Stalin goaded the two Allied leaders, particularly Churchill, who at one point, incensed at Stalin's criticisms, walked out of the meeting.[2]

Churchill saw the Italian campaign not only as a strategic thrust into the underside of Nazi Europe, but also as a means of diverting German forces away from France and OVERLORD. An amphibious landing at Anzio would get around the Gustav Line and open up the route to Rome. Although the Americans were making OVERLORD the pre-eminent priority for attacking Germany, both Roosevelt and Churchill wanted Rome captured before the Normandy landings planned for June.

Not only would it draw more German forces into the Italian conflict, but it would also provide a tremendous psychological boost to the American and British populations and their troops. Anzio seemed the only way to do that in the timeframe. Arriving in Tunis by plane from Cairo, Churchill went down with a bout of pneumonia, which extended his stay in a villa at Carthage. Nevertheless, it did not prevent him from finalizing the plans for Operation SHINGLE, the codeword for an amphibious landing at Anzio.[3]

Anzio is a fishing port as well as a summer seaside resort, on the Lazio region coast about thirty-five miles south-east of Rome. In Roman times it was known as Antium, where successive emperors such as Caligula and Nero built luxurious villas and where Cicero restored his libraries of scrolls. The flat hinterland of Anzio, and Nettuno to its south-east, was known to the Romans as the Pontine Marshes.

This marshy plain is ringed by mountains, from the Aurunci near Cassino in the south to the Alban Hills to the north. Not surprisingly armies from ancient times have always been wary of crossing this plain on its main north-south Highway 7, the Romans' Appian Way. In the 1930s Mussolini drained the marshes, built canals and constructed five new cities on the reclaimed land. In 1944 it seemed that the Allies' planners no longer harboured any fears of the once marshy terrain.

*   *   *

The aim of the Anzio landings was to strike inland some fifteen miles to Albano and the Alban hills, and so cut the two north-south Highways, 6 and 7. The thinking was that this incursion would force the Germans to retreat from Cassino and the Gustav Line. Combined with a breakout from Cassino, it could develop into an early thrust for Rome.

From Anzio's beaches two roads led inland over a flat coastal plain. The Via Anziate headed north from the town through railway lines at Carroceto and Campoleone, and then past Osteriaccia and Genzano to Highway 7. The other road, from Nettuno two miles or so east of Anzio on the sea front, led north-east through Conco, Cisterna and Velletri to Valmontone on Highway 6. On the maps the plan looked straightforward, a master-stroke to outflank and sever the Germans' supply lines.

Compared to the attack planned to commence on 12 January by Fifth Army on the Gustav Line at Cassino, the Allied Command saw the Anzio landings as the primary operation. The American Major General J.P. Lucas headed the Anzio taskforce, the US VI Corps, which comprised the 1st British Division, commanded by Major General W.B.C. Penney, and the 3rd US Division, led by Major General L.K. Truscott.

In the early hours of 22 January the 1st British Division, with 2 Special Service Brigade, landed seven miles to the north of Anzio. Although two days earlier at Cassino the US 36th Division had been cut down in its ill-fated attempt to cross the Rapido River, hopes remained high that Anzio would break the Germans' logjam of defensive lines.[4] The Americans' 3rd Division, with one Parachute and three Ranger battalions, came ashore largely unchallenged on the beaches to the east of Anzio. From there they reached out beyond their first goal, the Mussolini Canal, before their patrols were blocked by German forces.

To the west and north of Anzio the 1st Scots Guards and 2 Special Service Brigade also found no resistance, and by 2.45am were four miles inland at the Padiglione Woods. There they dug in as ordered, while patrols struck out further. At the beachhead 24 Guards Brigade, which included the 5th Grenadiers, were all safely ashore by 11.30am.[5]

Jack Chaffer, the 'would-be Surrey' lost to the 5th Grenadiers on joining up, was one of those struggling ashore. He had shipped across from Tunisia to Naples before embarking for Anzio. Despite the imminent landings, the stories he had heard about the Surreys' ordeals at Termoli, the Trigno and Sangro Rivers had made him think that the Guards had been the right choice. Now he was not so sure.

It was two in the morning, 22 January, and I was in the first group down the ramp at Green Beach. The water came up to my neck, as we struggled to the beach, holding rifles and everything we could above the waves. Once off the beach we dug in as fast as we could in a garden somewhere. Pouring rain meant there was no drying off. Sometime later we heard two officers talking outside a tent. One of them said, 'We must get on.' Later it was said to have been General

133

Alexander conversing with our CO, who was supposed to have said in reply, 'But I have not received any orders to move from General Lucas.'[6]

* * *

The Anzio taskforce had got ashore successfully, and the Alban Hills were beckoning. However General Lucas's orders from General Clark required him to consolidate his beachhead positions before striking out. Although the Allies' landings at Anzio took the Germans by surprise, Kesselring quickly ordered General von Mackensen's Fourteenth Army to attack and drive the Allies back into the sea. By 26 January von Mackensen had six divisions moving on Anzio. The Allies' advantage of surprise would quickly dissipate.

From the south of France, from Genoa, from Istria, from Florence and Trieste, came the 715th and 114th Light Divisions, the 65th and 71st Grenadier Divisions, and the 16th and 90th Panzer Grenadier Divisions. These reinforcements were deployed into two streams, into I Parachute Corps against British forces west of the Albano Road, and into LXXVI Panzer Corps to the east against US forces. The two corps came under the command of Fourteenth Army Group HQ, which Kesselring moved south from Verona.[7] Two more divisions were on their way, as Hitler released more reserves from the north. The German High Command thought Anzio could be a 'Second Front', and intended to destroy the Allies' beachhead.[8]

* * *

As early as 24 January, patrols of the 5th Grenadiers pushed out from the beachhead towards Campoleone and Albano. Three miles out they found Carroceto defended by the 3rd Panzer Grenadiers. General Lucas ordered the US 3rd Division to move towards Cisterna on the next day, and for the 1st British Division to do likewise in the direction of Albano.[9] Jack Chaffer was in that first drive towards the Alban Hills.

We now lived thinking we could be dead the very next minute, whether it be in the next German attack, from incoming shells and machine-gun fire, or in the next attack we made. We were ordered to attack some German positions at what was known as the 'Factory', one of Mussolini's fully enclosed modern towns at Aprilia.[10]

The so-called 'Factory' at Aprilia, covered a considerable area. Built by Mussolini's Fascist party, including a model housing village and shopping centre, Aprilia would soon become known more as a slaughterhouse.[11]

Before they attacked, Jack waited in his No. 2 Company for the preliminary artillery stonking of the complex to do its work. Suddenly the shelling stopped, and they got the word to rush forward.

As we ran I thought this is it, we are dead men. At last we reached their trenches, shouting and firing as we jumped in, expecting to be cut down by return fire. Then we were in the German trench, untouched. Two Germans were huddled down shell-shocked, one still with a Spandau on a fixed line, pointing at us through an archway. They could have easily killed all of us. Somehow no one shot them, and they were led away as PoWs, both trembling with fear. Funny thing is we were shaking just as much![12]

Together Alexander and Clark visited the beachhead on 25 January and heard that 5th Grenadiers had taken both Carroceto and Aprilia. The two towns were about five miles from Campoleone and a similar distance beyond was Albano. Despite putting pressure on Lucas to press on faster to the Alban Hills, the Generals must have thought everything was going well.[13]

Beyond Carroceto and Aprilia lay a dead flat plain stretching to the Alban Hills and known as Campo di Carno, which translates as 'Field of Flesh'. For those who knew some Italian, it must have stirred a sense of foreboding.

On 26 January the Germans counter-attacked at Carroceto and Aprilia, which the 1st Irish Guards and 5th Grenadiers withstood at great cost. The Grenadiers lost a whole platoon dead or captured, and their No. 3 Company was reduced to around only twenty men. Then the Grenadiers' dwindling survivors lost their second-in-command, before their CO was wounded and evacuated. This left another wounded officer, a Major 'Dusty' Miller, to step up and take command.

In his diary for 26 to 29 January, Corporal E.P. Danger at 5th Grenadiers HQ, recorded how the Battalion's CO and his staff held on in a commandeered garage building. In an increasing artillery bombardment, the Germans even had a gun firing 250lb shells from a distant rail track. It had their range, and although one shell landed very close to the garage, luckily it did not explode. A direct hit, however, by one of those on the garage, would obliterate the building and everyone in it.

When there was a pause in the shelling, they would relish another brew of tea, and with rather less enthusiasm take out more of their American K rations. Typically these included a tin of ham, chocolate, cigarettes, sugar, a coffee bag and biscuits which had a flavour reminiscent of chewing gum. Despite catching some wild chickens in one respite, Corporal Danger could see that men's nerves were fraying. And the casualties continued to mount.

During the afternoon of 28 January, someone rushed in to say that some ammunition boxes, next to a petrol dump were on fire. He dashed out again with a fire extinguisher, but at the precise moment a shell landed and took his leg off, and by this time things were well ablaze.[14]

In the midst of this damage and loss of supplies, orders were received for the 5th Grenadiers to make an attack that same night. In response the CO left the garage with a group of officers to undertake some reconnaissance. By mistake they got too close to the German lines. Five officers were killed, including all of the company commanders. With the resulting command structure in shock and disarray, and a dwindling number of men becoming ever more exhausted and bomb-happy, to try and organise an attack now seemed like a suicide mission.

Fortunately providence intervened, when Brigade HQ gained intelligence that some forty Panzers waited in the positions to be attacked. Good sense prevailed. The attack was cancelled, and the depleted Grenadiers pulled back, to be replaced by the Foresters.

In the midst of the killing and a dire battle situation, Jack Chaffer told of how a soldier's humour survived:

The time came to be relieved by a northern battalion, whose troops were much shorter than us. One of their sergeants appeared, told a couple of his men to take over our trench, and walked a short distance away. Because in the Grenadiers every man is over six feet tall, slit trenches were dug deeper than most other battalions. In one place the shelling with airburst shrapnel was so bad, that one of our men, an ex-miner, had dug down extra deep again.

He had dug the trench some eight feet deep, and at the bottom sloped it into a side cavity and overhang of some three feet with timber props, that gave full cover from air bursting shells.

The two new men, small northerners jumped in, and disappeared out of sight into the cavity. At that moment their sergeant strode back, looked down into the trench, and exclaimed, 'Bloody hell! Where the hell have they got to?' The confusion on his face gave us all a rare laugh.[15]

* * *

Beginning during the night of 29 January, 24 Guards Brigade went forward again and fought their way out of Aprilia. Typically it was as much a struggle against the confusion of the battlefield, as well as enemy fire, as Jack Chaffer remembered:

To get to the planned attack point, we were told to follow the white tape laid out for us. Huh, what a joke! Most times the tape just disappeared in the middle of nowhere – destroyed by shelling, ground into the mud, or just blackened so much we could not see it. And there we were under fire, scrabbling around looking for this bloody tape to check we were going in the right direction.

They were finally held up less than a mile from Campoleone's railway line. An advance on their left by the US 1st Armored became blocked at some ravines while, on their right flank, the US 3rd Division came to a halt a mile from Cisterna. Political dissatisfaction at not advancing the fifteen miles to occupy the Alban hills was increasing. Alexander visited the beachhead again from 31 January to 2 February and, because of warnings of an imminent German attack, he and Lucas ordered defensive positions to be prepared.

Despite the pressure from London and Washington to get forward to occupy the Alban Hills, the reality on the battleground was stark. In less than two weeks the US 3rd Division had lost more than 3,000 men and the British 1st Division more than 2,100. For those who were left in the British 2 and 3 Brigades, and 24 Guards Brigade, the order to dig in meant they were now stuck in an exposed salient reaching nearly to Campoleone.[16]

* * *

In the foremost, and most northern, bulge of the salient's front line, 3 Brigade's three battalions, 1st Duke of Wellington's, 1st King's Own Shropshire Light Infantry and 2nd Sherwood Foresters, were only just south of the railway at Campoleone town. On 3 February 3 Brigade were outnumbered and overwhelmed as six battalions of the Germans' 3rd Panzer Grenadier and 65th Infantry Divisions forced them to withdraw. This left 2 Brigade and 24 Guards further isolated, holding Carroceto and Aprilia. Worse was to come.

The 5th Grenadiers, and their fellow guardsmen of 24 Brigade, held part of the Buonriposo Ridge on the left side of the salient. In scrubby hills in north to south order were 1st Irish Guards, 1st Scots, 5th Grenadiers, and 2nd North Staffordshires. The 2nd North Staffordshires suffered the first onslaught, taking heavy losses in A and B Companies and having C Company totally destroyed.

By the end of the first week of February the German Fourteenth Army had swollen to around 100,000, while Allied troops were still only some 76,000. On the evening of 7 February, General Schlemm with nine Panzer Grenadier battalions, launched a massive assault to take the two towns of Carroceto and Aprilia.[17]

The 5th Grenadiers then came under attack from both the front and the rear where the North Staffordshires had been broken. After losing their Nos 1 and 3 Companies, those Grenadiers still standing in No. 2 and HQ Companies pulled back into a quarry called the Gully. Jack Chaffer was

137

one of those Grenadiers still left, holding a narrow salient between the Buonriposo Ridge and the Via Anziate:

On 7 February an attack by twelve or more German battalions began, or so it was claimed. It certainly felt like it. We and the rest of the bridgehead were very close to being driven back into the sea. From then on we were stuck in those trenches under continuous attack and constant rain.

Near the entrance to the Gully was the Carroceto Creek, known as the Ditch. The gap between the creek and the Ditch offered the Germans the opening to bring forward their tanks to gain the Anziate Highway. A breakthrough would enable the Panzers to drive onto Anzio, and also cut off the Scots Guards and 1st London Irish Rifles. To defend this gap, and save the beachhead, all that was left were a few paratroopers of H Company of the US 504th Parachute Infantry, and the surviving men of 2 and HQ Support Companies of the 5th Grenadiers.

Photographs of troops in the Anzio trenches are reminiscent of the Great War. In the chaos of mud, bodies and equipment, some men are caught looking at the camera, their eyes frozen in a mixture of despair and hate.

'Stuck in those rain filled trenches, our feet were always sodden and rotten,' said Jack Chaffer. 'During the night, if we were lucky, a lorry came around, and they would throw out fresh boots and socks. It was a lottery to get anything close to a reasonable fit.'[18]

The next German attack began when Lieutenant Heinrich Wunn's No. 7 Company, of the 147th Regiment of the German 65th Division, charged through the night of 7/8 February, intent on crossing the Ditch and reaching the Via Anziate. Facing them were Major W.P. Sidney and his HQ Support Company of the 5th Grenadiers. The Germans ran into an unexpected obstacle in the gap between the creek and the Ditch, dense and razor-sharp brambles. Only a narrow farmer's path had been hacked through them.

If Lieutenant Wunn and his men broke through they would gain control of the Anziate Highway and cut off Carroceto and the Factory. There would be an open route for the Germans and their Panzers to drive all the way down to Anzio itself. Major Sidney and his men held their ground with a frenzied fusillade of fire and grenade throwing.

As the German troops became entangled in brambles that were worse than barbed wire, their shouts turned to tortured screams. The rifle fire of Major Sidney's men found them in the dark, entangled by the brambles, and cut short their struggles. Major Sidney, despite being wounded by a 'friendly fire' grenade and bleeding profusely, led their stand, firing his Tommy gun and also hurling grenades. About 3.30am some more American paratroopers arrived to give support. By the end of the night

...nturipe. The mountaintop town, which was defended by German paratroopers, had to be taken ... 78th Division. (*Private collection*)

...he road to Centuripe, indicating just how tough was the task that faced 78th Division. ...ichard Doherty)

Into Italy. 1st Surreys move up to Larino. (*Linda Standen*)

Lt John Woodhouse leads the Surreys' Battle Patrol. Note that the 78th Division badge, a golden battle-axe, was worn over the left breast pocket of the battledress jacket by members of the Patrol. (*Michael Woodhouse*)

An aerial photograph of the Cassino area, showing Cassino town, Monte Cassino and the Abbey and the nearby Monte Cairo, which towers over Monte Cassino. (*US National Archives*)

The bombing of Cassino town on 15 March 1944. (*US National Archives*)

Cigarette, the codename for the smokescreen which was maintained over the Cassino battlefront by Allied artillery. (*US National Archives*)

Castle Hill, overlooking Cassino town, provided a strongpoint for the German defenders. (*US National Archives*)

The Abbey on Monte Cassino in the winter of 2011/12, covered in snow and evoking the horrific conditions of early 1944. (*Damiano Parravano/Associazione Linea Gustav (Gustav Line Association), Piedimonte San Germano, Italy*)

A view from Monte Cairo, showing the Abbey on Monte Cassino, the town and, beyond, the mass of Monte Trocchio. (*Damiano Parravano/Associazione Linea Gustav, Piedimonte San Germano, Italy*)

Soldiers of 1/6th Surreys in Cassino town. (*Linda Standen*)

German prisoners are marched in during the fighting in the final battle for Cassino. (*Private collection*)

he Commonwealth War Graves Commission Cemetery at Cassino with Monte Cassino and the bbey overlooking it. (*Richard Doherty*)

s the battles for Cassino raged, so too did the fighting in the Anzio beachhead. British soldiers look t for danger in Anzio. (*Linda Standen*)

A convoy makes its way through the ruins of a town in the Liri valley as Eighth Army pushes through towards Rome. (*Private collection*)

Lake Trasimene where Hannibal destroyed a Roman army and where the Germans planned to delay the Allies in the summer of 1944. (*Author's photograph*)

Orvieto Cathedral.
(*Author's photograph*)

lied soldiers had to
dure a second winter
war in northern
aly. Conditions were
ery difficult and
ovement was often
stricted while
pplying troops in
ountain positions
quired mules.
rivate photograph)

Soldiers of 5th Grenadiers in the Gothic Line in that final winter of war. (*Jack Chaffer*)

Death of an army group. Some of the detritus of the Germany Army Group C in Italy lies south of the River Po. (*Private photograph*)

attack, only twenty-nine of Major Sidney's company and forty-five paratroopers were left. When hit in the head by a German stick grenade, Major Sidney finally became a casualty himself. He survived to be awarded the Victoria Cross.[19]

*   *   *

The 5th Grenadiers' No. 2 Company still held their positions on the Buonriposo Ridge, and even as they were ordered to withdraw with Major Sidney's survivors on 9 February they incurred further losses. On their last day in the line they lost their fourth CO in three weeks, Lieutenant Colonel A.C. Huntington. Out of some 800 men the Grenadiers had lost 606 killed, wounded or missing. These losses effectively destroyed the 5th Grenadiers as an offensive fighting force, yet their stubborn resistance proved pivotal in successfully holding up the German onslaught.[20]

Although the Grenadiers and others had bought time, by 10 February the Allies had been pushed back out of the salient. On 16 February the Germans' Operation FISCHFANG (Fish-catch) forced them even farther back down the Via Anziate until, on 18 February, the German attack was finally stopped on the defensive lines of the original beachhead. Operation FISCHFANG cost the Germans 5,400 casualties, the Allies 3,500, to bring total casualties in only four weeks since the landings to a staggering 20,000 on each side. The next attempt by the Germans was on 29 February, by LXXVI Panzer Corps, on the Cisterna southern front. It was stopped, inflicting on them another 2,500 casualties.[21]

In the first week of March the fighting became a stalemate, a war of attrition. The Germans had turned off the pumps draining the land so that it was fast returning to its marshy origins, severely restricting any movement by tanks or other vehicles. It is alleged that the Germans' flooding of the land also aimed to foster mosquitos and malaria for the spring and summer.

From the ring of surrounding mountains, the Germans maintained an incessant artillery bombardment on the Allies' bridgehead, reaching into the town of Anzio itself. For both sides it became a desperate battle to hold onto positions while, at the same time, it was a race to build up force levels for the drier weather to come in the spring. Contrary to the original plan for Anzio to take precedence over the attempt to break the Gustav Line, it was now the reverse. Efforts must be redoubled to break through at Cassino, where grand strategy was also in tatters.

The surviving remnants of 5th Grenadiers, including Jack Chaffer, were pulled back on 6 March. By this time they had lost more than 75 per cent of their strength in casualties. They were shipped back to Naples for recovery and to rebuild with replacements. As they sailed into the Bay of Naples, smoke was spiralling from the summit of Vesuvius. To Jack it seemed like a peace pipe, signalling a welcome respite.[22] On 19 March Vesuvius erupted. The age-old volcanic forces were a symbol that the war continued.

Notes

1. Veterans' Accounts, Chaffer.
2. Fenby, *Alliance*, pp. 236–7.
3. Carver, op cit., p. 108.
4. Ibid.
5. Ibid, p. 118.
6. Veterans' Accounts, Chaffer.
7. Linklater, *The Campaign in Italy*, pp. 194–5.
8. Carver, op cit., p. 123.
9. Ibid.
10. Veterans' Accounts, Chaffer.
11. Linklater, op cit., p. 192.
12. Veterans' Accounts, Chaffer.
13. Carver, op cit., p. 123.
14. Ibid, pages 124–6.
15. Veterans' Accounts, Jack Chaffer.
16. Carver, op cit., p. 126.
17. Ibid, pp. 128–33.
18. Veterans' Accounts, Chaffer.
19. d' Este, *Fatal Decision, Anzio and the Battle for Rome*, pp. 208–10.
20. Ibid.
21. Carver, op cit., p. 153.
22. Veterans' Accounts, Chaffer.

Chapter 10

Cassino's D-Day Imperative

On Sunday afternoon 19 March, the desperate fighting for the piles of rubble at Castle Hill and Hangman's Hill must have hidden a sub-conscious symbolism for the troops of both sides. Castle Hill and Hangman's Hill were dwarfed by the surrounding mountains, most notably Monte Cairo and Monte Cassino. Yet the two hills were crucial to the occupation of Cassino town and Monte Cassino, and the consequent domination of the Liri Valley. Three times the German paratroopers of the 1st Parachute Division climbed out of Cassino's and the Monastery's rubble, to try and capture the two hills, and three times the 4th Indian Division troops, including the Gurkhas on Hangman's Hill, stopped them.

On Sunday evening the Allies called off their plans for an attack by 5 Indian Brigade. In five days the New Zealanders had lost more than 1,600 men, and the Indians more than 3,000. All immediate offensive plans were shelved and orders given to consolidate on existing positions.

Those German troops who were still alive crawled back to the ruins of Cassino town and the Monte Cassino monastery. A company commander in the German 1st Parachute (Fallschirmjäger) Regiment, Martin Pöppel, saw it as an heroic action, and said:

> Despite the onslaught of many enemy divisions, of shell fire which frequently lasted all day, despite carpets of bombs, the men held firm, crawled out of their holes and returned the fire. Singly, in pairs, sometimes a few more. Like Crete, this month long battle took a high toll in the blood of our men. What a Parachute Machine-Gun Battalion, and what men.[1]

Because of the difficulty of sustaining troops on Hangman's Hill, the Gurkhas were withdrawn from the exposed ruins. It was living up to its name, a place of dread which tormented both sides. Who had lost, who had won? When could the Allies try again to breach the Gustav Line? When would the Germans launch another of their typical counter-attacks? Monday 20 March dawned and, of course, no one had any answers to those kinds of questions.

141

What had the Third Battle of Cassino, as it has since been described, achieved in return for its heavy loss of life and casualties? Three incursions, which at the time may have seemed a paltry reward, were made in the Gustav Line. A bridgehead had been made across the downstream Garigliano, about half of Cassino town and Castle Hill captured and, in the east, the Americans and French at great cost had taken more mountains. It was the end of the third battle for Cassino, but its real meaning was not clear.

On 21 March General Alexander met with Generals Clark and Leese and their staff of Fifth and Eighth Armies. They agreed to consolidate and plan for a new, combined attack in May. The real question now, as in the Tunisian Winter of 1942/43, was which side could build its forces to a level which could exploit the drier weather of spring and the early summer. On 23 March, to replace the Indian Division across a sweeping range of mountain positions, that included the Bowl and Castle Hill, 78th Division including 1st Surreys received orders once again to climb.[2]

*   *   *

To achieve a decisive three to one superiority, General Alexander planned a build-up with a number of deceptions. The vast bulk of Eighth Army was gradually moved during night-time from the Adriatic coast to the Cassino front. False information on planning for another sea-borne landing northwest of Rome, at its port of Civitavecchia, was leaked to the Germans. It must have had an effect for Kesselring kept strong reserves north of Rome until a few days after the start of Operation HONKER, the next attack on Cassino and the Gustav Line.

The French Expeditionary Corps of four divisions, which included 12,000 Goumier troops from North Africa, were secretly moved into the Garigliano bridgehead. The Canadian Corps of two divisions was brought into Eighth Army's Reserve without announcement. At the same time fictitious information was issued that indicated the Canadians were re-locating to Naples, to embark for the fake amphibious operation to land at Civitavecchia.

The Allies' overwhelming air superiority reduced reconnaissance by the Luftwaffe to a minimum, strengthening the cloak of secrecy. Some anti-aircraft units never saw a Luftwaffe plane at all during their time in Italy, and were deployed to provide covering and diversionary fire.[3]

The concealment of forces was not just to give the benefit of surprise, it would hide the reserve capability to exploit the capture of Cassino and Monte Cassino so as to surge forward up the Liri Valley to combine with Operation BUFFALO, an Anzio break-out. The overall Army Group plan was codenamed Operation DIADEM.[4]

*   *   *

1st Surreys go back into the mountains

While the New Zealanders and Indians had fought to make the initial break in the Third Battle of Cassino, the 1st Surreys, and 78th Division generally, had waited, poised to follow through and drive up the Liri valley. The other two battalions of the Surreys' 11 Brigade, 2nd Lancashire Fusiliers and 5th Northamptons, had stayed concealed during the excruciating wait while the Surreys continually patrolled both sides of the Rapido. It was another of the many ploys to confuse and deceive the Germans. The order to attack never came and, on 23 March, the Surreys withdrew back to Mignano and enjoyed a four-day break.[5]

The four days at Mignano seemed to fly and then, with 11 Brigade, the 1st Surreys were sent back to the Cassino killing grounds. This time, as they might have guessed, it was up into the mountains to relieve 4th Indian Division around Monte Cairo, only a little to the north of Monte Cassino.[6]

'It was a bleak and desolate place,' said Daniell, 'made horrible by the number of American, Indian and German dead lying about as reminders of the bitter battles that had already been fought in that place.'[7]

Captain Toby Taylor was in the 1st Surreys' Battalion HQ, located in a natural amphitheatre known as the Bowl:

It was a small level area, set into a steep hillside, with a few olive trees here and there, about the size of a tennis court, containing the graves of a dozen or so Gurkhas. As all movement had to be carried out after dark, it was ideally suited to receive the nightly mule train. Nothing could move by day, and it was here that all supplies, including water, were issued to the carrying parties from the rifle companies. Everything had to be brought up a steep narrow track by mules or Indian porters the five or six miles from B Echelon, the other side of the Rapido at San Michele. Sometimes the mules, or porters, never reached the Bowl, as the nightly shelling tended to scatter them far and wide, so at times even drinking water was severely rationed.[8]

To assault Monte Cassino without attempting a suicidal climb up its single approach road, a zig-zag track of hairpin bends, or a mindless death on its steep rocky slopes, the only other way was to traverse along the Snakeshead Ridge. More like a boomerang in shape than a snake's head, it was narrow with steep sides, and 1,945 feet high at its pivot point. In the freezing cold of January and February the US 34th Division had lost more than 2,000 men fighting for Snakeshead Ridge. Despite the difficulty of being supplied only overnight by mules, in a hazardous journey of seven miles under fire, the Americans captured the ridge, established the bridgehead on the north side of the Rapido and understandably left it with its reptilian name.[9]

143

Now it was the turn of the Surreys' rifle companies to take over the bridgehead from the Gurkhas of the 4th Indian Division. To reach their forward positions they first climbed at night up through the 'The Valley of Death'. Then, amongst the bloodstained rocks of Phantom and Snakeshead Ridges, the Surreys deployed to cling on in either one- or two-man sangars.[10]

During the day they crouched or lay in such sangars, which were little more than scooped-out depressions, with surrounds of loose stones and rocks scrabbled together to give a gesture of cover. Only at night could they dare to stand, when the porters and mules brought up supplies and a hot meal could be cooked.

Some of the Surreys' positions were in full view of German troops in the monastery's rubble. In the evenings they could sometimes hear the Germans singing in their own rat holes amongst the monastery's ruins. One song that was often heard was 'Lili Marlene', the adopted song of both sides. At night both sides might sing the same song but during the day the close proximity often brought a cacophony of incoming fire, and a bumper harvest for both sides' snipers.[11]

On 24 April, after four weeks clinging to the mountain slopes around Monte Cassino, the Surreys were relieved by the 5th Polish Division and pulled back to Capua for rest and training. It brought hot baths, clean clothing, beds under cover, and bars and entertainment in Capua town. Some men were lucky to draw lots for a day or so of leave to Naples, Bari or Maiori. The mud had become dust in the warmer weather and training concentrated on river crossings, street fighting, and attacking with support of tanks. It could only mean one thing, preparation for the next major battle.[12]

The latest mail was distributed and older letters pulled out and re-read. Inevitably, aware that another massive battle for Cassino was imminent, some men found some time in the lull to sit down at last and scribble a few lines to family and loved ones at home. Most tried to sound cheerful, despite the feelings of foreboding at the thought of yet another major battle for Cassino.

In the brief respite Sergeant Gostling in the Surreys' Battalion HQ found time to write another of his letters to Captain Payne, who was rehabilitating still in England:

Dear Captain Payne,
    Yes, we are sweltering now and are back in tropical kit. The weather has been very fickle recently though, and we haven't known whether to put on shorts or a scarf! One day recently we started off by having a minor snow and hailstorm, followed by a terrific wind (and it can

144

blow out here), and finishing up with sunshine in the afternoon! I shall never complain of English weather again I'm sure!

I managed to have a week's leave, my first, at Bari a little while back. I was amazed the way the people in the back areas live. They haven't the slightest idea there is a war on. Still, someone has to be back there, I suppose.

We have had a go at the Cassino battle and saw too much of the town and the Monastery for my liking! The Monastery is all they say about it. It's orrible! But we'll have it soon I hope!

Cheerio from the Orderly Room staff who all send their best wishes.

Very sincerely, Eric Gostling[13]

Gostling's cheerful optimism about yet another imminent battle for Cassino hinted at the horror of battle and the thoughts and longings for home of many men.

Sergeant Frank Oram wrote to his wife, Winifred, recalling their wedding in January 1943. They had snatched only a few days together, before he had been posted out to the Surreys' front lines in Tunisia.[14]

Harry Skilton sent the typical aerogram letter to Jessie, his wife of less than a year, and remembered the summer of 1942 when they had met at the Annan town fair, in Dumfriesshire, Scotland. When Harry somehow got some leave, they had married on 23 June 1943 and just a few days' honeymoon was all they too had had together. It would soon be their first wedding anniversary.[15]

At last Frank Weston got round to replying to a letter from his brother, Les, who had reminded Frank that he would be twenty in a few days' time. Frank had completely forgotten his own birthday and the day had now passed. Les had also said that his girlfriend, Maude, had a friend called Doreen and they had suggested the four of them could get together, once the war was over. Like his birthday, Frank found it hard to grasp, and pondered what to say. It seemed so far away in the future.[16]

Many men struggled to put pen to paper when they faced the dismal outlook of never-ending days of fighting. Some men like Frank Gage wrote home rarely. He sat cleaning his gun again, an obsession he had acquired with Lieutenant Woodhouse in the now disbanded Battle Patrol. If he survived the next battle for Cassino maybe he would write then. Frank harboured the thought of so many others – he would never see England again.[17]

* * *

In February 2006 at Cassino railway station, my taxi driver, Giacomo, grey and wizened, looked a bit of a risk for driving me to the top of the 1,700-feet-high Monte Cassino mountain. The morning was still full of incessant rain, overcast with a biting wind. From the station forecourt looking up at the rocky peak, its slopes bare from the ravages of winter, I could not see where a road could make a climb that seemed nearly vertical. In summer the trees and vegetation appear to give Monte Cassino a softer, greener look, which brings hordes of tourists.

In the Cassino battles, Major Fred Majdalany of the Lancashire Fusiliers described it as it was in the winter of 1944: 'But in winter, when the slopes are bare, and the gales and the black thunderclouds sweep across from the wild hinterland of the Abruzzi, the Abbey of Montecassino hardens into a gaunt symbol of defiance, a great fortress in the sky.'[18]

It was just that kind of day for my visit, and for the Surreys in 1944 when they must have cursed as they crouched seeking any slight cover on the bare, rocky mountainsides.

The taxi turned from Cassino's main street and drove past the ruins of the ancient Roman amphitheatre at the mountain's base. In his few words of English, Giacomo assured me he knew every inch of what proved to be five miles of twisting road, climbing through a series of hairpin bends.

We came around the last turn and pulled into an empty car park. As I stepped from the taxi into the driving rain, the cold, thinner air made me gasp, and wish for another layer of clothing. Now I could see why the four drawn-out battles for Cassino, with the troops on both sides fighting, living and dying in the open, has been likened to the horrors of the siege of Stalingrad.

* * *

In the spring of 1944 the next attack on Cassino and the Gustav Line, Operation HONKER, was planned for early May by the combined forces of Fifth and Eighth Armies. Once Operation HONKER had gained sufficient penetration of the Gustav Line, and the hope was it would be within days rather than weeks, Operation BUFFALO would break out from Anzio. The timing was significant. There would be less than a month before the planned D-Day landings in Normandy. The aim was that the offensives would draw German attention and their forces to Italy, and away from Normandy and north-west Europe. The overall Army Group strategy, Operation DIADEM, just had to succeed. Further stalemate or defeats in Italy could be catastrophic, and allow the Germans to divert divisions to Normandy. A strategic loss in Italy would be a huge psychological blow to the Allies, and could even lead to failure of the D-Day landings. It was not even to be contemplated.

The night of 11 May 1944 was set for the fourth battle to begin, the hoped for final battle for Cassino and the Monte Cassino Monastery. With the bulk of Eighth Army now added to Fifth Army, the Allies planned to throw overwhelming force at the mountain bastion. In a concentration of numbers, firepower and a massive artillery bombardment, they intended to smash their way through the Gustav Line and north onto Highway 6.

* * *

1/6th Surreys in the first crossings of the Rapido

After the third Cassino Battle the 1/6th Surreys had withdrawn with 4th Division for rest and recovery at Barracone in the valley of the River Volturno. At first there were hot baths, decent meals, real beds, and even a day or two's leave in Naples. Then the grim reality returned, as they commenced training in river crossings of the Volturno in small assault boats which could be carried in pieces and assembled near the river bank. Once across the river they exercised in both infantry and tank support attacks. The rifle companies repeated the training ad nauseam, until they could assemble, launch, embark, cross and land, quickly and quietly in the dark, over the fast flowing Volturno, to be ready for the similar Rapido River.[19]

With 10 Brigade the 1/6th Surreys would lead 4th Division on the right, to cross the Rapido River, in places up to eighty feet wide, and seize a bridgehead between Cassino and Sant'Angelo. The Surreys' crossing point, codenamed 'Rhine', was a mile and a half below Cassino town, where the banks were up to seven feet high. Another mile or so farther downriver at the 'Orinoco' crossing point, 28 Brigade would enter the river at the same time as the Surreys. Behind 4th Division, ready to cross and exploit either bridgehead, was 78th Division including 1st Surreys. The orders for the river crossings by 1/6th Surreys, and other battalions to follow them, were to push out through their bridgehead a certain set distance, then to swing to the right towards Cassino, which lay about two miles from the river crossing.[20]

On the evening of 9 May 1/6th Surreys drove for two hours up Route 6 to stop near Monte Trocchio, their base for launching the river crossing. Secrecy regarding their move was maintained by leaving their camp with no indication of their departure. Their training boats and other equipment were left as if they would be returning.[21]

During 11 May everyone remained concealed, weapons were cleaned and oiled, letters were written home and everyone rested. It was a beautiful day and very peaceful, and as the operation orders were given and every point explained, the contrast between the quiet of the day and the fury of the battle to come was very marked.[22]

However, training to cross a fast-flowing river at night, without anyone trying to shoot you was all very well, thought Harry Skilton in 1st Surreys. To attempt it under fire, then get ashore and fight for a bridgehead, was an entirely different kettle of fish. Being attached to 1st Surreys' HQ Company, he knew something of the plans for 1/6th to be in the forefront of the coming attack. He had friends in 1/6th, and wondered if he would see them again.

Once across the river 4th Division had to gain four sequential lines of advance, each at intervals of some 1,000 to 2,000 yards. But lines drawn as objectives on a map could not show the reality of the terrain, or the terror, the certain casualties and the German troops to be overcome. It was known that there were mines on both sides of the Rapido and enemy snipers were hiding anywhere in the trees. On the far side of the river stretched flat fields interspersed with drainage ditches. Overlooking this killing ground, to the left across the Piopetto stream in Square Wood, and to the right on a rocky bluff, Point 36, the Germans watched and waited in strength.[23]

On the right of 10 Brigade and 4th Division, 1/6th Surreys led the Rapido crossing. The Surreys' Beachmaster, Major Charles 'Banger' Nash, and a group of his men managed to porter the components of the assault boats to a spot very close to the river.

As this party could not leave the lying-up area until dusk they had to do their job very quickly. Major Nash and his sixty-two men ran the mile and a half to the boats, and then worked feverishly at their task, erecting and laying them out ready for the assault parties. It had to be done in absolute silence, only 400 yards from the river, with the enemy in positions right up to the river's edge.

It was a warm-scented night, and very quiet. As the companies moved stealthily down towards the river, the nightingales were singing. At ten minutes to eleven, however, the peace of the lovely Italian night was shattered by the sudden roar of the massed guns of Eighth Army. It was a most awe-inspiring manifestation of power, the loud continuous thunder of the guns, the screech and whine of the shells in the air, and the explosions as they landed amid the German positions. The sky around Monte Trocchio was illuminated by thousands of gun flashes, and the air vibrated from the continuous explosions.[24]

When the Surreys' A and D Companies reached the river bank, right on time at 11.45pm, and began to launch their boats, German fire began to rake the river. Two of A Company's six boats were caught midstream in the glare of a chance flare, and the German mortars chopped them and their boats into a frothing vortex. Only the men from four boats made it across. Once across the river it was desperate close fighting in seemingly suicidal advances to take the German machine-gun pits with grenades and bayonets.

As soon as they breasted the top of the bank they were met with a hail of bullets from enemy posts around the southern tip of Point 36. Some of the Germans were standing up in the open pumping fire from their automatic weapons and hurling grenades. Under command of their platoon and section commanders the Surreys fanned out from their landing point, went

148

to ground and returned fire vigorously. Gradually platoons and sections groped and felt their way forward through fog and fire and noise towards Point 36. They kept coming up against strongly defended weapons posts, surrounded by barbed-wire and mines.[25]

While A Company fought towards Point 36, the six boats of D Company were pulled off course by the strong current so that where they made landfall the bank was around seven feet high. Despite the use of grappling irons two boats then capsized and several men drowned. It got worse when they lost many more in a minefield. Eventually, once they had found a way out with mine detectors, the survivors were ordered to go left to join up with A Company. Smoke and dust turned the night into a smog which blotted out any light from the moon or stars. The filthy murk did help to hide a cable ferry that shuttled B and C Companies, and men on foot from the Carrier Platoon, across the river to reinforce A and D Companies.

It was extremely confusing. The fog thickened and direction could only be kept by following the lines of tracer fired overhead. The attack against a very determined enemy in well-prepared positions was made by a series of isolated assaults by small groups of men. An enemy post would be spotted by the firing of its machine gun. The attackers would then crawl up to the wire, cut it, hurl in grenades and follow up with the bayonet. It was violent, desperate fighting, but the Surreys' blood was up and, despite their losses, they kept groping forward.[26]

* * *

On the night of 11 May 1/6th Surreys' Lieutenant H.G. Harris led a platoon in D Company across the Rapido river and into the hell of the fourth battle for Cassino. Because he was an accomplished swimmer, Harris would go first, and carry a rope across to the north bank. Once secured and pulled taut, it would allow his men in the assembled boats to shuttle themselves and their supplies across. He looked at the river, and in the dark he thought it to be no more than half the length of a cricket pitch. The problem was the current was flowing fast.

The far bank rose up in a mound like a dyke at the water's edge, and Harris knew that the Germans would be dug in on the other side. Would they have a lookout on watch? The night was eerily quiet, as if it sensed the impending artillery bombardment of Eighth Army. Gazing at the black, swirling water, he hoped against hope he could make the swim with little or no sound.

Surprisingly Harris chose to dive in. It was a clean dive, with hardly any splash, and after a few strokes he reached the other side with minimal downstream drift. Almost at once he found and grasped hold of some half-submerged tree roots. Now even more conscious not to make any noise, he tied the rope around them.

Up against the bank and hugging the tree roots, Harris forced himself to stay still, the icy water reaching up above his waist. From the other side of the bank he could now hear the muffled chatter of German troops. There were only a few minutes to go, he knew, before the shelling began. Hopefully the enemy did not.

Would the shells land the planned ten yards beyond the river's northern edge? That kind of accuracy he found hard to believe. Then the first salvo hit, and it was on target. Immediately the first of the assault boats began to ferry across men and supplies. Under the bombardment's cover, and not least its noise, the men of Harris' platoon joined him, either onto the bank's slope or into the water's shallows.

There they waited. The shelling would lift fifty yards farther on after five more minutes. The moment it did, Harris was thinking, they had to be into the Germans before they had lifted up their heads. He peered at his watch, and wished them to be slow to react. Before the final seconds had ticked over, he slapped the man next to him, and went into a rolling kind of dive over the bank's brow. Once over, it surprised him. The closest German positions were well visible, lit up in the incessant shell explosions.

> I spotted a dug-out about five yards to my right. I had come over the bank with a grenade in either hand, the pins already out as I pulled them from my webbing belt. The grenade in my right hand went into the dug-out, which I thought was the source of the voices I had heard while hugging the bank. The one in my left hand went in the general direction of a machine-gun pit ....[27]

The grenade explosions ignited an instant response from an uncountable number of Spandau machine guns. As previously ordered the platoon sections following his lead then spread out, and went to ground where they could, pinned down by the hail of fire descending on them. Their perilous position prompted Harris to radio Battalion HQ, for mortars to shell the ground between them and the German positions with smoke. It was the only way to give them a chance, he thought, by rushing each enemy dug-out under the cover of hopefully dense smoke, and using grenades to fight a way forward.

By first light Harris learned the depressing news that only two sections of the other two platoons of D Company had crossed the river intact. In fact the D Company commander, the other two platoon commanders, and the Company Sergeant Major of HQ Platoon were all dead. When he informed Battalion HQ by radio of this catastrophe, Harris was promptly informed that he was now in command of D Company. He must at once bring the other sections of men on his side of the river, into his area, and was ordered to try and enlarge the fragile bridgehead as much as he could.

They soon found themselves in a murky fog of confusion. Smoke from the bursting mortars and other shelling soon obscured anything beyond about ten yards away. Firing seemed to come from everywhere, whether it was their own Bren guns or the Spandaus. Rope pulleys were rigged to drag supplies of rations and ammunition over the river bank in sandbagged packs. Anyone foolish enough to clamber over the bank would surely be riddled with bullets.

From thereon day after day, Harris and the remnants of D Company who eventually got across the river to join his new command began to fight their way forward from one German trench or machine-gun pit to the next. It was all crawling, clambering and slithering, until they were near enough to throw grenades. Only the odd extra-deep dug-out gave them an opportunity to stand upright. They did it for seven days and nights, until they reached Highway 6 in the Liri Valley.[27]

* * *

In the Surreys' HQ Company the role of Sergeant H.J. James was to stick close to the CO, Lieutenant Colonel Thompson, and keep in touch by radio with all the forward companies' movements.

'At 11.55pm I had shaken hands with Corporal Knight,' said James, 'as it would be both our birthdays in five minutes. He remarked, "I hope we live to see many more."'

Shortly after midnight, Lieutenant Colonel Thompson, with some staff officers and Sergeant James, managed to cross the Rapido and establish an HQ Command Post in the bridgehead.

> I was sent forward with a telephone line to Major Newton to maintain contact in the attack as most of the wireless sets had failed or been knocked out. D Company lost theirs in the crossing. All companies attacked Point 36 under heavy mortar fire from Jerry, but our lads gave them a real bashing. I was with Major Newton and Lieutenant George when both got hit. I found two men and myself in the open, so I went in with the others and took a machine-gun post and three prisoners.
>
> After a lull in the battle I returned to Lieutenant Colonel Thompson with the three Jerries, and reported that Point 36 was now clear of the enemy. Then the pounding starts. Jerry puts everything on our area, Nebelwerfers, 88mm guns and machine guns by the hundreds. The earth literally lifts around us and there are quite a few casualties.[28]

Dawn broke early at 4.30am. Word got around that A Company was still holding a position on Point 36 and the remnants of B, C and D Companies were fighting on to link up with A Company. By 6.30am the Surreys had captured the whole of Point 36, taking forty-five prisoners. No-one counted the German dead. To the south and rear of the Surreys the other battalions of 10 Brigade had also got across the river and established a shallow bridgehead.

As expected the Germans began to counter-attack and, when the smoke and dust lifted around 11.00am on 12 May, the German artillery began again to target Point 36, Battalion HQ, the ferry sites, and anything that moved. A massive two-way artillery battle opened up. The tenuous bridgeheads had to be held while bridges were built across the Rapido. The Surreys and 10 Brigade had to withstand everything throughout the day and night of 12 May and beyond, so that armour, reinforcements and supplies could move across the river and drive through Cassino and the Gustav Line. Operations HONKER and DIADEM were in the balance.

When there came a lull in the German shelling, the Surreys' Beach-master, Major W.C.E. Nash, crossed on a ferry, and was making his way forward to contact Battalion HQ when enemy shells began falling again around Point 36.

> On looking about for cover, I spotted a weapon pit a few yards away. I jumped in just as a salvo of shells landed nearby. A German soldier was crouched in the bottom and I landed on top of him. He mumbled something like 'Don't shoot, Johnnie', and raised his hands, making no attempt to pick up his Schmeisser. This was just as well, because I had lost my pistol. My prisoner was very frightened – he could not have been more than seventeen years old.[29]

Losses had been very heavy, but a little before midnight the justification and encouragement the 1/6th Surreys needed was received in a message from the brigade commander:

> Own tanks are across the river and are advancing north as fast as possible, location not known. All tanks will cross as soon as construction completed. Hold hard to present positions. Defensive fire forms solid ring round you. Supplies, water, ammunition will come somehow. You have done magnificently. Corps, Division, Brigade Commanders intensely proud of you. If you require further information ask me.[30]

While under fire the Royal Engineers built Bailey Bridges at three crossing points, codenamed Amazon, Blackwater and Congo. The Surreys and 10 Brigade clung on to their fragile bridgeheads. At 3.45am on 13 May more infantry, and tanks of the 17/21st Lancers, began to cross at Amazon. With the support of reinforcements, new battalions and tanks, 10 Brigade began to push out the bridgehead salients. Yet again they had to forget their heavy losses. In just two days the Surreys alone had three officers and twenty-nine men dead, eight officers and 102 men wounded or missing.[31]

On 18 May at 9.00am the Surreys attacked Cassino town, while the Polish Division put in another assault on Monte Cassino. The town was just a mess of ruins, and only pockets of resistance, but it held more heartache for the Surreys. The rubble was embedded with unexploded bombs, shells, mines and booby traps. More men went down. Three more officers were killed, Major Geoffrey Maggs MC, Captain Geoffrey Sloan, and Lieutenant James Hawkins. The Surreys were not deterred and by 10.30am had gained their objectives in Cassino.[32]

* * *

1st Surreys exploit the breakthrough

On the night of 11 May, 1st Surreys had helped to bring forward the assault boats, and hide them on the river bank, for their sister battalion 1/6th Surreys to cross the Rapido. Now they themselves waited for the word to go, to follow across the river and exploit the first bridgehead.

On 14 May the order came, and 1st Surreys' lead companies began to cross the Rapido over the Orinoco Bridge. At the Surreys' Battalion HQ that evening, a signaller, Corporal H.E. Rolph, had just had some dinner, and was settling down with a blanket near their recently dug slit trenches.

> For the troops making the attack there was no sleep, and, as if to show his annoyance, Jerry started lobbing over his long distance shells. A particularly near one woke me up, and I believe I rose to suggest to my signallers that they took to their trenches. I cannot remember if I got back to mine, when I heard this tremendous bang, and for all the world felt as if I had received an almighty punch on the jaw. Possibly I passed out but came to quickly, feeling my mouth full of blood and seemingly full of loose teeth. As I lay there I realized I had been hit. I felt that I wanted to swallow, but feared swallowing the loose teeth and gum floating about in my mouth.[33]

Once across the Rapido the Surreys concentrated their position under long-range shelling near the village of Sant'Angelo. Over the next day as the companies probed forward, they encountered intensifying shellfire. While the bridgehead ranged from the Rapido a distance varying between 500 to 1,500 yards, the goal of 78th Division and the Surreys was to surge forward, bypass Cassino Town, crash through any resistance, and get to Highway 6 ready to drive up the Liri Valley.

It was perfect country from a defender's point of view, criss-crossed by hedges, walls and ditches, and all the better for snipers and ambushes now that the trees and vines were in full leaf and the grass knee-high. Visibility was seldom more than 500 yards: the frequently heavy ground mist – often succeeded by a heat haze – was made thicker by the artificial smoke, by

153

shellfire, by the smoke of burning bridges and buildings, and by the dust raised by tanks and lorries.[34]

In the path of 78th Division were other natural obstacles such as a tributary of the Rapido, the Piopetto, marshy fields from the German insti- gated flooding, hills such as the Massa di Vendetti, the town of Piumarola, mines and the Germans' well-prepared defensive positions. In places they had installed new steel pill-boxes, which sat above three underground rooms stocked with supplies, food and ammunition.[35]

The Battleaxe battalions, reinforced with some armoured support of the Sherman tanks of 16/5th and 17/21st Lancers, began a scrappy, bloody fight to smash their way forward. The Irish Brigade's Inniskillings led the way, before a full scale divisional assault went forward on 16 May.

A leading company of the Lancashire Fusiliers became exposed with no tank support, before they could even dig in. A German counter-attack of infantry and two Panzers found them, and opened fire at close range. Men went down, a PIAT anti-tank section was destroyed, and the company was facing disaster.

Somehow, Fusilier Jefferson got hold of another PIAT anti-tank launcher, and despite being untrained in its use, ran at the tanks. Ignoring a hail of fire, Jefferson stood in the open less than twenty yards from the leading Panzer and fired. When it burst into flames incinerating the crew, he reloaded and headed for the second tank as it turned away.

The arrival of some Lancers' tanks resulted in the Germans pulling back, averting a massacre. Even so the Lancashire Fusiliers' losses were heavy, and C Company lost forty men out of ninety. Jefferson was awarded the VC, becoming the Battleaxe Division's third of the war, to add to those of Major Anderson and Major Le Patourel in Tunisia.[36]

Behind Eighth Army's artillery bombardment, the Surreys pushed forward under heavy German shelling, still directed from Monastery Hill, as described by Sergeant Manning:

All around us were blazing trucks and exploding dumps of ammu- nition. Around us also eddied clouds of dust, from our tanks moving up into the assault. Through this area of fire and smoke streamed the long columns of German prisoners, arrogant parachutists, strutting grenadiers, and shambling infantry. They came in groups of twenty to forty or so, each group escorted by a couple of British soldiers. The Gustav Line was cracking.

It cracked still further the next morning, when we gained the last of the hills overlooking Route 6. Opposition had become slight, and the reason for this was not far to seek. Every country lane, every cornfield, every little farmyard, held its sprawling groups of unburied German dead, smashed and twisted by the unforgettable fury of the British artillery fire.[37]

On 17 May the Surreys and their fellow Battleaxe battalions overran the last remnants of resistance, to break through to the Liri Valley, and Highway 6. On the next morning came news that the Monte Cassino monastery was in the hands of the Poles. Driven by revenge for the horrors inflicted on their country by the Nazis, from the start of D Day on 11 May, despite giving up some early gains and incurring heavy casualties, the Poles recovered to drive the Germans from the ruins of the Monastery in a final assault. On the morning of 18 May the Surreys A Company patrol met with Polish troops of the Kresowa Division on Monte Cassino's slopes.[38] In their own surge through to the Liri Valley, the Battleaxe Division left in their wake approximately 800 enemy killed, wounded or prisoners, forty tanks destroyed, and amongst many other honours won, was that third VC of the war to Fusilier Jefferson.[39]

*　*　*

Today the thought of those terrible battles in 1944 contrasts with the rebuilt Monastery's tranquility, the beauty of its courtyards, cloisters and enclosed gardens. I walked into the entrance cloister to find a garden with its own resident white doves, fluttering and cooing around a sculpture of St Benedict, which commemorates his death on this spot in AD 547. In the second open cloister, named Bramante and reflecting the style of this Renaissance architect, there is another statue of St Benedict, left miraculously intact despite the destruction in 1944 of everything around it. Also still standing from the time of St Benedict himself is the original entrance arch and its Latin word of welcome 'PAX' (peace).

Looking out through the cloister's arcade I glimpsed through the swirling mist a view of the Liri Valley far below. To the west I could see the Polish war cemetery of more than a thousand graves set into the slopes of Snakeshead Ridge.

Walking around the Monastery today, from the ethereal Paradise Loggia that leads into the central Benefactor's cloister, to the opulence of Baroque art and decoration in the Basilica, and to the mosaic and marble of the underground crypts and chapels, one can only marvel at how it was rebuilt from the rubble of 1944 to such perfection by 1957.

Having read so much about its destruction, and seen those pictures of its bombed-out remains, the Monastery's restoration seems almost unbelievable. There must be something else I thought, as we left on the drive back down to Cassino. So when taxi driver Giacomo suggested that he drive me to the English Cemetery I had no hesitation in saying yes. How had it slipped from my mind?

155

Just a few minutes from the town we stopped outside the cemetery. The rain continued to beat down as I walked up some steps to the cemetery entrance, and I thought I would look for any graves of the Surreys. But as I came into full view of the cemetery, I was not prepared for what I saw.

Just thousands of graves – in excess of 8,000, more than at El Alamein. All were immaculately maintained, and tears welled in my eyes. So many graves all appearing the same, it seemed it might take some time to find any from the Surreys. The rain continued to lash down, bitterly cold, no doubt as it was in February 1944. I took a few steps down a path between the rows nearest to me, and there the very first grave in only the second line was that of a soldier in the East Surrey Regiment, and so was the first grave in the next line too. And the next two the same. It was as if an unseen hand had led me here.

The cemetery's graves marked the fallen from across what is now the Commonwealth, as well as the many British Army regiments like the East Surreys. Those whose bodies were never found are commemorated by inscriptions on stone monoliths at the cemetery's centre. And overlooking the cemetery, like a father figure, is Monte Cassino and its monastery, rebuilt perhaps grander than ever.

But more important of course than the Monastery's rebuilding was that those values of the Christian faith, of the Hellenic culture, and those beliefs in individual freedom and in democracy, drawn from its many books and manuscripts, were the foundation of the Allies' motivation.

The final battle for Cassino and the Gustav Line breakthrough took its toll on both sides. The 1/6th Surreys with 4th Division endured fighting so torrid, it took them seven days to advance less than a mile to finally take a position on the Cassino–Rome road. When it was over, the 1/6th Surreys had lost 40 per cent of their force in casualties.

That was the inevitable price, but with a three to one superiority the Allies' Operation HONKER was at last able to burst through the Gustav Line. Cassino and the Monastery were taken, and by late May the Germans were streaming north in another retreat. Could the trap be closed, so that combined with Operation BUFFALO, the break-out from Anzio, the Allies' pincer strategy, could crush the German Tenth Army as if in a vice?

Notes
1. Pöppel, *Heaven and Hell, the war diary of a German paratrooper*, p. 171.
2. Smith and associates, op cit., p. 1.
3. Veterans' accounts, Presland, 91st Light AA Regiment
4. Smith and associates, op cit., pp. 6–7.
5. Daniell, op cit., p. 196.
6. Ibid, pp. 197–8.
7. Ibid, p. 198.
8. Veterans' accounts, *A Pocketful of Time* (unpublished), p. 56.

9. Neillands, op cit., p. 315.
10. Daniell, op cit., p. 198.
11. Ibid, pp. 197–8.
12. Smith and associates, op cit., pp. 12–13; Squire and Hill, op cit., p. 24.
13. Surrey History Centre, ESR/25/PAYN/9.
14. Veterans' accounts, Oram.
15. Veterans' accounts, Skilton.
16. Veterans accounts, Frank Weston.
17. Veterans' accounts, Gage.
18. Majdalany, op cit., p. 6.
19. Daniell, op cit., pp. 202–4.
20. Ibid.
21. Ibid.
22. Ibid.
23. Ibid, p. 205.
24. Ibid, pp. 205–6.
25. Ibid, p. 206.
26. Ibid, p. 207.
27. Carver, op cit., pp. 179–82.
28. Squire and Hill, op cit., p. 40.
29. The Surrey History Centre, ESR/1/14/5/5, 'Recollections of the Beachmaster'.
30. Daniell, op cit., pp. 208–9.
31. Ibid.
32. Ibid.
33. Squire and Hill, op cit., p. 29.
34. Ray, op cit., p. 126.
35. Ibid, p. 130.
36. Ibid.
37. Surrey History Centre, Manning ESR/25/PAYN/8.
38. Smith, and associates, op cit., pp. 12–13.
39. Majdalany, op cit., p. 249.

Chapter 11

Operation DIADEM: Break-Outs from Cassino and Anzio

The break-out from Cassino, like a diamond finally cutting through German steel, came on the morning of 18 May 1944. At around 10.30am troops of II Polish Corps, after their heroic assault had driven out the last of the German defenders, came down from the rubble of Monte Cassino monastery.[1] Once the Poles had joined forces with 78th Division at the mouth of the Liri Valley, four divisions of Eighth Army with more than 20,000 vehicles began to move north, in pursuit of the Germans' Tenth Army, which was retreating up Highway 6.

In order to join up with Allied forces also breaking out from Anzio, it was urgent to quickly reach and take Piedimonte, six miles north-west of Cassino on the Adolf Hitler Line. The core of the planning of Operation BUFFALO was to quickly follow up on the break-outs at Cassino and Anzio and take on the Germans again before they could re-establish their defences on the Adolf Hitler Line.[2]

The Allied Command in Italy argued for the rapid exploitation of the victories at Cassino and Anzio, by requesting a commitment of more forces to defeat and destroy the German armies, so as to then accelerate the offensive drive into northern Italy. Their motive was to draw German forces away from Operation OVERLORD, the Allies' planned invasion of north-west Europe, which was known to be imminent. The D Day landings in Normandy, their precise date still held secret at the time, was scheduled in early June, less than three weeks after the breakthrough of Operation DIADEM.

General Alexander, with his usual confidence, advised Churchill that nothing, except an extra ten or more German divisions, could prevent Fifth and Eighth Armies from taking Vienna early in 1945. Clark recorded a similar view in his diary. If they were blocked by such a level of German reinforcements, Alexander argued, that would be exactly what was needed to assist OVERLORD.

However, Eisenhower and the American Joint Chiefs of Staff had their own quite different plan, Operation ANVIL. They believed that Operation

ANVIL, a landing in the south of France, would draw even more German troops away from the OVERLORD landings. Conversely, the other consequences would be that Operation ANVIL would draw troops and supplies away from Allied Armies in Italy, and play into the hands of Kesselring.[3]

* * *

For Operation DIADEM to succeed, and with it any hope of quickly advancing on Rome, Eighth Army must race north from Cassino, and immediately smash through the Adolf Hitler Line. Acting as a back-up defence to the Gustav Line, the Adolf Hitler Line stretched from the coast through Aquino and close to Piedimonte, to join the Gustav Line near Monte Cairo. It held the Allied troops' usual nightmares. Minefields and barbed wire sought to channel attackers towards killing grounds, which were covered by artillery and machine-gun positions embedded into rock and concrete emplacements. In concealed locations, Panzers and Panzergrenadiers were waiting, ready to rush forward to counter Allied thrusts.

The main attack on the Adolf Hitler Line, a Canadian assault named Operation CHESTERFIELD, began on 23 May. It was coordinated with a break-out from the Anzio bridgehead farther north up the coast. On 24 May the Canadians drove through at Pontecorvo and Aquino, and the next day Polish troops captured Piedimonte.[4] The Adolf Hitler Line was now breached. Alexander's plan to cut off and destroy the German Tenth Army as it retreated from Cassino appeared to be coming to fruition.

The plan required Truscott's VI Corps, part of Clark's Fifth Army to emerge from Anzio in Operation BUFFALO and move inland from the coastal Route 7. Then, as Eighth Army pursued the German Tenth Army up the Liri Valley on Route 6, Truscott's VI Corps must block them at Valmontone. The trap was being closed when, on 25 May, Clark sent orders to Truscott, to change the axis of advance of his VI Corps, and head north up Route 7 towards Rome. Only a small force was to be left in the path of the Germans.

At first Truscott could not believe it and, not wanting to carry out the orders, tried to get in touch with Clark. By the end of the day, unable to do so, he had to comply reluctantly and order his troops north. The result was that the German Tenth Army brushed aside the small, residual contingent of VI Corps troops and made its escape northwards. Later, in his memoirs, Truscott accused Clark of being disloyal to Alexander's orders and causing the failure of the Allies' plan to destroy Tenth Army in the planned pincer movement.

This left the question as to where the Germans would make a stand. Hitler feared that if Tenth Army sought to defend Rome, it could be enmeshed in another 'Stalingrad-like' defeat. He approved the retreat to continue past the Italian capital and declared it an open city. Apart from the Germans' customary rearguard actions, Kesselring continued to with-draw his forces to the north of the Italian capital.

Subsequently, on 4 June, Fifth Army entered Rome. Clark duly had his photograph taken in front of a sign reading 'Roma' on the city's boundary and many have alleged that this was Clark's motive, to be seen as the 'conqueror' of the Eternal City. Meanwhile German forces streamed northwards past Rome in retreat and so were able to regroup, to fight on at a place and time more to their choosing. Two days later Clark's snapshot of his conquest was forgotten by the media when, on 6 June, D Day, the Allies in Operation OVERLORD landed in Normandy.[5]

Clark later argued that his orders were flexible enough to allow him to make the switch of direction towards Rome. There was some rationale in his decision. Eisenhower and Washington viewed it as important that US troops were seen capturing Rome. It would be a major psychological boost for the American people, and for the troops readying themselves for their D Day ordeals.

Despite the failure of Operation BUFFALO to trap and destroy the German Tenth Army, Allied forces pressed on in pursuit. They had twenty-eight divisions and unchallenged air superiority against the badly-mauled and retreating twenty-one divisions of the Germans. Alexander still had every hope of reaching the Po valley, or even the Alps, before winter set in. From there he could plan to drive on to Vienna in the spring, or even into the Balkans to beat the Russian advance.[6] The long-held vision of Churchill and Alexander was to expand the Italian Campaign into the Balkans and Austria, perhaps even into southern Germany.

To support this strategy with more men, guns and equipment, was unacceptable to Roosevelt. The Americans' insistence on the priority of Operation ANVIL, the invasion of southern France, and originally intended to be simultaneous with Operation OVERLORD, won the day. By early July seven divisions, the 3rd, 36th and 45th Divisions of Truscott's VI Corps and four French Divisions of mountain troops, General Juin's entire French Expeditionary Corps, had been transferred to ANVIL, which later came to be known as Operation DRAGOON, in recognition of the forces commandeered from Italy.

The loss of the experienced French mountain troops, who had excelled in the high terrain around Monte Cassino, accentuated the blow. Ahead of Fifth and Eighth Armies between Rome and the Po stretched the Tuscan Apennines, which swing across country from the west coast north of Florence to the east almost to the Adriatic shore. Farther south there was a closer barrier, Umbria's mountains around Lake Trasimene, where German defences along the Albert Line would first impose another blood toll.

To compensate for the loss of these forces, Clark's Fifth Army was reinforced with the US 92nd Infantry Division, a Brazilian Division and the

British XIII Corps from Eighth Army. Even in the face of this disruption, and the difficulty of integrating disparate units, Alexander meant to press on hard after the retreating Germans.

The first objective was Florence on the River Arno. However the real imperative was to prevent Kesselring consolidating his forces once again. While Fifth Army nearer the west coast was making for Pisa, Eighth Army tackled the Umbrian hills heading for Florence. Could the Germans be caught before they reached the Tuscan Apennines, where for a year or more they had been preparing their Gothic Line defences?[7]

From the start of their retreat from Cassino and Anzio, the Germans had their eyes on making for the Gothic Line. They saw it as their final defensive line in Italy, using the Tuscan Apennines to guard the Po valley and Italy's industrial north. Even so, it was still the Germans' usual practice to withdraw at night leaving booby-traps, mines and rearguards to provide covering fire during the next day to obstruct and slow down the Allies' pursuit. For they knew that the months of stalemate at Cassino and Anzio, and every day they gained, was enabling the Gothic Line to be built into their toughest defensive barrier.[8]

But first the Allied armies had to overcome yet another defensive barrier, the Albert Line. Kesselring had built the Albert Line from Grosseto on the west coast along the River Ombrone, around the southern edge of Lake Trasimene and across to the east coast north of Pescara. It was meant to delay the Allies reaching the strategic ports of Livorno (Leghorn) in the west and Ancona in the east.

* * *

1st Surreys drive north

In the front lines of Eighth Army's pursuit of the Germans from Cassino, the 1st Surreys, once again in 11 Brigade of 78th Division, drove northwards up Highway 6 through the Liri Valley. The constant difficulty for Eighth Army was to maintain the rapidly extending lines of communication and the supply of petrol, ammunition and food. With only one viable route north, the traffic congestion was appalling. In contrast the Germans were falling back along established supply depots and prepared defensive positions.

At times the enemy withdrew at high speed, and Allied forces had to take great risks in order not to lose contact. Every now and again German rearguard units would turn at bay and make their stand, usually on a line of hills. Almost always the leading infantry would take a hard knock, for it was not possible to take even normal precautions, so invariably the first platoon to bump would get caught right out in the open.[10]

The first contact with a strong defensive position would trigger heavy German shelling. Then, following a counter by Allied artillery, the Germans would often withdraw during the night. The grind of hard fighting went on day after day.

To keep getting the job done, the gallows humour of the British soldier played its part. While stopped near Aquino the Surreys' Sergeant Frank Oram was surprised to be summoned in front of the Battalion's commanding officer, Lieutenant Colonel Hunter, and requested, not ordered, to form and command a Sniper Group.

> This rather threw me. It appeared that, for the first time in my Army career, as a pre-war soldier, I was being given an option and with the usual caution of war-time it brought me down to earth with a bump. However, being a Platoon Sergeant/Platoon Commander, there couldn't be a harder life, so I decided to take the job, and thus the Sniper Group was formed which I commanded for the rest of the War.

When Frank told his fellow sergeants of his 'volunteering', 'They all fell about in fits of laughter.' For Frank however, because the intensity of fighting and loss of men prevented any transfers at that time to the Sniper Group, it became no laughing matter. He alone had to respond to every request for a sniper patrol, 'I became a "lone ranger" spending my days moving from company to company whenever a German appeared.'[11]

The likelihood of being hit by bullet, mine or shell was ever present, so that nerves were constantly on edge, and some incidents are only amusing in recall. In the advance on Highway 6 beyond Aquino towards Rome, Major Toby Taylor at one place took part in a reconnaissance patrol with the CO and his new second-in-command.

> Our new 2 i/c was a Major 'Vino' Fisher, a keen lepidopterist. He suddenly yelled, 'Stop!' We all hurled ourselves to the ground thinking he had seen a German patrol, and we were about to be shot up. Vino however, had merely called a halt to examine a butterfly, which happened to be passing.
> The CO's reaction can only be imagined.[12]

By 2 June the Surreys had pushed up as far as Torrice and Frosinone and their patrols were stretching out farther north probing the German positions. Frank Weston recalled that around Frosinone, in the hills, were many partisans.

> They were carrying out raids against the Germans, and an officer from special ops, SAS or something, Roy Farran, parachuted into no man's land to help coordinate their attacks with ours. Frosinone was famous for sword making, and most houses still had their own forge. We wondered if they still used those swords![13]

Around this time one Surreys' patrol, led by Sergeant Thomas Carter, overcame and captured a German artillery crew. After fighting off repeated enemy counter-attacks, Carter and his men even brought back the 88mm gun. For this and a long series of prior brave actions, Carter received the DCM.[14]

While front-line units such as the Surreys were putting in the unseen hard slog in Italy's endless inland mountains, other more momentous events were taking place. On 5 June there came the news of Clark's Fifth Army entering Rome, and on the next day it was the Normandy D-Day landings. But the good news made no difference to the Surreys, apart from quickening the pace of advance. On 8 June, despite the traffic jam of Eighth Army's trucks and armour, the Surreys managed to motor sixty-five miles up Highway 6 and by nightfall had entered Rome.

Almost every yard of the road's surface was scarred by bomb craters, big and small, and with both sides of the highway littered with the wreckage of German transport – heavy trucks, light AA guns, staff cars, the ever present Volkswagen, which had been strafed day by day by the Allied air forces. Towns and villages along the way were mere heaps of rubble. It was early the next morning when the convoy passed through the southern outskirts of Rome and over one of the intact bridges across the River Tiber.[15]

There was no sightseeing, however, just straight through to stop on the edge of the city's northern suburbs.

* * *

That same day farther north than 1st Surreys on Highway 6, the 5th Battalion Grenadier Guards were pushing on through the hills a little to the east of Lake Bolsena towards the hill town of Orvieto. Lance Sergeant Jack Chaffer was back in the line with the 5th Grenadiers, pressing forward to catch up with the retreating Germans.

Highway 6 was head to tail with vehicles, tanks and thousands of soldiers. The Germans were in full retreat. On 8 June we were heading for Orvieto, when our Battalion was held up at Bagnoregio, where an infantry battle took place. My company took about 50 per cent casualties, eleven killed and the remainder wounded. In my platoon four killed, twelve wounded. Quite a blow to the system. On 11 June despite our weakened strength, and as the Germans had withdrawn once again, we headed for Chianceana in an 'Advance to contact' mode. That meant we had to move forward until we were shot at.

I was leading a platoon in No. 4 Company. The time was 1400 hours, 25 June 1944, implanted firmly in my mind, when an anti-personnel booby trap or buried mine, nowadays you would call it an IED, blew me off my feet. One of my Guardsmen pulled me into a ditch to get me below ground level, for now we were under very heavy mortar fire.

163

Thankfully after approximately thirty minutes the mortaring eased and they got some dressings on me. But then I lay there for seven hours. Some of the stuff from the mine was a spray of ball-bearings, which had peppered me. Because of our forward position at the time, stretcher-bearers were unable to get to me until 21.00 hours. Having been picked up by stretcher-bearers, they carried me and three other wounded to an ambulance, approximately one mile away, a horrendous journey. For one reason or another, maybe a close shell-burst or machine-gun fire, I was dropped four to five times.

But this was not the end of my ordeal. Once in the ambulance, I was laid next to another wounded soldier, who was in a bad way. The medic said they would have to take some blood from me, to give to him, because one of his arteries had been severed. They said I would be all right, I would live. How they thought I had enough blood left to give, I do not know, but I guess they were right.

Then they moved me into the front passenger seat, with my legs sticking out of the front window for the drive, so they had more space to attend to the other wounded in the back. Eventually we arrived at Orvieto, where I was taken into an Advanced Dressing Station. It was in a church in the market square, and the bad state I was in, I thought this is it, they won't have to move me from here at the end. I do not know what happened to the other soldier, I have always hoped he pulled through with my blood. Many of the ball bearings have remained embedded in me.[16]

After their brief stop outside Rome, the 1st Surreys, many to be Jack's future comrades, made their next stop also at Orvieto. In places on their sixty-mile drive through Umbria, cheering Italians lined the route holding out wine and flowers. In contrast to the Grenadiers' deadly firefights, the Surreys' journey in the warmth of summer must have seemed like a dream.

When they got to Orvieto, some of the Surreys would have stood and stared at the Piazza del Duomo and its renowned Romanesque-Gothic cathedral. Unknown to them Jack Chaffer lay with other wounded in a drugged fever in a nearby church. Even Jack's two friends from school days in India, Frank Oram and Harry Skilton, may have walked within a few yards of his sick bed. But it would not be until after the war that he would see them again, and rejoin the Surreys, when they would welcome him back at last into the 1st Battalion. For now reality was pressing in on the Surreys again, to catch up with the main force of Germans, who were making for the Albert Line and the southern shore of Lake Trasimene.[17]

The toughest German resistance on the Albert Line waited patiently for the Surreys and the Battleaxe Division, first at Citta della Pieve then at San Fatucchio near to the lake's south-west shoreline. A few miles south of

Lake Trasimene on 15 June, 78th Division approached Citta della Pieve. The town had actually been captured earlier by a platoon of the 1st Royal Irish Fusiliers, who were then ordered to leave it.

The Germans re-occupied the town and strengthened its defences to make another stand. Another battle would soon be on again.[18] The Surreys' engagement at Citta della Pieve on 16/17 June was typical of the increasing intensity of the fighting. It was an important junction for a network of roads running south from the city of Arezzo.[19]

It was dusk as the Surreys, with the support of tanks from 9 Armoured Brigade, were sent climbing once more. Citta della Pieve was a mountain town at a height of 1,670 feet. Despite earlier patrols reporting a clear approach, at about three miles distance shelling by a German rearguard caught them by surprise, sending everyone to ground to wait for the cover of the night.[20]

Next morning around 4.00am the Surreys' B Company deployed through the cornfields to attack the town. In his sniper role Frank Oram had a vivid view of the initial engagement.

Things became quite hectic and the rush culminated in our arrival just before dusk at a spot overlooking the town of Citta della Pieve – Germans seemed to be everywhere and just before dawn companies moved forward ready for an early morning attack on the town. From the observation post I occupied I had a panoramic view of the area. There was an approach road with cornfields on either side with broken ground and cover on the left. A and B Companies were carrying out a frontal attack, and C Company were moving around the left flank. Just short of the town the companies came under heavy machine-gun and small arms fire. Had it not been for the tall corn, casualties would have been much higher, for in a very short time the companies had taken advantage of its cover.[21]

Caught in the open many men were lost, including B Company commander, Captain George E. Alden.[22] Unbelievably it turned out that they were once more up against their continual foes, the Germans' 1st Parachute Division.[23]

When both A and B Companies made the next attack with supporting tanks, some troops managed to occupy about twenty houses. But more men went down, including two more officers killed, and could move no further. To try and exploit A and B Companies' fragile positions on the town's edge, C Company, led by Major Edward Bird, attempted a flanking attack from the south-west. A German counter-attack forced them back, killing Major Bird.[24]

It was a precarious position for the three companies. For those men who had been hit, as time ebbed away, it must have seemed the end was near.

The evacuation of wounded was a great problem as stretcher-bearers approaching them came under machine-gun fire. The Medical Officer, Lieutenant W.A. Smurthwaite, and the Padre, the Rev H.C.C. Lannigan, arrived together, and the German-speaking Lannigan remonstrated so forcibly with the hidden machine gunners, that they agreed to hold their fire while the wounded were collected and taken to a nearby house.[25]

That the clergyman's shouted pleas in German for a ceasefire were heeded is incredible enough, but something even more unexpected was to follow. During the night, while they waited for an ambulance to reach them by next morning, the three German machine gunners came up to the house, where the Padre somehow persuaded them to surrender. Not surprisingly Lieutenant William Smurthwaite and Padre Henry Lannigan were both awarded the Military Cross.[25]

Another night and day passed with the Surreys held down in static positions, as more troops and artillery were brought up. Not surprisingly on the next night, to avoid being outflanked, the Germans withdrew. After the intercept of a German communication, the 78th Division artillery targeted some of the retreating paratroopers' exit routes. The morning light disclosed a high toll of enemy dead, yet it did not deter them from their practice of leaving further rearguards and snipers in carefully selected positions. Citta della Pieve had been taken, but at a high price.[26]

*   *   *

1/6th Surreys get to Citta della Pieve another way

Once Cassino had fallen 1/6th Surreys, in contrast to their sister battalion, were given some rest. Some took leave back to Naples and Sorrento, where a few attended a concert by Marlene Dietrich. That came to an end on 5 June when the battalion motored up Highway 6 and the next day re-formed with 10 Brigade and 4th Division close to Tivoli, some fifteen miles east of Rome. The next move would be north into German-held territory.

At first light on 7 June 1/6th Surreys led 10 Brigade's left flank, crossed the east-west Tivoli–Rome Highway 5 and threaded their way north on a winding country road into the hills towards the village of San Angelo Romano. Nerves jangled for German rearguard positions and snipers could be hidden anywhere. It was also tentative going in the face of collapsed sections of road, demolished bridges, booby-traps and mines. Suddenly the rumble of the vehicles was blotted out as an explosion blew apart a lead vehicle of the column.

As was his way, the CO, Lieutenant Colonel Robert Thompson, raced his jeep forward to assist. Farther back in the column watchers dived for cover when, from the front a second explosion rent the air. Unbelievably another hidden mine in the road exploded under Colonel Thompson's jeep, killing him, Lieutenant G.H. Gudgeon, Corporal Harold Efford, and wounding driver Private V. Kinnard.

In his letter from HQ 10 Infantry Brigade to Thompson's wife, Brigadier S.H. Shoesmith said:

> He had gone forward, most gallantly as usual, to see what he could do to help the men in the vehicle which had just gone up on a mine. On the way up the road, his own vehicle struck a mine. I can assure you that death was instantaneous, and that your husband would not possibly have known a second's pain or dread. I myself was the despairing and horrified spectator of the whole tragic episode.[27]

Many of the Surreys must have had a flashback recollection of Tunisia. Lieutenant Colonel Thompson had replaced their previous CO, Lieutenant Colonel Bruno, who had died leading them to the top of Djebel Djaffa. Incredibly within two hours a new CO Lieutenant Colonel C.G.S. McAlester arrived and took over. Over the rest of the day they pushed on north a further twelve miles to Moricone, only to find 12 Brigade already there and blocked by enemy positions.[28]

The Moricone bottleneck and the opportunity to reinforce gains being made to the west resulted in 4th Division and the Surreys retracing their steps, first back south to Highway 5, then eastwards through Rome non-stop to a staging area some fifteen miles north-west of the city. As they drove through Rome's sunlit streets, every girl they passed was dreamlike to the truck-loads of troops. Their raucous calls and wolf-whistles brought many a smile and wave, and a recall of the normal life they had left behind.

Some did get leave to visit Rome's sights, but on 16 June the 1/6th Surreys moved on again to Viterbo, a further fifty miles to the north-west. Their new orders were to strengthen 6th South African Armoured Division, which was making faster progress west of the Tiber River. Then on 21 June, with the whole 4th Division, it was on again north towards Lake Trasimene, and first to Citta della Pieve, where a few days earlier the 1st Surreys had fought for its capture. Flanked by the South African Armoured Division on their left, and the Battleaxe Division on their right, who were already in action, it was clear to everyone that there was another major offensive building up to punch through the Albert Line.[29]

* * *

1st and 1/6th Surreys reach Lake Trasimene

Kesselring meant to halt the Allies at the Albert Line. Perhaps he hoped to repeat the famous battle success of Hannibal over the Roman General Flaminius, 2,200 years ago on the shores of Lake Trasimene. On 20 June the 1st Surreys and their 11 Brigade fellow battalion, the 2nd Lancashire

Fusiliers, with tank support attacked the village of San Fatucchio, only to be repulsed.

In the next attack 2nd London Irish Rifles of 38 Irish Brigade, with additional Sherman tanks of the Canadian 11th Armoured Regiment, came up as reinforcements. While the Surreys and the rest of 11 Brigade mounted a frontal attack, the Irish Rifles and a number of tanks went around the flanks. In bitter house-to-house fighting through San Fatucchio, first artillery and tanks blasted a building apart, and then the infantry went in to shoot it out with stubborn German rearguard defenders, who were still alive and refusing to give in.

As the day wore on the Surreys and their other battalion comrades suffered heavy losses, and those still on their feet were exhausted. By early afternoon the dead, wounded or just exhausted of both sides littered the streets. Fortunately, in the end German troops and their commander emerged from the town's rubble with their hands in the air. San Fatucchio was occupied. The Germans did not have the numbers to emulate Hannibal.[30]

Heavy rain slowed the bringing forward of supplies and reinforcements, and hampered the movement of artillery and armour, helping the Germans' main forces to make a gradual withdrawal. Not until 24 June were the 1st Surreys, supported by two tank troops from 9 Armoured Brigade's Warwickshire Yeomanry, able to attack northwards along the western edge of Lake Trasimene. It was a full 78th Division offensive, and at the same time on their western flank were 1/6th Surreys in 10 Brigade of 4th Division.[31]

German resistance in scattered pockets grew steadily stiffer until 29 June at Po di Mercanzia. In the surrounding countryside German rearguards in isolated farmhouses fought to a bitter, maddening end. The blood price on the 1st Surreys' assault companies was another toll of twenty-nine dead and wounded.[32]

Meanwhile, from Citta della Pieve 1/6th Surreys had moved north through the hills skirting Chiusi, so that on 24 June in heavy rain they joined in the Battleaxe Division's advance up the western side of Lake Trasimene. Over the next week 1/6th Surreys overcame German defensive pockets in village upon village: Strada, Lopi, Gioiella, Casamaggiore and Pozzuolo. Each village came with the expected hidden booby traps and mines. In his diary Sergeant James noted the loss of Private Fleet on the ridge above Lopi, and the number of men cut off after a counter-attack, dead or captured was not known.

By 30 June the Eighth Army had pushed the Germans back from Lake Trasimene. The cost for 1/6th Surreys was seventeen killed and forty-three wounded. In that last week of June, around the northern shore of Lake Trasimene, the first troops of XIII Corps joined up with X Corps, who had moved up the eastern lakeside. While the Germans were being forced to withdraw north again to Arezzo, on 2 July the 1st Surreys and 78th Division reached Cortona, and were there pulled out of the line for much a much needed recovery in Egypt.[33]

*   *   *

1/6th Surreys fight on through Arezzo to Florence

There was no respite for 1/6th Surreys. Once more they had little time to mourn their losses and, on 5 July, with the return of some men recovered from their wounds, the Battalion motored north and to the west of Arezzo, through which the Germans had established another defensive line. Like all the others it had to be overcome, for now the Allies' goal was Florence on the River Arno. The next night, 6/7 July, the Surreys' A and B Companies climbed through the hills passing through the village of Touri, and headed for the Arezzo–Florence road. Despite the non-appearance at staging points of promised support from both a tank squadron and the 2nd Somersets, the Surreys kept up their advance. It was as if the night was cloaking their forward rush.

At dawn on 7 July the Surreys were brought to a bloody halt. A German trap with Spandau machine-gun fire from three sides caught B Company in the open and cut them down. At the same time A Company took fire on its right flank. The officer commanding B Company, Major Allan Paskins, was wounded, captured, then rescued, while another forty men went down dead or were taken prisoner. Some survivors of both companies managed to pull themselves back to positions where they could dig in and try and hang on. The cinema newsreels in England may have been giving total coverage to the Normandy invasion, but the killing in Italy went on unabated.[34]

Fortunately, during that day of 7 July, C Company with tank support climbed up mountain tracks under German shelling to relieve A and B Companies and regain some lost ground. At night C Company cleared the ridge of remaining enemy positions. Yet predictably on the night of 8 July came the German counter-attack. This time the Surreys were ready and it was met with stronger supporting artillery and tank fire. Before dawn on 9 July the Surreys got the word to pull back to recover. They had lost another three killed, twenty-three men wounded, and in all fifty dead or missing.

It was the shortest break imaginable when, at 9.00pm the same day, they were recalled to the front lines. Another week of increasing the pressure and forward momentum forced a German withdrawal on 17 July and enabled the Surreys to advance up the Florence road.

After taking hill towns such as Chianti, Poggio and Montevarchi, by 22 July they were about half-way to the Tuscan capital at Ricasoli. Then they were able to pull back to Montevarchi with other battalions for some rest. During their recovery stretch there of two weeks, a number of Surreys found themselves marching in a Divisional parade for General Alexander. One can imagine the surprise in their eyes when they saw, next to Alexander taking the salute, their sovereign Commander-in-Chief, King George VI. Among the awards presented by the King, was the posthumous DSO to their former CO, Lieutenant Colonel Thompson.[35]

By late July some other elements of Eighth Army had reached the banks of the River Arno.[36] On 6 August 1/6th Surreys went forward again towards Florence. At first they were able to look on, as others such as the Durhams assaulted the strongest German position, the Incontro Monastery. Only a few miles from Florence and the River Arno, Incontro was like a mini-Monte Cassino dominating the surrounding country. While the Incontro Monastery was captured, the Surreys cleared out some ridges between Incontro and the Arno. The cost was high, however, the Durhams alone losing three officers and ninety-three other ranks.[37] When 1/6th Surreys captured some hills on 9 August, they, too, looked down onto Florence and the Arno River valley.

Kesselring began pulling his forces out of Florence in the first two weeks of August, to begin a withdrawal up into the Tuscan Apennines and the Gothic Line.[38] North of the city, the Gothic Line stretched along the Tuscan Apennines from the north-west to the south-east, then due east across the breadth of Italy to skirt the principality of San Marino, before reaching the Adriatic coast above Pesaro. The German retreat was the trigger for 4th Division and 1/6th Surreys to be rested, and sent back to the south of Lake Trasimene to recover near Assisi.[39]

* * *

Earlier on 4th July, when 1st Surreys and their Battleaxe Division had pulled back, it was to Tivoli in the Sabine Hills, fifteen miles from Rome, from where some made a visit to Hadrian's Villa and some to the Vatican. A week later it was Rome to Taranto by train. But the carriages, hot, filthy and lacking any sanitation, were little more than cattle trucks. So it came as a welcome relief, on 14 July, when they embarked at Taranto and sailed off into the fresh air of the Mediterranean. On arrival at Port Said, Egypt, on 22 July, it was first to a tented camp in the Suez Canal Zone, then to a camp of huts near the Pyramids.[40]

As usual there was an ulterior motive behind these respites from the front lines. Both 4th and 78th Divisions, hardened, experienced mountain warfare infantry, were not being rested as some kind of generous reward. They were going to be needed in the Tuscan Apennines against the Gothic Line. The Allies' Fifth and Eighth Armies faced their final, and perhaps toughest, challenge, a battle which had the potential to be worse than Alamein, Salerno, Cassino or Anzio.

170

In Europe all eyes were on the Allied armies breaking out of Normandy and battling through northern France. At the same time, yet relatively unacknowledged, the ultimate titanic struggle of the Italian campaign was rapidly approaching. It would pit, so to speak, an unstoppable attacker against an unbreakable defence. The Germans would wait now in those Tuscan mountains, like wounded animals at bay more dangerous than ever, and some of them would even see the Gothic Line as their own *Götterdämmerung*.

Notes

1. Neillands, op cit., p. 344.
2. Ibid, p. 345.
3. Ibid, p. 361.
4. Ibid, pp. 345–8.
5. Ibid, pp. 349–53.
6. Ibid, pp. 354–60.
7. Ibid, pp. 362–3.
8. Ford, op cit., pp. 229–30.
9. Carver, op cit., p. 216.
10. Daniell, op cit., p. 210; Journal of the East Surrey Regiment, Nov 1948, pp. 126–9.
11. Squire and Hill, op cit., p. 57.
12. The Surrey History Centre, ESR/25/Taylor/2, Major R.C. Taylor.
13. Veterans' Accounts, Weston.
14. Daniell, op cit., p. 211.
15. The Surrey History Centre, ESR/2/15/6/7, Manning.
16. Veterans' Accounts, Chaffer.
17. Veterans' Accounts, Jack Chaffer; Daniell, op cit., p. 211.
18. Daniell, op cit., p. 212.
19. The Surrey History Centre ESR/2/15/6/7, Manning.
20. Ford, op cit., pp. 230–1.
21. Squire and Hill, op cit., p. 58.
22. Daniell, op cit., p. 212.
23. Ford, op cit., pp. 230–1.
24. Daniell, op cit., p. 212.
25. Squire and Hill, op cit., pp. 30–1.
26. Ford, op cit., pp. 230–1.
27. Veterans' Accounts, Shoesmith letter 12 Jun 1944, ref Robert de Gavre.
28. Squire and Hill, op cit., p. 44.
29. Ibid, p. 45.
30. Ford, op cit., pp. 232–3.
31. Squire and Hill, op cit., p. 31; Daniell, op cit., p. 212.
32. Squire and Hill, op cit., p. 31.
33. Ibid, p. 45; Carver, op cit., p. 217.
34. Squire and Hill, op cit., p. 45.
35. Ibid, pp. 45–7.
36. Neillands, op cit., p. 364.
37. Daniell, op cit., p. 219.
38. Neillands, op cit., pp. 367–8.
39. Squire and Hill, op cit., pp. 45–7.
40. Squire and Hill, op cit., p. 31; Daniell, op cit., p. 212.

Chapter 12

Assault on the Gothic Line: A Destiny for Both Sides

Those who have never seen the Apennines in Italy cannot hope to appreciate the formidable obstacle they present to a force advancing from the south. This great range of mountains, rising to nearly 7,000 feet, stretches across the peninsula from the Mediterranean to the Adriatic. To the south of this great barrier the mountains tumble into foothills as far as the River Arno.

For over a year the Todt Labour organization had been working for Hitler on the construction of a line – the Gothic Line – a highly developed series of strongpoints stretching for about 200 miles across the peninsula, from Spezia on the Ligurian Sea, to Pesaro, south of Rimini, on the Adriatic. The line blocked every route north.[1]

In this Apennine mountain range, which barred access to the Po Valley and the industrial heartland of northern Italy, the Allies faced a ferocious struggle. It can be seen in retrospect that, early in the Italian campaign, even before the tumultuous battles at Cassino and Anzio, decisions were made which brought unforeseen and unintended consequences. The die had been cast in November 1943 when Kesselring had convinced Hitler to give him overall command to fight the Allies in southern Italy.

At first Hitler had favoured giving the Italian command, an Army Group comprising Tenth and Fourteenth Armies, to Rommel who advocated an immediate and fast withdrawal to the Tuscan Apennines. This would have resulted in a German withdrawal with a hint of panic, and perhaps might have taken on the feel of a morale-sapping retreat. The Allies would have been buoyed, and the German armies would have arrived at an unprepared defensive line.

Conversely Kesselring argued that he could hold the Allies south of Rome for at least nine months while the Gothic Line could be fortified into an impenetrable set of defences. Swayed by Kesselring's logic as well as his optimism, Hitler countermanded an order appointing Rommel. Kesselring was empowered to withdraw only grudgingly to the Gothic Line. The result was that the Germans would fight for every mile, every day in Italy.[2]

172

In the Allies' strategic deliberations, the Americans, unlike the British, viewed the Italian Campaign as secondary to the invasion of Normandy, Operation OVERLORD, and the subsequent offensive through north-west Europe to Germany. This caused bitter argument between London and Washington. Eisenhower proposed an invasion of the south of France, Operation ANVIL, to support the Normandy landings. This was opposed by Churchill and his Chiefs of Staff, who for a time thought they had reached agreement for its cancellation, but were over-ruled by Roosevelt. On 1 July 1944, the US President approved the order for the invasion of the south of France, resurrected as Operation DRAGOON, to go ahead.

While Hitler imposed his will to fight for every inch in Italy, these decisions rightly or wrongly condemned the Allies in Italy to always being short of the minimum two to one superiority in forces and supplies to achieve decisive dominance. This strategic difference was to be felt most acutely in the autumn of 1944 in the Battle for the Gothic Line. The defensive line of the Apennine mountains stood, in Hitler's view, as the Germans' final barrier to the Allied armies in Italy.[3]

In July 1944 even after receiving instructions to transfer seven divisions to Operation DRAGOON, for the invasion of southern France, Alexander received orders to break through the Gothic Line, cross the Apennines and then the River Po. He would receive further orders when he had reached the line of Venice–Padua–Verona–Brescia. In comparison with the Americans' priorities, for Operations OVERLORD and ANVIL, it could not be said that there was anything secondary about these objectives.[4]

The German High Command's strategy was to make the Gothic Line and, to its north, the Po valley into an unbreakable defensive barrier. Yet as late as June 1944 Hitler had forbidden any further retreat to the north. He demanded that the Allied advance be stopped on an east-west line that ran from south of Florence and around Lake Trasimene to the Adriatic – the Albert Line. Kesselring assured his leader that his forces would resist the Allies for every yard, and only as a last resort bring them to a complete halt in the Apennines' Gothic Line.

To deter any thought of a rapid withdrawal to a perceived safe haven, the Germans tried to rename it as the Green Line.[5] Even so, in the same month, despite Hitler's orders to stop the Allies at the Albert Line, the German High Command issued the Gothic Order to continue the building of stronger defences in the Apennines. If necessary it would be the final battle, where at last the Allies would be defeated.

Lieutenant Douglas Orgill, who served in an armoured division of Eighth Army, said of the Gothic Order:

It called for thirty 88-mm Panther gun turrets embedded in steel and concrete bases, a hundred Todt steel shelters, rock-tunnelling of

173

defence positions, the carving out of fire embrasures, deep minefields, and the creation of an obstacle zone some ten miles wide. The whole of the Italian populace was evacuated from ... a belt between twelve and fourteen miles deep.

The defences were about two hundred miles long, a steel chain threaded through the mountain range. They began in the valley of the River Magra, a few miles south of La Spezia, and then stretched south-east through the Apuan mountains to a series of strongpoints blocking the various passes through the Apennines, being especially formidable at the Vernio Pass north of Prato and at the Futa Pass north of Florence. The eastern end of the line ran along the valley of the River Foglia to the cliffs between Pesaro and Cattolica on the Adriatic. The Adriatic corridor, ... was thick with defences, and ... lines of hills and ridges which lay cross-grained to the Allied line of advance.[6]

In June 1944 in accordance with Hitler's demands, the Germans had made a major stand on the Albert Line, with three and a half divisions concentrated in a line between Chiusi, San Fatucchio in the centre, and Lake Trasimene's south-west shore. Not until 28 June, after a week of heavy fighting, when 78th Division took San Fatucchio, had the Germans begun to withdraw.[7] On 16 July the armour of 16th/5th Lancers took Arezzo, and the 2nd New Zealand Division crossed the River Arno and headed towards Florence. The German High Command declared Florence an 'open city', which they would not defend. Yet, what did that really mean?

They withdrew to the north of the city and established formidable rearguard positions in the Chianti region. Every vineyard seemed to hide the lethal 88mm anti-tank gun or a Tiger tank.[8] As predicted, the Germans were heading for the Gothic Line, and they intended that no one would stop them. On the Gothic Line, a final battle for Italy had become the destiny for both sides.

*　　*　　*

The German commander of Florence, Colonel Fuch, of the 10th Parachute Regiment, said that he would not make a futile last stand, which would see the city's antiquities destroyed.[9] Nevertheless, such a sentiment did not stop him ordering the destruction of all the bridges over the River Arno, apart from the world famous Ponte Vecchio. In 2010 I stood on the Ponte Vecchio and gazed along the Arno, and tried to visualize the devastation in 1944 of the other bridges.

It is bizarre, perhaps a miracle, that the Ponte Vecchio was spared. It was built in 1345, the last successor of bridges on that crossing site since Roman times. Tourists flock to the Ponte Vecchio, not only for its unique jewellery and antique shops, which date back to 1565, but to also take in the panoramic view of the city, the river and its bridges.

The other bridges, which were blown up, were such as the Ponte Santa Trinita, built in timber in 1290 then rebuilt in 1567, and the Ponte alla Carraia, Ponte Amerigo Vespucci, Ponte alla Grazie and Ponte San Niccolo. That the Germans could bring themselves to destroy these bridges seems impossible to imagine, but perhaps it gives an insight into their desperation, as they fled like a harried, wounded animal, making for its mountain lair. Just like the Allies were driven to destroy the Benedictine monastery at Monte Cassino, it provides a fleeting glimpse into those times, into the horror, fear and hate, that lay at the heart of the war.

* * *

Alexander's initial strategy for the next phase beyond Florence was to make a concentrated onslaught by both Fifth and Eighth Armies combined on the centre of the Gothic Line north-west of Florence between Pistoia and Dicomano. Air strikes were launched in mid-July destroying nineteen bridges over the River Po so as to cut German supply routes.

The plan's aim was to inflict a decisive defeat on Kesselring's Tenth and Fourteenth Armies before they could be reinforced and embed themselves in the Gothic Line. Speed was of the essence, before Alexander's forces were further weakened with little hope of any significant reinforcing. There was even an operation to deceive the Germans, to make them think that the offensive would fall on the Adriatic Coast. On 26 July the plan was sent to General Clark of Fifth Army and General Leese of Eighth Army.

It was fated to be stillborn. Leese, who was said to distrust Clark, disagreed so strongly that on 4 August Alexander flew to meet him at Orvieto. There on the runway at the Orvieto airfield, Leese argued with Alexander against the plan. He wanted Eighth Army to launch a separate, first attack up the Adriatic coastal corridor, where he believed their armoured warfare experience from North Africa could exploit the flatter terrain. The loss of the French Expeditionary Force and their Goumier mountain troops certainly weakened the case for a central attack through the Tuscan Apennines. Leese also saw difficulties, even from competitive distractions, in Fifth and Eighth Armies attempting to fight side by side on such a narrow front. Despite the extensive preparations and logistics already underway, based upon the original plan's classical principle of concentration, Leese convinced Alexander to his alternative way of thinking.

Even the contrary argument that deception efforts had been succeeding in making the Germans think that the offensive would come in the east on the Adriatic where, under Leese's change of plan, the Eighth Army's main assault would indeed now come was dismissed. Surprisingly Clark also agreed that there would be two separate hammer blows at the Gothic Line,

Fifth Army in the centre but preceded by Eighth Army in the east. It was a startling turnaround from orthodox planning. But could it work?[10]

By mid-August, making great efforts to hide the re-deployment from the Germans by travelling mainly at night, Eighth Army had moved across to the Adriatic. On 25 August with a simultaneous attack on the Gothic Line by three Corps, V British, I Canadian and II Polish, General Leese launched Eighth Army's attack, Operation OLIVE.

Within the first few days of September it was clear that, the concealment of the redeployment had worked. Too late, Kesselring was forced to hurriedly transfer three divisions from north of Florence to the Adriatic coast. This was the cue for Alexander to order Clark's Fifth Army forward in the centre of the Apennines for an attack on the Il Giogo Pass. The mountain pass led to Bologna, and held out the opportunity for a break-out into the plain of the Po valley.[11]

The Il Giogo Pass was taken by 17 September, but the price for Fifth Army was more than 3,000 casualties.[12] The two separate battles for the Gothic Line quickly left both sides desperate for reinforcements. At the end of September even Kesselring, who was normally so optimistic in adversity, felt his position untenable. He requested approval to withdraw his forces not only from the Gothic Line but back to the north side of the Po. Hitler rebuffed him, and insisted once again that the Gothic Line through the Apennines chain and all of upper Italy south of the Po must be held indefinitely.[13]

At the beginning of October losses in Fifth Army had already reached an average of 550 per day, and 750 per day in Eighth Army.[14] The Fifth Army assaults were being made with progressively under-strength forces. Clark reported on 6 October to General Marshall, the US Chief of Staff:

> My troops have been negotiating the most difficult mountain terrain we have had to face in Italy, involving the bitterest fighting since Salerno …. The decision which has faced me is one of halting our attack in order to rest, or of pushing on in an all-out effort to gain our objectives before winter catches us in the Apennines.[15]

Clark also informed Alexander that at this rate by the end of October, Fifth Army would be 8,000 men short in their US divisions alone.[16] Likewise in Eighth Army their strength was literally bleeding away. Since 25 August 14,000 had been killed, wounded or missing, which was even greater than the losses at El Alamein. Alexander's consequent request for 3,000 more troops was quickly approved by Eisenhower, but unfortunately delays in logistics and bureaucratic inflexibility meant the reinforcements would not arrive before winter took hold.

Weakened as they were, success for Fifth Army appeared maddeningly close. If they could break through to Bologna, only twenty miles away, it would rupture the German defences. Kesselring would be forced to retreat from the Po to avoid having his forces surrounded. On 5 October Fifth Army's American and British divisions began a gambler's offensive to reach the Po valley before the end of October. They had a little over three weeks before the inevitable losses would weaken their strength, and before the rain and mud would first slow them, then quickly turn to snow and ice to bring everything to a standstill. Four divisions of US II Corps attacked across a fourteen-mile front straddling Route 65, aiming to burst through the Il Giogio pass.[17]

By 8 October Fifth Army had taken Loiano and was only ten miles as the crow flies from Bologna. On the ground it was different in every way. The American and British troops now faced a natural fortress, the Livergnano escarpment, named by the Germans as the Caesar Line, which completely blocked the frontal approach.

This daunting, southward-facing barrier consisted of a virtually sheer rock wall nearly three miles long, and in places more than 1,500 feet high. Behind it stretched a row of hills, from the peaks of which any troops who finally stormed the escarpment would immediately come under the fire of well-sited German guns. There were two small breaks in the great wall – one where the road cut through it at Livergnano itself, and another through a footpath two miles to the east.[18]

It was a barrier which had to be overcome if Fifth Army was to reach Bologna and the Po valley before winter set in.

* * *

While Fifth and Eighth Armies strained to make the decisive break-through, Alexander had held back his one remaining card that might make the difference – his most experienced mountain warfare troops of the 78th Battleaxe Division.

Following the pursuit of the Germans as far as Florence in July, the 78th Division and the 1st Surreys had been withdrawn to Egypt for recovery. Their eight weeks of re-equipping, the intake of reinforcements and training, some of it close to Cairo and the Pyramids, came to an end on 9 September when they embarked once again for Taranto and Italy.[19]

From Taranto on 16 September the Surreys travelled north for a second time up the Adriatic Coast. This journey was now through Allied liberated territory, Bari, Termoli and across the bitterly-remembered Trigno and Sangro rivers, to rejoin Eighth Army at Fano, some forty miles south of Rimini. The Surreys and their 78th Division were scheduled to join V Corps on 4 October. Then, on 2 October, came a change of plan. New orders required the Battleaxe Division including the Surreys to move immediately westwards into the Tuscan Apennines to join Fifth Army's British XIII Corps.

To capture Bologna before winter arrived Alexander was throwing 78th Division, his last fresh division, into Fifth Army's attempt to break through the Gothic Line.[20] To commit his last main reserve, albeit the Battleaxe Division, shows how close Alexander thought Fifth Army was to reaching Bologna. The three generals believed they could make that breakthrough.

One can imagine the groans of disbelief when the Surreys heard of the circuitous route, over which they would have to drive to reach Fifth Army. First, they had to drive south back the way they had just come to Assisi, then turn around and travel north past Lake Trasimene again, through Arezzo, Perugia, Florence and Firenzuola. Next they climbed up into the central mountains to Castel del Rio, from where they moved into the front lines, to an assembly area at Sant'Apollinare before going forward to relieve American troops.[21]

The road climbed up the mountainsides crossing and re-crossing the Santerno River, and had to be shared between the US 88th Division, a Guards Brigade, and the other battalions of 78th Division.

There was barely room for two-way traffic along it and only room for one-way traffic over the Bailey or timber bridges. The forward troops and observation posts in the heights had to be maintained by mule from the beginning, and as the roads deteriorated and the line advanced, the mule-routes became longer and longer. Between the rivers mountain spurs ran down to the plain, all of them bleak and bare. The mountains consisted of clay, shale and loose stones and presented enormous precipices of slippery grey mud; many of the slopes were 300 feet high and in wet weather movement on them became almost impossible, deep as they were in sloppy, cloying mud. Into the sides of the spurs were cut deep gorges that carried tributaries to the main rivers.[22]

At Sant'Apollinare, a small hamlet a few miles north of Castel del Rio, Frank Oram recalled how the Surreys relieved an American battalion:

We had to live in half a slit trench and half a sangar under mortar and shell fire, together with American dead still in their old slit trenches. It brought back to mind the days on Snakeshead Ridge and the Bowl at Cassino. I now established Observation Posts for my Sniper Group, in each company area. Continual visits to these OPs made me very familiar with the mountain paths and tracks in the vicinity.[23]

The weather and battleground also had similarities to the rain and mud of Tunisia as well as Cassino. On 8 October Sergeant Gostling, clearly missing the sun and heat of Egypt, wrote another letter to Captain Payne:

Dear Captain Payne,
We are once more in this wretched and 'orrible country Italy. The rain hasn't stopped for more than an hour since we have been here,

and I really think this is the worst country in the world for rain, including Manchester! Remember Goubellat? Well that was a mere nothing to this place! The mud is over a foot deep in places and everything is well under it. I understand that up at the front the Yanks are firing the guns until they have embedded themselves right in the mud, and then they cover them up with earth (or more mud) and go and draw some new ones.[24]

The task of the Division was to advance astride the Imola road, protecting the right flank of an American Division, as part of the major operation to break out into the Bologna Plain. The objective of 11 Brigade was Monte Pieve, or Point 508, some 3,000 yards north-east of Apollinare, a stocky outcrop of rock with an almost cliff-like face which must be climbed to get at the Germans. After Point 508 the next objective was Mount Spaduro, which ran north from Monte Pieve, a massive razor-backed ridge stretching north and south for two miles.

While it was in enemy hands there could be no progress towards the Lombardy Plain and the town of Castel San Pietro between Imola and Bologna on Highway 9. The Spaduro Ridge was of particular importance in the offensive as it overlooked the line of advance of the American Division on the left. First however, Monte Pieve had to be taken. The approach was such that only one battalion, on a one company front, could be deployed against the feature.[25]

The Surreys' Sergeant Manning described Monte Pieve as, 'an ugly looking brute of a mountain, strongly defended and ringed around with mines.'[26]

Those Surreys who were veterans of the Tunisian mountain battles, must have thought back to the assault on Longstop Hill and wondered if they would soon be joining their lost comrades.

* * *

In the assault on Monte Pieve by the Battleaxe Division's 11 Brigade, the 2nd Lancashire Fusiliers made the first attempt on the night of 13 October. They were thrown back losing fifty-nine men to intense machine-gun and mortar fire.[27] The next day a second attempt by the 5th Northamptons, reinforced by the Surreys' A Company, was called off when mines and friendly fire helped the German defenders inflict losses of nearly 100 men on the combined force.[28]

Despite the losses from A Company's support of the 5th Northamptons, the Surreys were the Brigade's third and last battalion which remained still intact. At midnight on 15 October it was their turn to begin another attack on Monte Pieve.

The attack involved an approach march to the start line of over 3,000 yards along a narrow track with minefields on either side. Everyone was heavily laden as wireless sets, weapons including Vickers machine guns and tripods, ammunition, picks, shovels and hard rations for the following day had to be carried. The companies moved in single file and sustained some casualties along the route from enemy defensive fire.[29]

The Surreys fought their way up the approach slopes until, like their fellow battalions, they came to a halt at the sheer cliff face. This time the Surreys reeled from a barrage of explosions in their midst. The Germans were throwing and rolling hundreds of hand grenades down the cliff. Unbelievably one platoon, or rather those in it who remained in one piece, somehow fought its way to the top of the cliff. Not surprisingly its losses were such that it had to retreat back down again.[30]

To add to their earlier casualties supporting the 5th Northamptons, the Surreys lost one man killed and another twenty-one wounded. The latter included Major Ricky Seymour, commanding B Company, Lieutenant Bob Guest, and company sergeant majors Charles Rosoman and Bill Attewell. Attewell had won a DCM at Citta della Pieve.[31] It was some consolation that two days later the Germans, obviously weakened by holding off the Surreys, withdrew to the Monte Spaduro Ridge.[32] The German commander must have feared that his depleted force would not be able repulse a fourth assault. It seemed that the third assault by the Surreys, and one platoon's charge to the summit, may have made the difference.[33]

* * *

In the mountainous terrain, the incessant rain, shelling and military traffic soon rendered unrecognizable any road or track. Douglas Orgill witnessed how it all had a tragic impact on the evacuation of the casualties:

> For wounded men, this sometimes meant that an injury which in better country would have meant no more than a long time in hospital now meant death. A man shot on the steep, shaly slope of an Apennine crest first had to be reached by his companions, often climbing hand and toe, and then lowered down for as much as a mile before he could be brought to relatively open ground. Here he would be loaded on to a mule which carried two stretchers as it swayed and lurched down the mountain trails. Sometimes a mule would throw a wounded man down the steep slopes on either side.
>
> It often took six hours to get a man from the point where he was shot, down to the necessarily cursory attention of the Regimental Aid Post, and perhaps a further eight hours before he finally reached a vehicle waiting at the road head on Arrow route. Then it would be a further hour or more, as the ambulance splashed through the

quagmire of the road, before he could reach a surgeon. Thus a man often died from loss of blood or exhaustion before he reached proper aid.[34]

Every day winter closed in and, if the dead and wounded were to mean anything, the offensive to escape the mountains and descend onto Bologna must not slacken.

The Monte Spaduro ridge was initially captured by the Irish Brigade, but then under an intense bombardment and counter-attack they had been forced to withdraw. When the Irish then took Casa Spinello, it enabled 78th Division to make another plan to take the Monte Spaduro peak. This required the Battleaxe Division's 36 Brigade to attack from the south while 11 Brigade, including the Surreys, went around to assault Monte Spaduro itself at the ridge's northern end.[35]

It was barely a week after the mauling they had suffered at Monte Pieve, when the Surreys received their orders for the 78th Division's second assault on Monte Spaduro. Sergeant Manning saw it as a greater obstacle than Monte Pieve: 'It was a massive hog's back feature known as Monte Spaduro, about two miles long, reaching a height of about 1,500 feet.'[36] The divisional historian described it thus: 'Monte Spaduro stretched north from Monte Pieve, and its German possession blocked access through to the Lombardy plain, where the nearest town on Highway 9 was Castel San Pietro, between Imola and Bologna.'[37]

If the larger US forces on their left flank were to have any chance of bursting through to the Po valley the Battleaxe Division must take Monte Spaduro.

* * *

'Around 6.00pm on 23 October we left Sant'Apollinare,' said Sergeant Bill Woolley, 'and marched three and a half miles north to the 11 Brigade assembly area at Ripiano. The muddy mountain tracks were steep and slippery, so we really needed the hour's rest when we got there.'[38]

Sergeant Manning thought the march itself was a nightmare.

The night was fine but the ground was soaked by previous heavy rain. A rough track led over the high ridge from Sant'Apollinare, up one hill and down, then up and down again. A recce party had gone out at midnight to lay strips of white tape along the Battalion start line. This was a task well practised in field training, but a nerve-racking business in the presence of the enemy.[39]

Shortly after midnight the Surreys' A, B and C Companies began the attack. The assault was made under cover of heavy concentrations of Allied artillery fire but there were some casualties from shells falling short. The Battalion's objectives were two peaks, Points 289 and 298, some

15,000 yards north-west of the main Monte Spaduro feature, which was simultaneously under attack by the 2nd Lancashire Fusiliers. It was a tense moment as the two battalions passed their start lines, the Surreys diverging from the Lancashire Fusiliers' line of advance to fight their own battle. The night was violent with the noise of artillery, mortars and machine gun fire.[40]

At around midnight A and B Companies were in the lead and C Company following them. A Company had casualties after taking their positions from a machine gun position and sniper on the reverse slope

The attack lasted about one hour and included hand-to-hand fighting with the desperate German outposts. By about one o'clock in the morning both objectives, Points 289 and 298, had been taken.[41]

'Nevertheless, some pockets of resistance held out,' said Woolley, 'including a machine gun and a sniper, who were causing casualties in A Company.'

The Surreys' A Company, led by Major John 'Jake' Saunders, was pinned down by these snipers and machine gunners directing their fire from overlooking deep gullies. Earlier in the afternoon mortar fire onto the German positions had made no impact, so that the planned reinforcement by C Company remained on hold.

On one stretcher from A Company, a dead man's brains were exposed, from where a bullet had shattered his skull. On another a man lay dazed, an arm tourniqueted in a blood-soaked bandage. The company commander, Major John Saunders, looked at the two casualties, and something snapped. 'Peachy!' Saunders shouted to Frank Oram, his company sergeant. 'Let's go! Bring two men with you.'

After grabbing his rifle, Saunders led Oram and the two other men in an outflanking route to try and work their way behind the German-held gullies. When he felt they were above the enemy positions Saunders stopped them. All was quiet, nothing to be seen or heard. Yet he was sure they were down there.

Saunders told his men to fix their bayonets, follow him and shout like hell. The four men charged down into the gully, yelling like banshees. The German rearguard must have thought they had been outflanked by a full platoon. Three German soldiers emerged from their cover, and with hands in the air surrendered.

Two Spandau light machine guns were recovered and for his fine leadership in this action Major Saunders was awarded the MC. Despite the success of the Monte Spaduro battle, the Surreys lost thirty-five men.[42]

Losses were greatest in C Company, which had to be disbanded and the remaining men reallocated to the other companies.[43] The 2nd Lancashire Fusiliers also gained the Monte Spaduro summit itself so that on the next day, 24 October, the whole ridge was in the hands of the Battleaxe

Division. As the sky lightened, the men braced themselves for the inevitable German counter-attack. Instead, down onto the Surreys' newly-won positions came their other ever present enemy, torrential rain. It brought a halt to the American offensive on their left and the associated plans of 78th Division.

It was tantalizing to see in the brief interludes of good weather, the towns and villages of the Lombardy plain only a few miles ahead, and the flat country dotted with farms. To the troops huddled on the bare hillsides in rain and wind it was like a mirage.[44]

Added to the mounting casualties, the onset of winter weather further weakened the offensive capability of Allied forces. Between 9 and 15 October the four US divisions had lost 2,491 men in scaling and fighting their way up the mountainous escarpment of Livergnano. By the time the German defenders pulled back, American losses since 1 October had increased to around 5,700.[45]

Although the rain helped to dampen down German counter-attacks, it was on the side of the defenders. Winter was beginning to bite with a vengeance, and time was running out for the two Allied armies.

* * *

In addition to the worsening weather, other unforeseen forces were combining against a breakthrough by the four US Divisions and the British XIII Corps. Shortages of ammunition grew severe during October, limiting the Allies' artillery. Ironically on the German side there was an opposite effect. In their slow pull back towards Bologna, the 29th and 90th Panzer Grenadiers and 1st Parachute Division, three of Kesselring's best divisions, were able to shrink their front lines and shorten their supply routes, and consequently concentrate their firepower.

Inevitably the winter rain and mist also neutralized the Allies' air superiority. Yet above all manpower was being cut down. Since early September the four American Divisions had lost 15,716 men, and more than 5,000 alone in one division, the 88th.[46] There was a similar casualty impact and supplies shortage on Eighth Army. Alexander reported on 13 November that there was only sufficient ammunition for ten days in Fifth Army, and fifteen days in Eighth Army. Even if the weather improved, the lack of reinforcements and supplies was undermining the plans for a renewed offensive in December.[47]

The two Allied Armies' offensive capability had been severely weakened, particularly in officers lost. Furthermore, the priority demands of Operations DRAGOON and OVERLORD meant that they had no reserves to call upon.[48] Incredibly, the orders for Fifth and Eighth Armies remained the same: to break through the Gothic Line before Christmas. Brutal realities meant the odds against them were fast lengthening.

183

Notes

1. Alexander of Tunis, op cit., p. 135.
2. Orgill, *The Gothic Line, The Autumn Campaign in Italy 1944*, pp. 3–6.
3. Ibid, p. 9.
4. Ibid, p. 22.
5. Ibid, pp. 25–6.
6. Ibid, pp. 27–8.
7. Neillands, op cit., pp. 365–66.
8. Ibid, pp. 367–8.
9. Ibid.
10. Orgill, op cit., pp. 29–31.
11. Neillands, op cit., pp. 373–6.
12. Ibid, p. 377.
13. Orgill, op cit., p. 193.
14. Ibid, p. 194.
15. Ibid, pp. 200–1.
16. Ibid, p. 194.
17. Ibid, pp. 196–7.
18. Ibid, p. 198.
19. Daniell, op cit., p. 231.
20. Ibid, p. 232.
21. Ibid.
22. Ray, op cit., p. 162.
23. Squire and Hill, op cit., p. 58.
24. Surrey History Centre, ESR/25/PAYN/9.
25. Daniell, op cit., p. 233.
26. Surrey History Centre, ESR/2/15/6/7 Manning, p. 5.
27. Orgill, op cit., p. 203.
28. Squire and Hill, op cit., p. 54.
29. Ibid.
30. Orgill, op cit., pp. 203–4.
31. Surrey History Centre, ESR/2/15/6/7 Manning, pp. 5–6.
32. Daniell, op cit., pp. 234–5.
33. Ray, op cit., p. 169.
34. Orgill, op cit., pp. 204–5.
35. Daniell, op cit., pp. 234–5.
36. Surrey History Centre, ESR/2/15/6/7 Manning, p. 5.
37. Ray, op cit., p. 169.
38. Veterans' accounts, George Wilson and Bill Woolley, 1st Surreys.
39. Surrey History Centre, ESR/2/15/6/7 Manning, p. 6.
40. Ibid.
41. Ibid.
42. Squire and Hill, *The Surreys in Italy 1943–45*, p. 54, QRS Museum obituary Sir John Saunders MC DSO, and Veterans accounts, Wilson, and Woolley, 1st Surreys.
43. Ibid, p. 54, and Veterans' accounts, Major Frank Oram, 1st Surreys.
44. Ray, op cit., p. 175.
45. Orgill, op cit., p. 200.
46. Ibid, pp. 212–214.
47. Ibid, p. 215.
48. Ibid, p. 20.

Chapter 13

A Second Mountain Winter in Italy: The Dread of Spring

In the autumn of 1944 the coastal corridor south of Rimini, sandwiched between the Tuscan Apennines and the Adriatic, became the scene of another series of bitter battles for the high ground. The Gothic Line fortifications made good use of rivers, hills and ridges, of which the most formidable was the Coriano Ridge. While 1st Surreys and 78th Division joined Fifth Army in the centre of the Tuscan Apennines, 1/6th Surreys were called on by Eighth Army for their own mountain warfare experience to climb the Coriano peak.[1]

In early September 1/6th Surreys had left their rest camp near Assisi with 10 Brigade and 4th Division and moved up the Adriatic Coast to a staging area near Tomba di Pesaro, north of the port of Ancona. From there they went forward towards Coriano, ready for another attempt to break through the final tentacles of the Gothic Line.[2] After costly gains by the Canadians at the end of August and in early September, another assault to climb and take the Coriano Ridge was to be made. Named after the village on its peak, Coriano Ridge was the last barrier between Eighth Army and the Po valley.[3]

The plan was for three divisions to cross the Marécchia River ten miles south of Rimini, then to burst through the Rimini Line, part of the eastern Gothic Line. It began on 13 September, and the following day 4th Division attacked, crossing the Marano and Ausa rivers during the next week. On 19 September the Surreys were thrown into heavy hill fighting to assault San Fortunato at the end of the Coriano Ridge. Over two days scores of prisoners and two 75mm guns were captured as the Surreys duly gained San Fortunato and other hills beyond. Private Percy Brook was awarded the Military Medal and Major Walter Brown the Military Cross, yet there was the inevitable toll, as eight dead and fifteen wounded told the story.[4]

These gains enabled 4th Division to press the attack so that, on the night of 21 September, Canadian troops crossed the Marécchia River and then reached Highway 9, the Via Emilia. Just as the Gothic Line was breached, the Allies' other enemy burst upon the scene. Heavy autumn rains had begun early on 20 September. Streams quickly became fast-flowing rivers, rivers swelled into raging torrents, fields turned to swamps, and tracks to glutinous mud. Any ideas to immediately make a rapid armoured drive north-west towards Bologna and the Po valley, were put on hold.[5]

However, despite the rain and mud, Eighth Army began to fight its way along Highway 9, which runs north-west in a straight line, like the Roman road it once was, from Rimini to Bologna. Although the route takes advantage of the Lombardy Plain, it is dominated on its south side by a number of dorsals jutting out from the Apennines. The infantry would have to wrench every one from the Germans before Eighth Army could take each town along the way, Cesena, Forli, Faenza and Imola.[6]

After enjoying three weeks of respite based at San Aqualina, caused by the rain-induced slow down, on 17 October the 1/6th Surreys were ordered to the front to help 12 Brigade clear the hills overlooking Cesena. The immediate dilemma was that some troops had been cut off for more than three days across the flooded River Savio, over which the Surreys had to find a way. After some tanks had been used to build a ramped 'Ark' bridge, the Surreys crossed on the night of 23 October. By 3.00am the next morning they had climbed under fire to gain a village in the hills. Despite a preceding artillery barrage, the Surreys still lost three killed and seventeen wounded before it was done.[7]

*   *   *

In the next advance on 24 October the Surreys led 10 Brigade as far as the River Ronco, which was only two miles from their goal of Forli and its airport. Then the rain intensified. It halted any crossing until it ceased and water levels fell. When it did stop on 31 October the Surreys managed to get across, and fought their way forward to establish a bridgehead half a mile deep. They had reached the Meldola Road, which ran between the River Ronco and Forli airfield. A full divisional attack was planned for the night of 7 November to capture Forli town and its airfield. The first foray at Forli airfield was given to the Surreys. On their own, with no armour in support, they would have to gamble upon speed and surprise to overcome the German defences.[8]

From Forli and around its airfield the Germans maintained heavy shelling at the approaching Surreys, and threw out batches of the screaming Nebelwerfer mortar shells. Together with a like response from the Surreys' supporting artillery, airstrikes went in from the RAF 'Cab Rank'. The 'Cab Rank' comprised fighter-bombers cruising above the battle zone, and a system for ground forces to radio them for strikes on enemy positions.[9]

It was bitterly cold, with a boisterous wind blowing across the airfield towards them, when B and C companies went down to the forming up areas, but it was helpfully dark. To make for speed in the vital dash across the airfield the men had left their packs behind them and wore leather jerkins instead of overcoats. As zero hour approached the shelling of the airfield buildings died down and diversionary concentrations on other enemy positions increased.[10]

In C Company Sergeant Stanley Gibbs and his platoon moved towards the airfield for the attack. It was 11.00pm and the men shivered in a biting wind, and scarcely a muffled word was spoken. But it was not just the cold night. To attack the airfield buildings the men of B and C Companies had first to cross an anti-tank ditch, thirteen feet deep and six feet across, then advance across 700 yards of the airfield. The ground was flat airfield runways and open grassy surrounds, covered by the Germans' Spandau machine guns, almost certainly on fixed lines, with anti-tank and other artillery. Gibbs knew that the Surreys had to cross without the Germans hearing their advance, and before the moon rose.

Jerry had bags of Spandaus and could bring down defensive fire from his artillery. So there was only one thing to do, and that was to 'fox' him, and make a 'silent attack'. We reached the ditch without mishap, and started to cross it one at a time. I can tell you it was mighty cold wading through that water, but soon we were all across.

Somehow the two companies covered the airfield's open ground within ten minutes, without being seen or heard.

We got to within fifty yards of Jerry's lines before a single Spandau opened up. After that things became pretty chaotic. My platoon got dug in and my OC went off to see if he could raise reinforcements, leaving me in command.

One of my men was killed in front of me, and another beside me. The stuff was coming down from all directions. Suddenly I made out the shapes of two men coming towards me from our rear.

Gibbs felt the urge to just open up on them. He motioned to his remaining men to hold their fire, stayed low on the ground, and held his breath.

They were Germans. One was a big fellow with his Spandau tucked under his arm like a walking stick. I waited until they were within six feet, and then emptied my Tommy gun into them.[11]

But this was only the start. More buildings were seized, men went down, radios did not work, no one knew who was who in the dark, and heavy fire kept coming in from German positions somewhere. Some platoons somehow constructed sangars where they could hold their ground. The flat expanse with no cover made it a death trap. 'Movement in the open was impossible because of withering machine-gun fire which ripped across the airfield,' said Daniell in the Regimental History. 'The moon had risen and all the company commanders and their isolated platoons could do was to hang on to their positions.'[12]

The night wore on and doubts rose at the thought of how conspicuous they would be in German gunsights at first light. Nevertheless they stayed put. Then miraculously soon after 5.00am tanks arrived from the 51st Royal Tank Regiment and, after relieving the stranded platoons, shelled the buildings still in German possession. Air strikes were also called in on some outlying German positions on the airfield perimeter. Not long into the morning daylight of 8 November the Forli airfield was fully secured and in the hands of the Surreys.[13]

The Surreys' daring assault resulted in Major Allan Paskins, leader of B Company, and Captain John E. Hatt-Cook, leader of the Carrier Platoon, each receiving the Military Cross, and Sergeant Stanley Gibbs the Military Medal.[14] Although they lost four dead and eight wounded, if surprise had not been achieved, it could have been much worse in such an exposed location.[15]

Other units of the Battleaxe Division had attacked the town of Forli at 4.00am, while the Surreys held their positions and tight grip on the airfield. Later in the day the Surreys' patrols pushed out and found that Forli town had also been captured. Next day, 9 November, the Surreys pulled back to Cesena for recovery.[16] Forli had been the home town of Mussolini. Now he would never return.

*   *   *

On 11 November 1/6th Surreys left Cesena and rejoined 10 Brigade at Forli. In an offensive in which 4th and 46th Divisions were tasked to cross the River Cesena, at midnight on 20 November the Surreys' B and C Companies went into the attack.[17]

In the Regiment's record, the Surreys' Lieutenant Colonel Squire and Major Hill, described the two companies' attempt at a night crossing.

When the leading two platoons of B Company got to within 200 yards of the river they found themselves in a minefield and a number of men were wounded. The platoons also came under Spandau fire and Captain Ward brought them back about 200 yards, where they dug in until ordered to withdraw. Then C Company came to grief even more disastrously.

It followed up the barrage until it was about 200 yards short of the river, where two platoons lay up while the third went forward to clear a house at the end of a track which the company was to follow to the river. While the two platoons were waiting one of them suffered many casualties from mortar fire and the platoon commander, Lieutenant H. Stephenson, was wounded. Practically the whole of C Company Headquarters was wiped out.

Lieutenant J. Street, commanding 13 Platoon of C Company, went back to Company Headquarters for orders, only to find he was now in sole command. He collected the survivors of the company and gallantly attempted to advance, but they ran into a minefield and suffered heavy casualties.[18]

In the end it was to no avail and the Surreys' B and C companies were pulled back after losing six dead and sixty-three wounded. On 28 November the depleted 1/6th Surreys journeyed back to Pescara with 4th Division for recovery. From there it was back to Taranto. Their Italian campaign was over, but once again their rest was brief, and for a reason. On 7 December they embarked for Greece to counter a civil war.[19]

* * *

In the Tuscan Apennines in November and December 1944, winter began to tighten its grip. The US Fifth and British Eighth Armies both ran out of reserves. Losses of men could not be replaced and, as priority was given to the Allied Armies advancing across north-west Europe and into Germany, ammunition supplies were cut. The rain and mud bogged down vehicles, guns, tanks and the infantry. Meanwhile, the German defences pulled back around Bologna and, on a more compact front with shorter supply lines, were able to concentrate their firepower. With the help of the defenders' constant friends, rain, mud, ice and snow, relative to the Allies the Germans grew stronger.[20]

For 1st Surreys and the 78th Division, still deployed with Fifth Army after their taking of Monte Spaduro, they faced another, third winter in the mountains. For the veterans of the past two winters in Tunisia and southern Italy, the terrible rain and mud were back again to inflict their cold, wet torture. 'It became difficult to stand,' said Ray, 'let alone fight, in what resembled a foot or more of fluid porridge; tanks became quite useless; rivers rose at a phenomenal rate.'[21]

Clinging to their gains around Monte Spaduro and its ridge, the 1st Surreys and other Battleaxe battalions took shelter wherever they could. The Germans, however, had not given up hope of reclaiming lost ground, and were sending out probing patrols looking for weak points.

* * *

For the Surreys' Sergeant Frank Oram, the main task of his Sniper Group was to establish and man forward Observation Posts (OPs) for sniper hides and make night reconnaissance patrols:

Both tasks had their problems. Any movement in the area risked immediate mortar and shell fire, so I moved men into OPs and sniper

189

hides before dawn, and then they stayed there all day until dark for relief.

The extreme cold made life very hard, and we were grateful when extra winter clothing was issued. The good old gas cape we had carried on our backs for so long came into its own. It came down to the ground and not only kept the rain and snow out, but the body heat in. But nothing could take away the pain and discomfort of being cramped into a hole for ten hours at a time.

As anyone who has done patrolling knows, it causes reactions in mind and body unexplainable in words. Added to this the creeping and crawling about in mud and snow, and the intense cold gave one the feeling of the last straw, so to speak, and only the 'rum issue' brought us back to life.

Beyond the Spaduro Ridge there were two houses used by my Group as OPs. The most forward house was attacked by the Germans and virtually a complete platoon with two of my lads were captured. We did not reoccupy the house, but sent out a patrol nightly to a position on a small piece of ground overlooking it.

When the Germans occupied the house, the RAF 'Cab Rank' was called in. The 'Cab Rank' consisted of Spitfires, circling high up in the sky, ready to pounce on targets chosen by the ground forces. I watched from my OP the spectacular display, as the Spitfires attacked the house with cannon and machine-gun fire, and saw the Germans scuttling away.[22]

* * *

In the Surreys' D Company, Private George Wilson was deployed in early November near to the Spaduro Ridge, in a twelve-man platoon to counter such enemy patrols. George was nineteen. He had been born in Blackheath, joined the Home Guard Infantry at sixteen and then had a period in an anti-aircraft battery before being transferred into the 1st Surreys in November 1943.

We had taken over a deserted farmhouse, Casa Bernadi, on flat ground between the base of Monte Spaduro and the Sillaro River. We were forward of D Company HQ, who were in another ruined farm-house, Casa Aquabona. We were really some 500 yards or so into no man's land, using the farmhouse as a listening post, for advanced warning of enemy activity, and sometimes as a start point for a patrol.

Casa Bernadi was a typical small Italian farmhouse, one room up and one room down, with an open lean-to barn against the back of the house, from where a dirt track led down to the river. There was only

190

one door in the front of the house. Its surrounds were a few trees and bushes, and agricultural land now overgrown.

By day we stayed in the house, no fires or cooking; smoke would have given the game away. At night defensive positions were taken up, two slit trenches outside front and back, manned three men each with Brens. Three of us stayed upstairs in the house, the other three downstairs.

On the night of 1/2 November a German patrol from the 1st Paratrooper Regiment (Fallschirmjäger), of more than twenty men appeared like apparitions in the dark, walking eerily towards the back of the farmhouse. They made no attempt to scout it out first, they came straight up to the building. They must have thought it unoccupied.

Those Surreys crouched in the slit trenches held their breath, and held their fire, hoping that the Germans were just passing through. They did not wish to give away their occupation of the house. Then some German paras began preparing explosives, and others began to make their way around to the front of the house. They intended to blow up the house. It was time to act.

The first I knew of the German patrol was when the Brens opened up. We also opened fire from the upstairs windows. Downstairs when Ted (the Germans) tried to kick the door in, Sergeant Frary, fired at them through the door. There was a lot of firing from both sides, and Ted tried to lob stick grenades through the windows.

In the dark all we could see was fleeting shadows. Taken by surprise, Ted retreated to the back of the house, possibly to take stock and consider their next move, which brought a lull in the firing.

In the uncanny silence the quandary was: what were the Surreys to do next? The six men in the house could see no movement in the blackness outside. What had happened to their comrades in the two slit trenches, front and back? Had they been killed by the Germans? Were the Germans at this moment about to launch another attack from the back, or bring in more support and firepower? Did they have their guns trained on the house's only door, just waiting for the Surreys to come through it? 'That's when Sergeant Frary gathered the five of us together,' said Wilson, 'and after a quick briefing we dashed out of the house and took the firefight to Jerry.'

Wilson and the others followed Frary, and charged around to the back, firing in the general direction of where they guessed the enemy may be.

Enough was enough for them, the Germans must have just took to their heels, for the next minute they were gone. After a check around the area and making sure that the lads in the trenches were OK, we made our way back to the farmhouse to take stock of the situation. When morning came, since secrecy did not matter anymore, we carefully had a good scout around.

The Germans as usual had evacuated their wounded, so we had no idea how many had been hit. But going by the equipment discarded we knew that some had been, like a para's steel helmet with the chin strap cut through so it could be removed, and various leather straps from their equipment.

That's when we found the explosives in the barn, also placed against the wall of the house. They included a glass mine, a type of Teller Mine, because it was made of fibreglass and few metal parts, it made it difficult to detect. We were told it was one of the first found. We'd had another lucky escape.

Later that morning Ted gave us the benefit of a mortar stonk. One bomb did make a direct hit on a disused slit trench, but we all survived with no casualties. For some of us it was a third escape from 'cashing in our chips'![23]

Wilson and his platoon were relieved the following night, and did not return to that outpost again. For his initiative and fearless leadership in fighting off the patrol of German paratroopers, Sergeant Jack Frary was awarded the DCM.[24]

Not that there was any reward for Wilson and his comrades for repulsing the German patrol. They were repositioned to spend the rest of the winter on the summit of Monte Spaduro. Typically Wilson made light of those times:

We spent Christmas Day on the top of Monte Spaduro with only the promise of Christmas Dinner when we came out of the line! We had up to eighteen inches of snow at one time, and we were issued with snow suits, and white overalls when we went on patrol ... it was one continuous round of patrols, every night, either standing, fighting or listening.[25]

In that contested area between Monte Spaduro and the Sillaro river, Frank Weston went out in another patrol to occupy a deserted farmhouse. 'We set off soon after dark,' said Frank, 'an eight-man patrol led by our new sergeant. The rumour was that he had not seen much front-line work. It made us more unsettled, more jittery than usual.'

Frank thought of the many comrades he had lost, since that day he had joined the Surreys in March 1943. Was this going to be his time? Tonight it seemed harder to dismiss that thought.

After trekking for an hour or so, we came upon the farmhouse we were ordered to occupy for a couple of days. Two men went forward, and soon signalled back that it was empty. Our new sergeant then stunned us. He ordered all eight of us to go upstairs in the farmhouse. Unbelievably, no-one was to remain downstairs, and no-one outside in a slit trench.

Three of us, the older hands, objected in pretty blunt language. But this know-all sergeant would have none of it. Now we were really on edge.

It was a very cold night, and in the relative warmth of the upper floor, some men were asleep quickly. Frank lay awake for a long time, his sense of foreboding growing stronger. He felt for his gun, and unusually made sure the safety was off. Like so many, Frank had a paranoid fear of being taken prisoner. Better if your number comes up.

As the night wore on, we must have all fallen asleep, even the look-out on duty at the window. Then the shouts, bawling out from below, brought me awake with a start. The first light of dawn was seeping in.

The Germans were downstairs, shouting out *'Komm herunter!'* – Come down! Or something like that. They would have had their Schmeissers trained on the ceiling, and the stairs. We had no option but to do what they said, before they blew us apart.

We came down in single file. My mate Bob behind me whispered to me, 'Get ready to run, as soon as we are all downstairs!' As soon as the eight of us were all down, I heard the ping, as Bob pulled out the pin of a grenade.

Bob threw it at the four or five Germans who were standing to one side of the room, and at the same time darted to the open door. I was right behind him. The Germans threw themselves to the ground. As soon as Bob was out of the door he opened up with a burst from his Tommy gun, at two or three startled Germans outside, who scattered for cover.

We heard the grenade explode back in the house, and then we just ran, boy oh boy, did we run. Somehow the rest of the patrol were right behind us. And we just kept running. I reckon I would have won any Olympic race that day.[26]

* * *

To the west of 1st Surreys, close to Monte Sole, No. 4 Company of the 5th Grenadier Guards prepared to attack a German position. On 2 December at 1.00am, Lance Sergeant Jack Chaffer, the would-be Surrey, crossed the start line with his platoon in No. 4 Company in bright moonlight.

Although almost at once the whole company came under intense fire from five enemy machine guns, the Grenadiers pressed on towards the German positions in the foothills of Monte Sole. Incoming fire took its toll and then, some seventy yards from the Germans' lines, many men were blown up by mines. The company commander, several platoon commanders and seven men from Chaffer's platoon went down.

Some way ahead Jack could see that his own platoon commander was down, and his seemingly still body must mean that he was at least seriously wounded.

> I did not think at all and I was oblivious to the continuing enemy fire. I just went forward to him, with another man, like anyone would. He was still alive, and between us we half-dragged, half-carried him back. I have a knack of knowing the right direction in the dark, and this time it must even have helped me avoid the mines!

Jack then took command of the surviving men of his platoon, who were spread out, exposed to being picked off by enemy fire, or, if they moved, blown up. Once again with a disregard for the mines and chattering Spandaus, he re-grouped his men so that they could support each other and return fire at the Germans. Knowing they were in a precarious position, Jack radioed in for new orders to move his platoon. Otherwise it would only be a matter of time before they would be wiped out.

The new orders were to move to some higher ground which Jack achieved without any further casualties. Lance Sergeant Jack Chaffer was subsequently awarded the Military Medal, for outstanding courage, coolness and efficiency, which, it was noted, had been displayed throughout the campaign.[27]

* * *

On 13 December came the first really serious fall of snow. The thermometer fell as low as fifteen degrees Fahrenheit, and even the fast mountain streams from the heights froze over. The cold, dry weather was less miserable for the men than the mud and the rain, but the mountain blizzards became a serious danger and the tracks, now sheets of glassy ice, were as difficult for vehicles as when they had been a foot deep in mud.[28]

Once again, as transport became immobilized, supplies of any kind could only be moved by mules. The jeeps drove up as far as they could, then transferred their loads to mules. The final stretch was on men's backs to the forward positions.[29]

More and more the Allied troops in Italy were starved of ammunition, in favour of the Allied armies in north-west Europe advancing on Germany. In contrast the Germans were increasing their artillery firepower, exploiting their shorter supply routes and the narrower front lines.[30]

The troops of 78th Division, and the rest of Fifth Army, spent the winter dotted across bare mountainsides, dragging themselves through the rain, mud, ice and snow, as they clung to the ground they had won. Not one yard could be conceded to any German probe, otherwise a spring offensive would be harder and bloodier.

The men would pass most of each day curled up in slit trenches or in small caves dug out of the hillside. Besides this, there would be a spell of sentry duty, a few hours' rest, an hour spent trying to clean the thick mud off the rifles or Bren guns, and periods of boiling tea over a Tommy cooker. They would sleep, covered in wet blankets, with their heads on sodden sand-bags, continually disturbed by the crump and whine of shells and mortars. At night half the men would man the forward positions, while the others would be prowling out in front on patrol or trying to ambush a German patrol.[31]

Yet again the troops struggled to survive and fight in the rain and mud, which was often more than a foot deep. Huddled and freezing in a sodden blanket, the escape came when exhaustion finally brought on an hour or so of sleep's oblivion.[32]

In another of his letters to Captain Payne, who had now been invalided out of the Army because of his maimed leg, Sergeant Gostling somehow found a way to express his despair, and at the same time his hope for the war to end:

9 December 1944
Dear Mr Payne,
    I expect you have read all about the glorious Italian mud on the front. As you can guess we are here in it as usual. Up to our eyebrows. I have never known such weather and mud. I went up to Main (I hope you know what this is!) the other night, and the mud came up to my knees. And this is no exaggeration. I have seen mules up to their bellies in it. And chaps have had to dig them out. It's awful. Orrible.
    By the time I get out of this army of ours I shall have had enough.
    Very sincerely yours,
    E.W.A. Gostling[33]

The men would read their latest letters from home and, for a few moments, would be transported back to that different world. It was a world of ordinary day-to-day life, jobs, wartime rationing, children, friends, families and the emotions of being apart. Soldiers would write a reply, and in some way try to hide the reality of random death with which they lived.

Then the sergeant's bark of new orders would interrupt. The preparations for the next patrol, the next fight were on again. Men would wrench their thoughts away from loved ones at home and seek the camaraderie of their mates. They would become automatons again, that was the way they functioned. They also yearned for that too, it was what they knew.

Christmas drew close and the winter seemed to stretch out like eternity. On Christmas Eve night, Lieutenant Dennis, of the 64th Anti-tank

Regiment Royal Artillery, had no thought of a visit by Santa, but still felt some kind of premonition. Were the Germans about to break an unofficial lull in the shelling and patrol skirmishing?

Within the last hour or so to midnight, Dennis could hear nothing, not even a distant shot or muffled explosion. It felt uncanny. Then a faint voice was heard from the German positions. A man was singing, growing louder, the words in German of the Christmas Carol 'Silent Night', 'Stilige nacht, heilige nacht'. When the singer finished, Dennis listened to one of his men make a dumbfounding reply, singing forth the Carol, 'God rest ye merry gentlemen.'[34]

The second winter of the Italian campaign, the third winter of the war for 78th Division, brought morale to a low ebb in both Fifth and Eighth Armies. The bitter fighting and heavy losses in the Gothic Line were taking their toll. Casualties from psychiatric disorders, commonly referred to as 'bomb happy', and desertions from both Allied Armies, were at record levels.

In an ironic way the dreaded spring offensive could not come too soon. However, the logistical challenge in massing troops and supplies to support an attack was bad enough, but on what date in spring should it begin? Early spring brought melting snow, flooding rivers, and mists that would hinder air support. Late spring and early summer would allow the Germans more time to organize and tempt them to divert forces to their homeland. The dilemma confronting Generals Alexander, Clark and McCreery, and their planners, was envied by no-one.[35] But spring and its looming battles would come. London and Washington demanded it.

Notes

1. Squire and Hill, op cit., p. 49.
2. Daniell, op cit., pp. 219–21.
3. Squire and Hill, op cit., p. 49.
4. Ibid.
5. Ibid.
6. Daniell, op cit., pp. 221–2.
7. Ibid.
8. Ibid, pp. 222–3.
9. Squire and Hill, op cit., p. 51.
10. Daniell, op cit., pp. 223–5.
11. Surrey History Centre, ESR/25/GIBBS/1.
12. Daniell, op cit., p. 223–5.
13. Ibid.
14. Squire and Hill, op cit., p. 51.
15. Daniell, op cit., p. 224.
16. Ibid.
17. Ibid, p. 225.
18. Squire and Hill, op cit., p. 52.
19. Daniell, op cit., p. 225.

20. Orgill, op cit., pp. 208–16.
21. Ray, op cit., p. 176.
22. Veterans' accounts, Oram; Squire and Hill, op cit., pp. 58–9.
23. Veterans' accounts, Wilson.
24. Squire and Hill, op cit., p. 59.
25. Veterans' accounts, Wilson.
26. Veterans' accounts, Weston.
27. Veterans' accounts, Chaffer; Military Medal Citation.
28. Ray, op cit., pp. 176–7.
29. Ibid, p. 178.
30. Ibid, p. 179.
31. Ibid, p. 183.
32. Carver, op cit., p. 268.
33. Surrey History Centre ESR PAYN 10/11.
34. Carver, op cit., p. 267.
35. Ibid, pp. 275–6.

Chapter 14

The Gothic Line, Argenta Gap, River Po: The Impossible Battles?

Wedged between Lombardy and Venetia in the north and the Tuscan Apennines in the south is the region of Emilia-Romagna. At its core is the Roman road, the Via Emilia, built in 200 BC by Aemilius Lepidus, which runs as a spine for 150 miles north-west from Rimini on the Adriatic, to cross the River Po at Piacenza. Emilia-Romagna has two distinct geographical features, the southern valley of the River Po and, farther south, the range of mountain spurs jutting northwards from the Apennines.

Most of the region's towns and cities such as Rimini, Forli, Faenza, Imola, Bologna, Modena, Reggio, Parma and Piacenza are connected by the Via Emilia, which is the main artery to Milan, Genoa and Turin in the north-west. For some 2,000 years, until more recent times, they were also connected by the canals and rivers of the Po valley. In summer the Emilia-Romagna can suffer a scorching heat while in winter the Apennines' winds bring a bitter cold.[1] In early 1945, Emilia-Romagna was also the wedge that separated the German and Allied armies and, as winter began to wane, the region threatened to become the ultimate killing ground, which would define the Italian campaign.

For Allied forces in the mountains of the Gothic Line, and in the south-eastern Po valley, the winter stalemate was a battle of attrition going nowhere. New thinking was required, not only to take the initiative and break through, but to prevent the Germans from moving some of their divisions back to confront the Allied armies fighting in north-west Europe. At the same time, for many in the Allies' Fifth and Eighth Armies, there was an unspoken dread of the coming spring. The warmer weather would bring a resumption of full-scale battles. The snows of the scenic Tuscan Apennines could melt into rivers of blood in the Po valley.

From Christmas 1944 Generals Alexander, Clark, McCreery and Truscott planned and plotted, and gradually built up their Fifth and Eighth Armies for the spring offensive. (Alexander had been promoted to be Allied Supreme Commander in the Mediterranean theatre; Clark had succeeded him as Army Group commander and General Lucian Truscott had been appointed to command Fifth Army.) Their goal was to gain the final victory in Italy. At the heart of the planning was the philosophy of General McCreery – deception, and surprise. And to achieve surprise, McCreery was a passionate believer in keeping the enemy busy, and guessing.

In February 1945 a feint attack by Fifth Army along the Mediterranean coast prompted Kesselring to move the 29th Panzer Grenadiers to the west. In March dummy guns, make-believe supply depots and misleading wireless activity on the Adriatic side caused a German motorized division to be moved out of reserve to Venice. The Germans had a paranoid fear of being outflanked by an amphibious attack. Another diversionary attack in the west on 5 April drew the 90th Panzer Grenadiers, and some additional battalions, into the Mediterranean coastal area.

General Mark Clark remembered the deception psychology:

We knew the enemy had developed tremendously strong defensive positions along all those natural river obstacles which stood between us and the Po. He knew that we knew, and consequently he was always expecting us to do the obvious, which was to make thrusts along the sea edge on either flank supported by amphibious landings.[2]

McCreery, Truscott and Clark were in full agreement on the priority given to these deception tactics for they knew full well the awesome strength of the German defences. In whatever way the enemy's positions were analysed, they appeared to be insurmountable. The transfer of the Canadian Corps to North West Europe, and a number of other British brigades and divisions to Greece, which had begun in October, severely weakened Allied forces in Italy. Facing the Allies' seventeen divisions, nine in Fifth Army and eight in Eighth Army, was the Germans' Army Group C, which across its Tenth and Fourteenth Armies could call upon twenty-seven divisions. As McCreery recalled:

It really was a ridiculous situation. Not only were we battle weary, depleted, depressed, out-numbered and generally mucked about, but we who could least afford to find manpower, were being asked to send whole formations to France and Greece, and at a time I may add, when we were being ordered simultaneously to nail down sufficient divisions of the enemy, to make a worthwhile contribution to the whole war effort.

But during all this agonizing period we had some things going for us. We had aerial supremacy. The support we had there was derived from the Desert Air Force, which I believe to be the most skilled tactical air power in the world. It was the key to our survival and to our attack.[3]

It was estimated that to break through the Po valley would require horrendous losses of men, and reserves of troops which the two Allied armies did not have. Furthermore to make it worse, as the snows melted in the mountains, and rivers rose, the Germans were flooding large tracts of the Po valley's low-lying land.[4]

On 24 March General Clark issued orders for the plan of attack to commence in early April. Phase 1 required Eighth Army to cross the Senio, Santerno and Reno Rivers in the east, then break through the Argenta Gap to its north. In Phase 2, a few days later, Fifth Army would surge down from their central mountain positions into the Po valley and strike for Bologna. The goal was to surround, then destroy or capture, all German forces south of the River Po. The language of Clark's orders conveyed the offensive's objective, as a final conquest of the Italian campaign. However, one single phrase which Clark used, 'If fully successful,' betrayed an underlying apprehension.[5]

General Alexander's Special Order of the Day in early April was also full of his typical confidence, even claiming that the battle for the River Po, 'will end the war in Europe'. Yet even the ever-optimistic and confident Alexander could not conceal a hint of doubt. He conceded: 'It will not be a walk-over; a mortally wounded beast can still be very dangerous.'[6]

*　　*　　*

For the crucial first strike by Eighth Army in the east to race for the Argenta Gap, the infantry had to be strengthened. With this in mind, on 25 February Alexander ordered XIII Corps including the 78th Division to transfer from Fifth Army in the central Apennines, back to Eighth Army on the Adriatic coast.

The 1st Surreys came down from the mountains around Castel del Rio and San Pietro, and with the rest of the Battleaxe Division halted first at Bivigliano.

> It was out of the mountains into a paradise of baths, fresh clothing, excellent food, abundant NAAFI rations and entertainment. From Bivigliano we moved to Forlimpopoli (which became known to the troops naturally as 'Fall in Properly'), which was near the city of Forli close to the Adriatic Coast. Here training began for what everyone felt would be the last campaign. The Battalion was brought up to full strength, the horrors of the winter receded and morale rose with the early Italian spring.[7]

> 'There was rest and recreation as well as training,' wrote Ray, 'clubs and opera and concert parties in Forli itself, and houses and green fields and vineyards instead of rocks and mud. There was spring weather, and roofs over men's heads.'[8]

200

In the November 1944 offensive to break the Gothic Line it had been the 1/6th Surreys in a night attack who had taken the Forli airfield. Forli town, which since then had been occupied by Eighth Army, was a prosperous agricultural and industrial centre of around 100,000 people, situated on the Via Emilia. Of its many historical buildings, perhaps the best known, dating from the fifth century, is the Abbey of San Mercuriale. Of course, less recognized today is that Forli was the home town of Mussolini, who was born close by in Predáppio.

For the Surreys in Forlimpopoli, and other 78th Division troops, the respite was also a time to catch up on a backlog of mail from friends and families. Men wondered if the next battle really would end the war. Sergeant Frank Oram read a letter from his wife Winifred, of her lessons in lace-making, and her work with the Kent Women's Institute. Sergeant Harry Skilton heard of his wife Jessie's lucky escape in a bombing raid on London. Jessie had been called up some time before to work in a munitions factory in London. She had been walking back to her boarding house from work one night when a bomb landed in the same street. The blast threw her into the gutter but, apart from a few bruises, she was unhurt.

Frank Weston wrote again to his brother Les and said he looked forward to his promised introduction to Doreen when he returned. In the officers' mess there was that song being played for the umpteenth time: 'We'll meet again', again and again.

The Surreys' training commenced in conjunction with their 11 Brigade, and the tanks of the 10th Hussars, with exercises in river crossings of the nearby River Montone. They were the Surreys' first formal joint exercises with armour. Together they had to fight their way across the marshy Po valley, with its countless other rivers, canals and tributaries.[9] On 27 March 1st Surreys and 11 Brigade travelled north a few miles beyond Ravenna, and moved up into Eighth Army's front-line positions on the River Senio.[10]

> It was unusual terrain for us. From the time of Tunisia, Sicily and through most of the campaign in Italy, we had become more accustomed to fighting in hilly or mountainous country. The ground was flat and cut through by the Senio, a narrow but deep stream, protected on each side by flood banks from ten to twelve feet high.
>
> The Germans were mostly dug in on the far bank of the river, and the Surreys' forward positions were in the floodbanks on the near side. It was a period of close contact with a lively enemy. There was little movement by day as enemy observation posts were efficient and well concealed. At night everything seemed to be on the move, ration parties, company reliefs, evacuation of wounded, patrols, and raids.[11]

One company was in trenches dug half-way up the flood bank on the opposite side of which the Germans had their trenches. Each side lobbed grenades over the bank, and holes were tunnelled practically through the flood bank, so that mines could be pushed through and exploded right up against the trenches of the other side.[12]

At the Division's workshops many of the Bren carriers had been converted into 'Wasps', mobile flame throwers, ready for the assault against enemy fortified positions. Farther back the armour was massing, tanks of all varieties, some armed with the new 17-pounder gun, others equipped with flails to root out and destroy enemy mines. Yet others were modified to carry portable bridges.[13]

Everyone knew. They were getting ready for the battle that was expected to surpass everything they had done before.

*   *   *

The Battle for the River Po, codenamed as Army Group Operation GRAPE-SHOT, would begin on 9 April. In the east in Operation BUCKLAND Eighth Army's four divisions of V Corps would drive across the Senio and Santerno rivers. Fifth Army, in Operation CRAFTSMAN, would drive out of the central mountains for Bologna. But it would be Eighth Army's V Corps, who would make the all-important first, and major, incision on 9 April into the German defences.

General von Vietinghoff's Tenth Army, despite losing two divisions to the western and eastern fronts, confronted Eighth Army with four divisions of I Parachute Corps and three divisions of LXXVI Panzer Corps.[14] On Eighth Army's left, the 8th Indian and 2nd New Zealand Divisions would be the first to cross the Senio, and then advance another eight miles to establish bridgeheads across the Santerno. While Lake Comácchio was seen by most on both sides as a major barrier, McCreery identified it as an opportunity. Amphibious DUKW and Buffalo (or LVT) vehicles were to be used by 56th Division to achieve surprise on the eastern and right flank, by moving troops across the lake and flooded areas. Then the 56th and 78th Divisions would exploit the crossings, and drive some ten miles north in a pincer to break through the Argenta Gap.

Despite the official air of confidence, the officers and men who were charged with leading the attack held misgivings and feared a disastrous defeat. Numerous canals and rivers, each protected by high earthworks and dykes, hid well dug-in German defences, which had first to be overcome merely to reach the south bank of the River Po. The attack could founder at any one. Even if the Po could be reached and crossed it was felt that, like so many previous river crossings, the Germans would escape again to fight once more on its north side, and subsequently retreat up into the Alps.

Many men, especially veterans of two years or more of the North African and Italian campaigns, were suffering 'battle fatigue' in varying degrees, or were described commonly at the time as being 'bomb happy'. Additionally the news of Allied forces' accelerating drive through north-west Europe into Germany's heartland was widespread. It was fertile ground for a little voice in men's minds which said, 'Why get yourself killed, when the war is nearly over?'[15]

For many in Eighth Army's 56th and 78th Divisions, who were to lead the attack, even the first goal of crossing the River Senio, seemed impossible. Either side of the Senio's huge floodbanks, British and German troops were dug in so close to each other that they had to talk in whispers.

The 1st Princess Louise's Kensington Regiment, which was the Support Battalion of 78th Division, provided companies or support groups to the Division's three brigades. In one of those support roles, Lieutenant Brian Harpur, summed up well the feelings of many men:

> We who were up in the front line could be forgiven for having a little scepticism about the outcome, because there was nothing to indicate that the pattern of the many previous river crossings, when the enemy escaped to fight another day, would not be repeated. Indeed a feeling of deep disquiet affected many of us because this was not just one more river crossing, it was an operation demanding at least half a dozen canal and river crossings before even reaching the mighty Po itself.[16]

So as to give their armies south of the Po even more protection, the Germans had flooded vast areas of the Po valley. The result was that a corridor of high ground about four miles long and up to three miles wide, was bordered on its west side by the flooded land south of the River Reno, and on its east by Lake Comácchio, which lay close by the Adriatic Sea. This narrow corridor carried the only route north, Highway 16, from Ravenna across the rivers Lamone, Senio, Santerno and Reno, through Argenta to Ferrara. It was to become known as the Argenta Gap.[17]

Both the Senio River and, a few miles to its north, the Santerno River, flowed north-east into the River Reno, which disgorged into Lake Comácchio. The first river in Eighth Army's path was the Senio.

It is a narrow stream between steep, muddy banks with flood banks ten feet high built on each side of the river, from sixty to eighty yards apart. The enemy held the west bank, and had some positions on the east bank as well, and it was over this narrow strip of river that the opposing armies faced each other.[18]

In the flat open terrain it was as if both sides were well dug in for static trench warfare. Any movement during daylight had to be severely limited whereas the night saw patrols engaged in firefights, and shelling by both sides. Throughout a network of tunnels and earthworks the Germans

203

had built in listening and observation posts everywhere, to support their dug-in gun positions. It gave the impression that to get anywhere near the south bank of the Po would be impossible.

A mouse could not move without being knocked off. In addition there were thousands of mines everywhere on both sides of the enemy's bank and on the ground beyond, plus pits, traps, barbed wire trip-wires, and just in case of real emergency, pre-arranged salvoes from mortars and artillery could be called on at any time, to saturate any section on either or both sides of the river. Yet somehow the troops had to get over the Senio sufficiently quickly and in such force as to be able to breach the next river, the Santerno, which was defended on almost identical lines.[19]

*   *   *

The morning of 9 April was a sunny spring day, with a cloudless sky, and after a few weeks without rain the ground was firm.[20] For the Germans it must have seemed just like any other in the near six-month stand-off. It was far from normal in Eighth Army. While routine aerial strikes and reconnaissance, artillery shelling and fire onto German positions was maintained just as normal, during the night and the morning of 8/9 April, all front-line troops were pulled back a few hundred yards from the Senio. It seemed that the Germans saw little of this, or took little notice. Even if they had begun to suspect a major offensive, in the time available there was little they could have done.[21]

At 1.50pm the combined Allied air forces, the strategic US Fifteenth, and the tactical US XXII Air Support Command and the RAF's Desert Air Force (DAF), began an unprecedented onslaught. For more than an hour and a half, 825 heavy bombers dropped 175,000 fragmentation bombs, 1,692 tons of explosives,[22] on enemy gun positions, and on defences which blocked Eighth Army's planned attack points. Simultaneously 1,000 fighter-bombers carried out pinpoint, low-level strikes on machine-gun and mortar positions, ammunition dumps, and anything trying to move.

An artillery bombardment followed for forty-two minutes, which was a normal precursor to a ground attack, which the Germans would now have been expecting. However, before they could emerge from their dug-outs, they were immediately hit for a further ten minutes by another wave of fighter bombers, flying so low they barely appeared to clear the flood-banks and dykes. Without a pause four more identical waves of artillery bombardment, followed by fighter-bomber strikes in similar duration, went in. From beginning to end the battering would last around five and a half hours. It was what we now term 'shock and awe'.[23]

During the afternoon, all the fighter-bomber wings dived enemy positions from Imola to the River Reno, firing rockets, strafing and dropping fuel tanks filled with incendiary jelly, whose liquid fire, more terrible than molten lava, bubbled unquenchably in trench and dug-out. On the V Corps front, successive waves of Spitbombers of 244 Wing broke across the Senio during ten-minute lulls in the artillery barrage. Four times the Spitbombers sprayed death over the river defences.[24]

After the fifth round of artillery shelling, when the Germans heard the fighter-bombers roar in once more, those enemy troops still unscathed must have continued to huddle heads down in their underground shelters. Many would have thought the alternating waves of shells and bombs would never end, and the paralyzing nightmare would pound on into the night.

This time, however, the wave of fighter-bombers was a dummy run, screaming low over the Senio without dropping a single bomb. After hour upon hour of incessant shelling and air strikes, it was enough to keep the Germans underground, each man no doubt grateful that he was not receiving a direct hit. While the planes flew in mock attack overhead, right on cue the 2nd New Zealand and 8th Indian Divisions drove forward with portable pontoon equipment, unseen and unheard, to make vital crossings of the Senio. It was a culminating master stroke of deception.[25]

At 7.20pm, as dusk began to darken the sky, the main ground attack commenced. Dykes were blown apart and temporary bridges of portable pontoons and even huge bundles of branches were hurried into place, to allow the first tanks to cross the Senio. Some of those tanks used flame-throwing guns to destroy close-in German positions. Despite the preceding massive bombardment, the Germans threw themselves into a fierce fight back. Although Eighth Army was across the Senio, next to come was the Santerno River, and this time without any element of surprise. The goal of the River Po was still a long way away.

Alexander's planners had clearly realized the dilemma posed by the Santerno. Before a critical mass of force and forward momentum had been generated, the Santerno could bring the offensive to a shuddering halt on only the second day. The attack must get across the Santerno, then accelerate to quickly reach the Argenta Gap before the Germans could concentrate their forces there.

Again the support of air power was seen as the only possible way ground troops might do it. During 10 April some 1,200 aircraft continuously bombed and strafed a ten- square-mile area on the Santerno River, to clear a path for Eighth Army's planned crossing.

From Forli, from dusk to dawn, eighty-three Bostons and seven Mosquitos took off or landed every two minutes. From Cesenatico, another sixty Baltimores rose into the air, not to attack bridges and pontoons, but gun positions running from Castel Bolognese to Bagnara, from Imola to

Massa Lombardo, bombing closer to our troops than DAF had ever attempted at night.[26]

The commander of the German 98th Division, General Reinhardt, a veteran of the Eastern Front, said it was the worst bombardment he had ever experienced. Planes peeled off in turn from their 'sky cab-ranks' to strike anything they could see, a vehicle, a tank, even a single German soldier.[27]

Yet this now made it quite clear to the Germans where the main thrust of the Allied attack would be directed – the Argenta Gap. The Allies had declared their hand.

* * *

On 9 April when, as planned, the air force bombing raids and the shelling finally ceased at 7.20pm, the Indian and New Zealand Divisions drove forward to cross both the Senio and the Santerno rivers.[28] Right behind the Indians and New Zealanders, the 78th Division and the 1st Surreys were poised to exploit their bridgeheads. First the Battleaxe Division's Irish Brigade, using Kangaroo armoured troop carriers and enlarged nearly to the size of a division, and 36 Brigade led by the 8th Argyll and Sutherland Highlanders, drove through to the front to exploit the Santerno bridge-heads.[29]

The Surreys' Sergeant Manning recalled what followed:

> Later that night forward companies of the Surreys crossed the river to occupy a bridgehead, which included the small town of Cortignola. There was a big haul of prisoners, all of them in a state of shock from the savage bombardment they had suffered during the day. It was again a battle of rivers, recalling those of the Trigno and Sangro in our early days in Italy.[30]

On 11 April two battalions of 56th Division's 169 Queen's Brigade used eighty amphibious Buffalo vehicles, to make the surprise crossing of Lake Comácchio. Although only lightly armoured with a single Browning machine gun, the Buffaloes were a large tracked vehicle, had a large troop carrying capacity and performed well over both normal ground, and in deep water. The operation for 2/5th and 2/6th Queen's was to cross the lake, and on its western side take the villages of Menata and Longastrino.

There had been delays launching the Buffaloes but they were able to lay down a smokescreen, fired from guns mounted in the vehicles, which hid them completely as they approached firm ground in full daylight. As the massive amphibians hit the rising ground below the water and seemed to mount higher as they emerged from the mud and floodwater, very few shots were fired at them. From each leading Buffalo emerged a platoon of

Queensmen, while Browning machine guns gave covering fire from the turrets of the ponderous vehicles.[31]

Not surprisingly the German troops of 42nd Jäger Division were stunned, and gave little opposition, some 300 being taken prisoner. The planned pincer movement by 56th and 78th Divisions, aimed at the Argenta Gap, was gathering momentum.

In stubborn fighting, the 56th and 78th Divisions, led by the Irish Brigade, drove on from the bridgeheads across the Santerno River and Lake Comácchio, until on 14 April a rapid thrust captured a partially-damaged bridge across the Reno. In four days Eighth Army had fought its way over the Senio, Santerno and Reno rivers, and across Lake Comácchio.

Also on 14 April in Operation CRAFTSMAN, Truscott's Fifth Army attacked out of the central mountains, to fight their way down towards Bologna. The three lead divisions, the Brazilian Expeditionary Force, 1st Armored and 1st Mountain Divisions, were at once making good gains.[32]

Suddenly the goal of the Argenta Gap, and with it the River Po, was within sight.[33] By the evening of 16 April the Surreys and their 11 Brigade had reached the suburbs of Argenta, which lay on Highway 16 close up against the flooded area to the west. To the south-east of Argenta, 167 and 169 Brigades of 56th Division were closing in on Bastia.[34]

The Argenta Gap was in effect a causeway high above the flooded land leading to Argenta town. The two divisions faced the Fossa Marina canal, which ran east from Argenta across to Lake Comácchio. German defences in the area had deployed in the canal banks, sown extensive minefields, and recently been reinforced by the 29th Panzer Grenadier Division, whose orders were to hold the Argenta Gap at all costs. Nevertheless, Eighth Army's plan called for the main rupture of German lines to be made by 56th and 78th Divisions, north-east of Argenta across the Fossa Marina.[35]

In this battle the most difficult obstacles were the thickly-sown minefields, covered by expert machine gunners and a still active German artillery. Numbers of Italian partisans led troops along secret paths through the minefields. Where there were no paths, the flail tanks rumbled ahead to clear a way.[36]

As night fell the Surreys went forward first and secured a base from which to launch a crossing of the Fossa Marina. This allowed the 2nd Lancashire Fusiliers, with their newly-appointed second-in-command of only two days, ex-Surreys' Major 'Jake' Saunders, to follow up and attempt a crossing of the canal. The aim was to outflank Argenta town.

In the face of furious German resistance, by midnight the Lancashire Fusiliers secured a slender foothold on the opposite side of the Fossa Marina. Then disaster struck. The Lancashire Fusiliers' CO was seriously wounded and evacuated. Major Saunders took over command and organized the consolidation and deepening of the bridgehead. At dawn came the inevitable German counter-attacks. The Lancashire Fusiliers, inspired by Saunders' calm and confident lead, threw back every German thrust. The Argenta Gap defences were pierced. Major Saunders was awarded an immediate DSO.[37]

In a bitter slog of firefights by dawn on 17 April the Surreys and the Lancashire Fusiliers were across the canal and into the north-east sector of Argenta. The Surreys lost twenty-two casualties, but took thirty-three prisoners, as the 11 Brigade assault pierced the Argenta Gap defence lines.[38] The advantage was then exploited by the Irish Brigade who drove through to fight their way into the ruins of Argenta, to sit astride Highway 16.

The Surreys and 11 Brigade pressed on farther north, across two more canals to the east of Highway 16, and by 19 April were west of the town of Portomaggiore. The next day was yet another hard one, as the Surreys fought their way across the flat orchard country. Snipers, Spandau machine guns and anti-tank guns, hidden in hedges, ditches and farmhouses, were putting up a bitter defensive fight everywhere.

Sergeant Harry Skilton watched as one of his platoon hauled himself up a canal bank. As the soldier eased his body over the top, a mine blast threw him backwards into the canal.

Two of my men rushed to him and pulled his body out of the water. One of his legs had been blown off. He was face down, and no movement. I bent down, a bandage roll already in my hand to apply a tourniquet. As they turned him over, I froze. He was gone. Half the front of his head had been blown away. Death was a common thing to us, but each time you saw it close up, one of your group, it hit you, and numbed you. I suppose it was the only way we coped.[39]

In another typical infantry firefight, like those taking place repetitively across Eighth Army's front lines, the Surreys' Sergeant George Charlton was wounded and lost his three Bren gunners, as they covered 13 and 15 Platoons. Despite being wounded, Charlton continued to lead his 14 Platoon in covering the rest of No. 4 Company, for which he was awarded the Military Medal.

On 20 April the Surreys lost Lieutenant J.C. 'Chips' Louis. When Lieutenant Louis went down, Private Stanley Gosling and Lance Corporal Leslie Morrish, who assumed command, both won Military Medals. The loss of Lieutenant 'Chips' Louis was a huge blow. Louis was a tough, charismatic New Zealander, who had joined the 1st Surreys in December 1942 in Tunisia. Despite being forty years old, and having been wounded three times, he had still seemed indestructible. Even today surviving veterans speak of him in the same breath as Lieutenant Woodhouse, with undiminished memories and respect. Louis was always loath to accept promotion, just wishing to get the job done. The Surreys lost eight dead including Louis, and ten wounded this day. The German dead were uncounted, but the Surreys took sixty-five prisoners.[40]

* * *

After capturing Gobbietta on 20 April, the Surreys found themselves pinned down by enemy fire some 150 yards short of the Canale di San Nicolo. Next morning Lieutenant R.R. McLean led 12 Platoon of B Company in open order, edging forward towards the canal bank, to seek a crossing point. Despite coming under heavy enemy fire from a nearby farmhouse, it seemed of every kind, they found a single plank footbridge still intact. Their orders were clear – 'Get across!'

Laying down as much covering fire as they could, one by one they ran across the footbridge. Miraculously they all made it. They now had to hold the crossing point and repel any German counter-attack. The incoming fire from the farmhouse left them with no choice. To hold the footbridge they had to take it out.

Once night descended and things fell quiet, Lieutenant McLean decided they must act. Listening for any sound, McLean and his men crept up close to the German-held farmhouse. They waited again, listening. McLean went forward first around the wall of the building, towards its door, peering for any movement that would betray an outside sentry.

Then he was at the edge of the doorframe and he could see the door was slightly ajar. He wondered whether to go for a grenade but he had his pistol in his right hand. There was nothing for it now, he thought, and, shouting '*Hände hoch!*', kicked in the door. In that first instant the first German he saw move towards him, he shot. Five others had their hands in the air.[41]

McLean and 12 Platoon had established a tenuous bridgehead across the Canale di San Nicolo, which B Company quickly exploited. They crossed the canal by the footbridge and advanced to within 500 yards of Lungurella, before being held up by Spandau fire. The casualties of B Company were remarkably light, yet they had killed fourteen Germans and taken twenty-eight prisoners. Nevertheless, they were coming under increasing counter-attacks and had to be reinforced. When night fell A Company also crossed and raced straight into Lungurella, closely followed up by B Company. For his leadership of B Company in the crossing of Canale Di San Nicolo, Major G.L.A. Squire was awarded the Military Cross.

The unrelenting pace of the Surreys' advance in continual engagements was not only felt by the front-line troops. At this point the Surreys' CO, Lieutenant Colonel H.M.A. Hunter, was ordered to the rear to get some rest. For seventy-two hours non-stop he had gone without sleep.[42]

Not surprisingly the German forces in Lungurella knew what was coming and had pulled out under cover of darkness. Next day, 22 April, the urgency resumed, with the Surreys ordered to cross the Po di Volano, a not insignificant tributary of the mighty Po itself. Bridgeheads were gained overnight on the north bank and, early in the morning of 24 April, the Surreys were crossing in rafts and boats.[43]

Despite the rapid advances, for many there still persisted the disbelief that final victory was within reach. On 23 April Lieutenant Harpur, of the 1st Princess Louise's Kensington Regiment, had attended an 11 Brigade conference to receive orders for the actual crossing of the Po itself. Like everyone else Harpur was not thinking that victory was close:

> I looked around at the faces of the Brigadier and his staff and the other commanding officers, and all I read with sinking heart was that they too were viewing this next confrontation with the enemy, with what I can only describe as a melancholy fatalism. ... We knew that as we launched our attack across the Po, the enemy with their customary legerdemain would conjure up from nowhere, more tanks, more self-propelled guns, more Nebelwerfers, and more Spandau teams, to bring about the slaughter, which their propaganda leaflets had depicted so graphically. It was not just one more bloody river to cross, it was *the river*.[44]

The Surreys found that getting forward out of the bridgehead positions across the Po di Volano was not easy. The flat countryside enabled the Germans to direct wide fields of fire from numerous farm buildings. Before noon A Company headed north-west towards Tamara, which was known to be defended by a strong German rearguard. Lieutenant Dennis Smith led an attack, taking fourteen prisoners and winning the Military Cross. Meanwhile B Company advanced more directly north towards the south bank of the Po and the immediate goal of the village of Corlo, and a nearby canal.[45]

*   *   *

Late in the day on 24 April, close to that village of Corlo, in a platoon of the Surreys' B Company, Frank Weston was out in front with his mate Bob Turner. They were taking turns to cover each other, in stooping runs from one hedge or clump of bushes to another. They came together in a particularly tangled thicket. On their stomachs and elbows they nosed their way through until they could see the next span of open ground. What they saw some fifty yards or so in front of them, was the twenty-foot-high dyke of a canal.

Transcript of Frank Weston's story:

Somehow we had got separated and ahead of the rest of the platoon, but Bob spoke before I did.

'It's the canal, what they told us about,' Bob almost whispered.

'And look through that gap in the dyke. There's a footbridge still standing.'

'Yeah, but where are the bloody Teds (Germans) hiding?'

'Just waiting to pick us off like at a fairground shooting gallery,' I replied. 'Where the hell is the rest of our platoon? Better get on that radio and tell the sarge' or that new lieutenant, or anyone to send some more support and firepower up here, bloody quick.'

It was probably only a minute or so for Bob to make contact, although it seemed an eternity. Then he switched off and said, 'That new lieutenant said to get across the bridge, and cover its approaches as best we can. They'll get some men with Brens up here as soon as they can, but we have to secure the bridge at once at all cost.

'Bloody hell! Is that really what he said, just the two of us to take that bridge?'

'That's it,' muttered Bob. 'We're the first men to reach the canal, and they've ordered us to cross it immediately, without waiting for further support. That sodding lieutenant is mad, we're dead men.'

I stared at Bob, then edged forward out of the thicket. I think I said something like, 'Come on, even dead men can crawl.'

We half slithered, half crawled on our knees and stomachs, towards the gap in the dyke, expecting at any moment to be hit by the crack and spit of a Spandau. Above our gasping I could hear a bird twittering. Near the gap in the dyke we lay flat, chests heaving, pushing ourselves into the ground. Now through the gap in the dyke we could even glimpse the water in the canal.

Bob spoke first. 'Our only bloody hope is to crawl up to the canal bank, and wade or swim across. That way there's just a chance the Teds may still not spot us. If we go across that footbridge, we're bound to be seen and picked off.'

'Now you're crazy,' I said. 'Look at that black slimy water, there's no knowing how deep it is, or how thick is the mud on the bottom. With all our kit and the radio, swimming is not on, we'd drown. Getting in might be all right, if we're not seen. But even if the water is only up to our necks, how would we haul ourselves up that steep bank on the other side?'

'Well, on that footbridge we'll be sitting ducks. I'm not doing that, its suicide.'

'Forget it, I'm not getting into that cesspit of water,' I insisted. 'I'm going to make a run for that bridge, there's no other way. You stay here and cover me.'

I scrambled to my feet, and was off in a crouching run towards the bridge. I left Bob with his finger tightened on his rifle's trigger, scanning left and right, for any movement or a burst of German fire. I had nearly covered the twenty yards or so to the footbridge. Surely I must be seen.

At the bridge, I stopped and dropped to the ground. Was I really going to run across that bridge? I turned my head each way, looking up and down the canal banks. My heart was racing. I could not believe there was still no enemy fire, no bullets that would finally put an end to my luck. Like many others I had long ago given up believing I would survive the war. I just did what had to be done.

I heard Bob swear. He must have thought I had frozen in fear. I could not stay there, I had to move. Seconds ticked by. Then in an instant I was on my feet, and running like a man possessed across the bridge. It seemed like a marathon, every stride a huge effort. To Bob's eye, he told me later, I seemed to fly across the bridge, like an Olympic sprinter. And then I was on the other side, and diving into some bushes. There was still no German fire.

'I'm coming over now,' shouted Bob, and he was racing across the bridge at similar breakneck speed. He collapsed into the bushes next to me.

That's when I laughed. 'What took you so long? I bet you could not see my arse for dust, when I ran across!'[46]

* * *

The luck of Frank Weston and Bob Turner had held at the eleventh hour. They did not know it, but for them their luck had held to the end. Shortly before 8.00am the next morning, 25 April, the Surreys reached Corlo, close to Ferrara, and on the south bank of the Po, where they stayed.[47] Day by day they waited for new orders to advance, as day by day news came in of Allied forces hammering forward through the German lines.

Meanwhile the motorized and armoured units of Fifth and Eighth Armies, swept on across the River Po into northern Italy, taking Mantua and Verona on 26 April, Padua and Milan on 29 April, and Turin on 1 May. On 2 May staff of General von Vietinghoff, at the Eighth Army HQ in Caserta, signed the surrender of all German armies in Italy, to Field Marshal Alexander.[48] Hostilities in Italy at least were at an end. It was later learned that Hitler had committed suicide on 30 April. Maybe there was

212

something in Alexander's claim made some weeks earlier, that victory in the Battle of the Po would end the war in Europe. On 4 May all German armies in Germany, Holland, and Denmark surrendered to Field Marshal Montgomery.

'It was all over,' wrote Daniell in the Regimental History, 'and like every other fighting unit, the Surreys, the 1st Battalion in northern Italy and the 1/6th away in Greece, found it all strangely unreal; the purpose of life seemed suddenly to have been taken away.'[49]

Inevitably, the Allies' 'Blitzkrieg' strategy in northern Italy, unleashed ironically upon the Germans themselves was so successful that it brought on a sense of anti-climax. It was also overshadowed, and still is today, by the conquering of Germany itself by the Russian and Allied armies. The real story is that the final victory in Italy by two Allied armies was astounding. They had achieved what many had thought to be impossible. In less than four weeks they had broken the shackles of the Gothic Line, fought their way through the Argenta Gap and the nightmare maze of canals and rivers of the Po valley, and then raced on to capture the whole of northern Italy.

General McCreery felt that the Germans became preoccupied with thinking about their own formidable defences, and the conundrum that the Allies must be fully aware of those defences.

> However, I think our real triumph at this time was [that] the enemy forgot the one thing which might have turned the scales against us. He forgot that the best method of defence is to attack. If he had come at us over the Senio or down the middle of the Italian front, I believe he could have blown us wide open.[50]

The battles for the Gothic Line, and the subsequent surge through the Argenta Gap to the Po, was an offensive that had begun in late August 1944. It had taken eight months of mountain battles and attrition, and the devastating onslaught of April 1945, before Fifth and Eighth Armies arrived at, and crossed, the Po. It was the end of the Italian campaign, which with combined casualties of both sides approaching 700,000, was the costliest in Western Europe. What had been the purpose of the Italian campaign? Like many others in retrospect after the war, Alexander came to see it as a gigantic holding operation, because it dragged German forces away from the offensives of North-West Europe, and the Eastern Front. Ironically, Kesselring saw it as diverting Allied forces away from the Normandy invasion, and the attack on Germany.[51]

What does seem clear, however, is that, without the victory in Tunisia and Italian campaign, the Allies' amphibious landings in Normandy would have faced much stronger German forces and defensive preparations. And the Allies would have been attempting to land on the

Normandy beaches without the bitter lessons learned in those landings in Morocco and Algeria, at Sicily, Salerno and Anzio. It is a hypothetical question but in such a scenario would the D-Day landings on 6 June have been repulsed?

What is beyond argument are the achievements and self-sacrifice of the individual soldiers in all Allied forces, like those in the two Surreys' battalions. The snapshots of the Surreys and other troops illustrated in this book show how even a single battalion, a company, a platoon, a single soldier, must succeed whatever the cost for battles to be won, and for grand strategies to end in victory.

Notes

1. Morton, *A Traveller in Italy*, pp. 108–9 and 208–9.
2. Harpur, *The Impossible Victory*, pp. 152–3.
3. Ibid, pp. 124–5.
4. Ibid, pp. 152–3.
5. Ibid, pp. 154–5.
6. Ibid, p. 156.
7. Surrey History Centre ESR/2/15/6/7 Manning, p. 8.
8. Ray, op cit., p. 191.
9. Daniell, op cit., p. 237.
10. Ibid, p. 238.
11. Surrey History Centre ESR/2/15/6/7 Manning, p. 8.
12. Daniell, op cit., p. 239.
13. Surrey History Centre ESR/2/15/6/7 Manning, p. 9.
14. Linklater, op cit., p. 419.
15. Harpur, op cit., p. 156.
16. Ibid.
17. Squire and Hill, op cit., pp. 62–4.
18. Daniell, op cit., p. 238.
19. Linklater, op cit., p. 425.
20. Harpur, op cit., p. 157.
21. Ibid.
22. Owen, *The Desert Air Force*, p. 300.
23. Harpur, op cit., p. 158.
24. Owen, op cit., p. 301.
25. Harpur, op cit., p. 158.
26. Owen, op cit., p. 301.
27. Harpur, op cit., p. 159.
28. Daniell, op cit., p. 239.
29. Ray, op cit., pp. 202–5.
30. Surrey History Centre ESR/2/15/6/7 Manning, p. 9.
31. Doherty, *Eighth Army in Italy 1943–45: The Long Hard Slog*, p. 201.
32 Ibid., p. 207.
33 Harpur, op cit., p. 160.
34 Doherty, op cit., p. 207.
35 Ibid.
36. Surrey History Centre ESR/2/15/6/7 Manning, p. 9.
37. Obituary, 'Sir John Saunders CBE DSO MC', *The Daily Telegraph*, 30 Jul 2002.

38. Squire and Hill, op cit., pp. 62–4.
39. Veterans' accounts, Skilton.
40. Squire and Hill, op cit., pp. 62–4.
41. Ibid, p. 63.
42. Imperial War Museum, Department of Books, *Battle for Lungurella*, pp. 46–7.
43. Squire and Hill, op cit., p. 63.
44. Harpur, op cit., p. 166.
45. Squire and Hill, op cit., p. 63.
46. Veterans' accounts, Weston.
47. Daniell, op cit., p. 242.
48. Linklater, op cit., p. 246.
49. Daniell, op cit., p. 242.
50. Harpur, op cit., pp. 154.
51. Orgill, op cit., pp. 3–6.

Epilogue

**Part 1: A Tour of the Battlefields of the East Surrey Regiment's
1st Battalion of 1943/44, by Captain John M. Woodhouse
(22nd Special Air Service Regiment), May 1955**

In October last year I left England by air for Tunis. After our flight from London to Paris in company with travellers who, by their seeming unconcern, must have made the journey many times, the passengers from Paris to Tunis seemed more interesting. Here obviously was the French colonial family returning home after visiting relatives in France. Army officer and wife returning from leave, government officials with the autocratic yet worried look, which seems to stamp government officials of all countries. We two Englishmen were no doubt more conspicuously obvious than anyone else in the aircraft, but of that, being English, we were at the time quite ignorant.

At El Aouina, the still bomb-scarred airport had a fine new building. The French police seemed rather surprised that we should give Medjez-el-Bab as our intended place of residence. Next day by bus to Medjez. The weather was fine and warm, and my first sight of the town, preceded by a familiar view of Longstop Hill across the valley, took me back eleven years and nothing seemed changed. The town itself has been tidied up, but many scarred walls remain. The yellow church still stands, and the smell of straw, animals and Arabs has changed not at all. There are still Frenchmen here who remember us; one old lady had letters and photographs of several British soldiers and spoke of them with affection, hoping they had survived the war.

We went round the 1st Battalion's positions facing Goubellat, which we had held from about the beginning of February to the end of March 1943. Here I found B Company positions looking towards Fort McGregor still in existence, though now only two to three feet deep. The view far over the Goubellat Plain to the mountains beyond in the purple distance was the same. Apart from a group of Arab huts, the country seems as silent and empty as in the war; and it seemed almost odd to see no soldiers of the Regiment sitting in the trenches writing letters, no sentry staring out over the plain, no groups of muddy khaki figures moving on the tracks.

216

Fort McGregor, the scene of a very gallant stand by D Company on 26 February against an equally brave assault by masses of German parachute troops, was unchanged. I had watched this battle, and was first to see that grim-looking hill when we reoccupied it at dawn on 27 February. It was hard to imagine such a pleasant, peaceful place could ever have witnessed these events.

The British military cemetery lies on the road west of Medjez. It is perfectly kept and its soft green grass contrasts pleasantly with the bare, stony brown slopes of the hills round it. It was remarkable and rather moving that the native caretaker refused a small monetary present after he had shown us round. The stone cross, which is to complete the cemetery, was being finished. To the relatives of the soldiers who lie there one can only say that, both here and in Italy, an impression of calmness and strength, peace and respect, seems to surround these memorials.

Generally the high peaks above Toukabeur, the Djebel Mahdouma, the Djebel Ang, are unchanged. The trenches, never deep because of rock, are perhaps now a bit shallower. Rusty tins still mark the path of our advance, but almost nothing else remains. On Longstop Hill the slopes are still scattered with fragments from shells and bombs, but the ground is more thickly covered in mimosa scrub than it was.

In Sicily we walked up the steep slopes towards Centuripe and visited Adrano, walking from there to Bronte along the road winding through old lava streams from Etna. The insanitary habits and insulting smells are quite unchanged, and perhaps worse. We were often asked if we were Germans, but our replies of 'No, English' were usually obviously welcome.

An old Dakota took us from Catania to Naples. The river battlefields on the east coast have none of the litter of war left on them, and a great deal has been done to clear up the shattered towns and villages. A Bailey bridge still crosses the Sangro, and the absence of new houses makes it easy to recognize the ground.

Cassino, now rebuilt, is a tourist centre and visited by many Germans. A terrifying taxi ride took us up the mountain to the monastery, and I was left feeling more surprised than ever that we had finally managed to capture the place. A visit to the village of San Angelo on the Rapido River, where I ended my otherwise very happy and perhaps rather lucky year with the 1st Battalion, seemed a suitable place to finish our battlefield tour.

Some of the mountain positions that the Regiment stormed so successfully in those eventful years now look impossible, yet at the time, there was never a man in the Battalion who doubted that we could and would succeed in every attack.

Perhaps that was the secret of so much success.

Part 2: Post-war personal stories, and biographical notes

For those Surreys who were fortunate to survive the Second World War, it was just the beginning, the beginning of the rest of their lives. Here are some glimpses of their personal stories.

Jack Chaffer MM

At the end of the war in Italy and Europe, Jack Chaffer was redeployed almost immediately with the 5th Grenadiers to Scotland. Whatever the Army's now forgotten reason for this move, it seemed that reuniting with his wife Doll, his family and friends in Kingston-upon-Thames in Surrey, seemed farther away than ever. Then in late 1946 Jack was promoted to Company Quartermaster Sergeant with the 2nd Grenadiers, and found himself moved to a station in Germany. Finally they returned to the UK in 1947.

At last Jack was back with Doll, from whom he had been separated, apart from brief snatches of leave, since March 1942. Like many women Doll had spent the war years employed in the munitions industry in the war effort. She had begun work at fourteen at a bus factory, which was converted to making parts for mortar bombs. Later, in 1947, Jack left the Grenadiers and the Army but, like so many others, faced the austerity of post-war Britain, and the scarcity of employment opportunities. Despite this he soon gained work in the locally based Hawker Aircraft Company, and Doll had a baby daughter Jackie. But that longstanding desire to join the East Surreys would not go away.

After being approached by the commanding officer, Lieutenant Colonel Tom 'Buck' Buchanan, who had been a company commander with the 1st Surreys in Tunisia, Jack also joined the part-time Territorial Army, as a company sergeant in the 6th Battalion of the East Surreys. The horrors of Djebel Bou Aoukaz, Salerno, Anzio and the Gothic Line were in the past, yet those experiences and the military bonds had changed him. The call of the military life, its more varied demands and challenges, were too ingrained, and in 1956 he re-enlisted in the full time Regular Army, as a sergeant in the 1st Battalion East Surreys.

Now he was again back with his pre-war boyhood friends, Frank Oram and Harry Skilton, from those days at the regiment's school at the camp at Rawalpindi. Their post-war service soon came under the Queen's Royal Surrey Regiment, after the amalgamation of the Queens with the East Surreys in 1959, and included deployments to Hong Kong, Germany, Somalia, Aden and Cyprus, where their operations countered the EOKA terrorist campaign. In 1972 Jack gained the rank of RSM, which he held until 1976.

The post-war years also saw Jack and Doll bring up two children, Jackie and Michael. In between the many overseas postings, they based themselves in their home town, Kingston-upon-Thames. Jack was a keen sportsman, and for many years was the goalkeeper for the Regiment's hockey team.

On leaving the Queen's Royal Surreys in 1976 Jack was invited to join the Yeomen of the Queen's Body Guard Extraordinary, popularly known as the select thirty-five Yeoman Warders, or Beefeaters, guarding the Tower of London and its Crown Jewels. After being sworn in at St James Palace, Jack and his Beefeater colleagues also performed a policing role within the Tower's grounds, and amongst the millions of curious tourists. On Jack's retirement from the Beefeaters he and Doll moved to Northampton, where Jack now lives with his daughter Jackie and husband Mick, and is also close to his son Michael. Among their many visitors are now also six grandchildren.

From the East Surreys, and its successor regiment, the Queen's Royal Surreys, Jack retains a wide circle of old comrades, who range from Generals to National Service privates. To this day he still carries the ball-bearings and shrapnel in his body, from the anti-personnel mine explosion which he survived in Italy. The field surgeon at the time, facing a constant queue of urgent cases, said they were too difficult to extract. Those ball-bearings are an ever recurring reminder of that nightmare journey of many hours, by stretcher and an ambulance laden with other wounded, which eventually saved his life.

Despite the trauma of losing his wife and life-long partner Doll on 16 August 2011, and the incapacities that come with advancing years, Jack continues to be an engaging character and personality in the regimental community, and a notable and stalwart regular at the Queen's Royal Surreys' Association's various functions and annual reunions. The resilience and spirit of Jack and Doll's lives, no matter what adversity, still shines through undimmed.

A former Lieutenant Colonel of the Surreys has said of Jack, 'He is the model of a Regimental Sergeant Major for any regiment.'

Lieutenant Colonel John Woodhouse MBE MC, SAS Commander

While in German PoW camps, first near Munich then at Braunschweig, John Woodhouse struck up a close friendship with a fellow officer, Eric Newby. Together they participated in a number of attempted escapes, breaking out of the PoW camps only to be re-captured. After their release in May 1945 by American forces, and return to London, John and Eric Newby sipped champagne together in London's Savoy restaurant.

For the moment they celebrated their survival and new-found freedom. They had no thought for tomorrow. Yet perhaps each of them must have secretly vowed not to waste their good fortune. Eric Newby would throw himself back into journalism, and become a best-selling travel author, while John would create a stellar military career, fully exploiting his experience and lessons learned with the Surreys, and later also become a successful businessman. The pair would remain close friends for the rest of their lives.

Once the euphoria of freedom diminished, John was unsure of what direction to take. The Army placed him into a basic training role with new infantry recruits, which after his war experiences was less than inspiring. He wondered what to do next. After coming to the realization that he enjoyed life in the field with soldiers, he decided to stay in the Army. In 1946 John undertook a Russian language course at Cambridge University. It was where in 1939 he had failed the University entrance exam, motivating him to enlist as a private in the Dorset Regiment. Perhaps he saw the Russian course at Cambridge as a way to make up for failing that earlier exam.

Gaining proficiency in Russian enabled him to take up an appointment as an interpreter with the Allied Control Commission in Germany and Austria from 1947–49. During this time he took the opportunity to apply himself to one of the foundation principles of warfare – 'get to know your enemy'. He studied how Communism used methods of subversion to take control of populations. These insights would prove invaluable in his subsequent development of counter-insurgency strategies, and training regimes for the SAS.

John served spells back with his parent Dorsetshire Regiment, and in intelligence in Hong Kong, before joining the Malayan Scouts SAS Regiment in 1950, first in an intelligence post then as a squadron commander. At first operations against the Communist insurrection in Malaya, because of poor tactics and a shortage of appropriately trained troops of the right quality, did not achieve much success. However Lieutenant Colonel Michael Calvert, a veteran of Chindit operations in Burma, recognized John's experience and professional standards of self-discipline and endurance, which he had learned and honed in Tunisia and Italy. He sent John back to England to establish a new selection process and training methods. The work John did at this time became the foundation for selection and training of the modern SAS.

In 1955 John returned to Malaya as a squadron commander, by which time 560 men in five SAS squadrons selected and trained by his new system, were making headway in the jungle against the insurgents. In 1957 John was awarded the MBE for his services in Malaya in command of D Squadron 22 SAS. The next year brought an even more momentous event in John's life, when he met and married Peggy, a nurse at London's St Thomas' Hospital, who had served in the WRNS in the Second World War.

Marriage was clearly good for him, for in 1958 John was made a company commander in the 3rd Battalion of the Parachute Regiment. Then in 1960 he was appointed second-in command of 21 SAS, and in 1962 was promoted to full command of 22 SAS. When the confrontation between Indonesia and the new Federation of Malaysia broke out, John arrived in East Malaysia in January 1963 in command of the SAS advance force.

Despite the pressures and strain of high command, he never lost his intense personal interest in his men, and wrote at one time to a subordinate officer, 'it is your duty, which should also be your natural wish, to do the best possible for your men ... You will never succeed unless you like soldiers.'

By the end of 1964, using John's tactics of long-distance patrols for up to three weeks, the SAS and other Commonwealth forces had defeated the Indonesian incursions. For John though, even at such a high point of his military career, the pull of family life and obligations to Peggy and their two sons, Michael and William, led him to retire from the Army.

Yet it was a change to a life of perhaps even more challenges. As well as devoting himself to support of his family, and management of forestry, the farm and house of his father's estate at Higher Melcombe near Dorchester, John took on the role of a security consultant with the Foreign Office. This brought him into a collaboration with his old colleague Colonel Sir David Stirling, and numerous clandestine missions abroad.

Later he took up a managing director appointment, then a board position, and eventually the role of chairman with the family-owned brewery Hall and Woodhouse. For eight years he served as chairman of the SAS Association. In later years John suffered from Parkinson's disease and chronic pain from curvature of the spine. Nevertheless he fought their growing onset, staying active and independent managing the farm and house of the family estate until the age of eighty.

After a drawn-out and debilitating illness, John Woodhouse passed away on 15 February 2008 aged eighty-five. Throughout his life even in the most trying times he could always see the funny side of things, and towards the end while enduring great pain, he told his son Michael, 'This is a bit like an SAS selection course!'

Both Colonel Sir David Stirling and General Sir Peter de la Billiere have acknowledged that John, through his new training techniques, tactics, and leadership with the SAS Malayan Scouts in operations in South East Asia, was effectively the founder of the UK's modern SAS. With a unique blend of kindness, generosity, and a wry sense of humour, John Woodhouse never sought the limelight, and lived a life of unselfish leadership and drive, for which succeeding generations will be forever indebted.

Acknowledgements: *The Times* Obituary of 21 February 2008, Michael Woodhouse, and the Appreciation read by Sir Peter de la Billiere at the funeral of Lieutenant Colonel John Woodhouse.

Major Frank 'Peachy' Oram

Frank Oram tucked into beef stew, mashed potatoes and cabbage, and he thought it the best meal of his life. He was back from Italy in the summer of 1945, in the canteen of the Surreys' Shorncliffe Barracks near Folkestone, and his wife Winifred was still in charge of the NAAFI catering. It was where they had first met. Their reunion was short however, before Frank went off with 1st Surreys to Greece. At least periods of leave now became more frequent, and luckily Frank and the Battalion were back for an extended stay by Christmas 1946, in time for Winifred to give birth to a son Michael in January.

In the Surreys' deployment to Greece, Frank had been appointed a Company Sergeant Major. Further overseas postings were to Mogadishu, Somalia, Cyprus and Brunswick in Germany, where Winifred was able to join him with the addition of their daughter, Linda. In 1959 Frank was appointed the first RSM of the amalgamated Queen's Royal Surreys Regiment, and subsequently Mentioned in Despatches for service in the Cyprus counter-terrorist operation.

Through his exemplary service, study and examinations, in 1964 Frank gained a commission. He subsequently attained the rank of Major, and served five years as the Quartermaster of the 5th Battalion the Queen's Regiment.

While Frank was progressing his military career, Winifred was busy raising their two children. She enjoyed the travelling of the overseas postings, and took on the many commitments of the wife of one of the Regiment's senior officers. Once their children Michael and Linda were grown up, and Frank had retired, Winifred was able to find more time for her life-long passion for drawing and painting. She became a staunch member and chair of the Women's Institute, and will be remembered by many members for her ability in painting, needlework, lace making, flower arranging and teaching in all these subjects. For many years she also used her talent to write elegant commemorations in the local church's Book of Remembrance for those who lost loved ones.

In 1976 when Frank retired from the Army, he launched himself into a new endeavour to exploit his aptitude for repairing machines. He built a successful business renovating cars, as well as restoring radios, TVs and other equipment. Through Frank's expertise the Oram household enjoyed satellite TV from all around the world, including the US Defence Forces' transmissions. But the Army did not forget Frank.

His son-in-law, Linda's husband Alan, was a regular driver of the coaches transporting the Queen's Regiment band, who were at that time stationed in Connaught Barracks at Dover. Their travel often took them along the main road past Frank and Winifred's house. On one occasion as they drove past, to Alan's surprise, everyone stood and saluted 'Peachy!' After that, whenever the coach passed Peachy and Winifred's home, the same salute was repeated every time.

In her later years Winifred suffered chronic respiratory conditions, and eventually lost her sight. Despite the constraints and pain, and increasing lack of mobility, she kept teaching and meeting her friends as long as she could until her passing in 2004.

Frank found himself alone, and having to fend for himself. He had been losing his memory for a number of years, and now he was without Winifred to monitor his diabetes regimen. With support from a home help and his daughter Linda, he was able to live alone in the house where he and Winifred had made their life.

On 28 February 2008 Frank died aged eighty-seven. Throughout their lives and to the end, Frank and Winifred overcame everything they faced, and lived their lives in the service of others.

Harry Skilton

In a blur of flashing coloured lights the carousel spun its riders around. While the strains of 'Wish me luck as you wave me goodbye ...' blared above the fairground noise, Harry Skilton could not take his eyes off one dark-haired girl. One evening during the Surreys' training in the spring of 1942, at Hoddom Castle in Dumfriesshire, prior to embarkation on Operation TORCH, Harry and many other Surreys were visiting a nearby fair at Annan. It was there he fell for the captivating beauty and laughter of Jessie. She was nineteen, Harry was twenty-one.

For Harry Skilton like many others, that chance meeting came amidst the confusing activities of war, and in the middle of a journey into the unknown. Soon after that Annan fair, the Surreys were gone, first to exercises in the Scottish Highlands, then embarkation to Tunisia. A year of letters later Harry somehow got leave, and in June 1943 he married Jessie in Annan, only a stone's throw from that fairground.

In 1945 with the Italian campaign finally won and the war over, Harry then saw service with the Surreys to counter civil war in Greece, to confront terrorism in Palestine, and to bring order to Cyprus. Further service abroad was to follow in the post-war years in Somalia, Tripoli, Tobruk, Germany, Aden and Hong Kong. In the Surreys' deployment to Brunswick in Germany, Harry gained promotion to RQMS.

It was now a journey together for Jessie and Harry. Over the years Jessie, soon with a growing family of three daughters, Jean, Carol and Karen, and a son, Jumbo, accompanied Harry everywhere on postings both within the UK and around the world. It was a time for Harry to take up once again some of the sports he loved, particularly boxing.

While based in Aden he trained and coached the Combined Services boxing team, and led them in a visit to Kenya for a tournament. Although losing the contest 8–2 against the Kenyan national team, it was said they gave the finest show of courage and fitness seen at that time in the Kenyan ring.

All his life Harry was a fitness fanatic and sports enthusiast. Many never knew that he was an excellent badminton player. Often when on leave he would visit the All England Badminton Club at Wimbledon, where his father was on the staff, and play against some of the best players in the country. Before leaving the Surreys he attained the position of RSM, then for the final three years he was posted to the Army's Outward Bound Training School in North Wales. After all those mountain battles in North Africa and Italy, there was some knowledge to pass on to others.

But on leaving the Army after thirty-one years of service Harry decided it was Jessie's turn to choose a home, and they settled close to her family in the county town of Dumfries. The Dumfries and Galloway Burgh Council called Harry into service again as the Burgh Officer, a position he was to fill with distinction for fourteen years until retirement. He became an active member of the National Mace Bearers' Association, took up regular golf, fishing, gardening and viticulture, and avidly followed most sports. But his first love was Jessie and his family, no matter that two of his teenage daughters rejected the Army's overtures and joined the WRNS and the WRAF!

Through all his later years, Harry maintained an exercise routine as well as many active pursuits which helped him overcome many ailments that would have struck down most other mortals. He lost a kidney from cancer, an eye through glaucoma, went deaf in one ear, suffered from chronic emphysema and asthma, underwent major operations for blood clots in his groin and leg, and broke his wrist, which required a steel support. Yet through all these debilitating conditions his spirit never failed him. He and Jessie continued to travel, to Munich and down the Rhine in Germany, to Italy and Spain, and numerous visits to their eldest daughter, Jean, in Australia.

When Jessie fell ill with cancer, it was Harry who took over on his own and nursed her through the ravages of chemotherapy till the end. Although his life's love was to be no longer with him, afterwards he also took over her role, and ensured the family came together regularly in the years that followed. It was that East Surrey grit, a determination to see things through against all the odds. He kept as active as he could, still following his exercise routine, gardening and doing all his own cooking and household chores.

Harry passed away on 27 May 2003 after five days in hospital. Yet in those final days, struggling for breath and in a semi-coma, Harry was still able when conscious to thank his doctor and nurses. To the end he fought his illness as if he was once again at Cassino.

Frank Weston
In December 1946 winter lay grey and cold across the London docks. Returning from helping to put down the Communist insurgency in Greece, Frank Weston found himself and the rest of 1st Surreys thrown immediately into moving freight stuck in the national Dock Strike. No matter he thought, he was home. When he could get a discharge, he would take up his old trade as a butcher. And Maud, the fiancée of his brother Les, had promised to get him a date with her sister Doreen.

On 23 March 1947, when Doreen accepted Frank's invitation to a dance at the Battalion's Kingston Barracks, he got his chance. Something clicked at once. Frank and Doreen began a whirl of a romance, going to shows, movies, speedway, racing, football matches and more dances.

Although Frank left the Army, and went back into being a butcher, the influence of those war years had not finished with him. In Italy he had fought alongside troops of the 2nd New Zealand Division, and listened to them talk with pride of their homeland. It sounded like a good country in which to make a fresh start. In September 1947 Frank sailed for New Zealand, and Doreen was left to wave goodbye.

For nearly two years Frank and Doreen wrote regularly to each other, with an occasional, expensive phone call. In June 1948 Frank proposed to Doreen over a crackly phone line, and sent her the money to buy an engagement ring. Doreen was only eighteen, and her parents were dismayed at her plans to marry Frank. Eventually they approved her passport application, and in August 1949 she embarked for New Zealand.

It was two years since she had seen Frank, and heart-wrenching for Doreen to leave her family. On the long voyage of seven weeks, she began to have doubts. When the ship was delayed in Fiji, she received a telegram from Frank, 'Sick of waiting ... suggest you start swimming!' It might have been cockney humour, but it told her that Frank was constantly thinking of her arrival. On 15 April 1950 they were married in Wellington.

In the fifties they had first a daughter Gillian, and then a son Colin. Into the sixties and seventies Frank owned and ran a series of butcher shops, each one larger and more prosperous. In 1990 Frank finally retired from the butchery business, and a few years later in 1997 Frank and Doreen moved to a house on the Kapiti Coast. A more relaxing lifestyle beckoned them.

It was not to be. A cruel twist of fate did for Frank what Hitler's troops could never do. They had been in their new house barely seven weeks, when Frank fell in the kitchen and hit his head on the corner of the stove, damaging his brain. His health gradually deteriorated, and in 2005 he needed to be admitted to a nursing home for round-the-clock care.

Despite his declining health, immobility and impaired speech and concentration, an indomitable spirit and sense of humour shines through. Doreen too has battled through, warding off cancer and traumatic injuries from a car accident. She visits Frank to sit with him every day, to talk and read to him, waiting for Frank to come out with some unexpected but hilarious comment. Their children, four grandchildren and a great grandson, also visit as often as they can.

To know Frank and Doreen is to see how the struggles of life must be faced. There is no better illustration of how the Second World War's forces of darkness were defeated.

Part 3: The Surreys' Second World War Commanding Officers – Biographical Notes

Of the seven commanding officers of the two Surreys' Battalions, 1st and 1/6th, in the Second World War, three were killed in action. Here are some brief biographical notes on the men who led the Surreys.

1st Battalion East Surreys Regiment – 1st Surreys:
Lieutenant Colonel W.B.S.J.A.E. 'Bill' Wilberforce DSO

October 1942 to May 1943 (killed in action)
William B.S.J.A.E. Wilberforce was born on 4 February 1904. He was commissioned in The King's Own Yorkshire Light Infantry in January 1924, and subsequently served in India, and in staff appointments in southern England.

In October 1942 he was appointed Lieutenant Colonel to command the 1st Battalion of The East Surrey Regiment. He took the 1st Surreys to North Africa in Operation TORCH, and in the Tunisian campaign led it with courage and dash. At the momentous battle of Longstop Hill, when all the other COs of 78th Division battalions had been lost, he took overall command of the operation, and his unflappable and confident manner was pivotal in gaining Longstop's capture.

Shortly after on 6 May, having been informed of the award of the DSO for his fine leadership, he was killed by one of the last shells of the campaign.

Acknowledgement: QRS Museum.

226

Colonel H.B.L. 'Harry' Smith MC
6 May 1943 to May 1944

Henry Brockton Lochart 'Harry' Smith was born on 2 February 1909, the son of Colonel H.L. Smith, who was a previous CO of 1st Surreys. Educated at Marlborough and Sandhurst, he was commissioned into The East Surrey Regiment in January 1929. He served with 1st Surreys in India until 1938. In 1935 Harry married Helen Douglas, and had three sons, Martin, Peter and Anthony. In France 1939–40 he commanded an Anti-tank Company of 11 Infantry Brigade.

In September 1942 Harry Smith rejoined 1st Surreys as second-in-command, serving with them in Operation TORCH and the Tunisian campaign, in which he was awarded the MC for his leadership in the successful capture of Longstop Hill. On the loss of Lieutenant Colonel Wilberforce in the final victorious drive for Tunis, he assumed command. Lieutenant Colonel Harry Smith led 1st Surreys in the Sicilian campaign, and then through the gruelling battles in Italy at Termoli, the Trigno and Sangro rivers, and Cassino. Following the capture of Cassino, and the breaking of the Adolf Hitler Line at the end of May 1944, he was appointed to the staff in the Middle East.

From September 1945 until August 1946 he commanded 1/6th Surreys in Greece. Following service with Sudan Defence Force, he commanded 1st Surreys again from 1951–53. Harry was promoted to Colonel in 1956, shortly before he was posted to a senior appointment at Supreme Allied Headquarters, Europe. There he served under General Spiedel, who had been Field Marshal Rommel's Chief of Staff.

Colonel Harry Smith retired from the Army in May 1961. All his life he had a love of field sports, particularly hockey and cricket, and enjoyed fishing and shooting into his late seventies.

Colonel Harry Smith died on 26 July 1997. His wife Helen pre-deceased him by twelve days, and they were buried together after a joint service at St Mary's Church Ellingham on 1 August 1997.

Acknowledgement: QRS Museum.

Brigadier H.M.A. Hunter CVO DSO MBE
June 1944 to July 1945

H.M.A Hunter, known as Michael, was born on 29 June 1913. Educated at Marlborough and Sandhurst, he was commissioned in The Wiltshire Regiment in February 1933. He served with their 2nd Battalion in India, before appointments in England in 1940.

Staff appointments with 78th Division HQ in Tunisia and Italy followed, then a tour as a company commander with the 5th Northamptons, for which he was appointed MBE. In early 1944 he was posted as second-in-command of 1st Surreys, until June 1944 when he took full command. For his fine leadership of 1st Surreys he was awarded the DSO. Brigadier Hunter died in 1981.

Acknowledgement: QRS Museum.

1st Battalion East Surreys Regiment – 1/6th Surreys

Lieutenant Colonel H.A.B. Bruno MBE
April 1942 to April 1943 (killed in action)
Hugh Alan Bruno was borne on 4 September 1897, and was commissioned in The Hampshire Regiment in September 1917. For his service in the First World War he was appointed MBE.

After service with The King's Own Royal Regiment, the Staff College, and 164 Infantry Brigade, in April 1942 he was appointed to command 1/6th Surreys. He led the 1/6th Surreys in Operation TORCH to North Africa, and in April 1943 was killed while gallantly leading an attack at Djebel Djaffa. For his services in Tunisia he was Mentioned in Despatches.

Acknowledgement: QRS Museum.

Lieutenant Colonel R.O.V. 'Tommy' Thompson DSO
April 1943 to June 1944 (killed in action)
Robert Oliver Vere Thompson was born on 6 January 1904. On leaving Sandhurst he was commissioned into the Royal Sussex Regiment in 1924, serving with them on India's North West Frontier in 1930–31. In September 1937 he married Teresa 'Tita' Cameron, the daughter of Commander Gordon McLeod Cameron DSO, Royal Navy. They met hiking in Ireland while Oliver, as he was known, was home on leave from India. Oliver and Tita had two sons, Timothy and Robert.

In 1940 he was badly wounded while serving with the Royal Sussex in Northern France and evacuated through Dunkirk. It was said at the time that if he had been physically a smaller man, the wound would have been fatal. Later while recovering from his wounds he was assigned as an Air Staff Officer with the RAF to help establish forces to defend airfields in the UK. Subsequently Major Thompson was transferred to the 1/6th Battalion of the East Surrey Regiment, with whom he was posted as second-in-command to Tunisia in March 1943.

When in April 1943 in Tunisia the CO of 1/6th Surreys, Lieutenant Colonel Bruno was killed in the Battle of Djebel Djaffa, Major Thompson was given command of the Battalion, and subsequently became Lieutenant Colonel. In the following weeks of April and May Colonel Thompson led the Surreys with great dash in the Allies' battles, which culminated in the capture of Tunis.

In Italy in 1944 Colonel Thompson provided the 1/6th Surreys with inspirational leadership in the final stages of the epic fourth Battle for Cassino, in which 1/6th Surreys, despite suffering some 40 per cent casualties, were one of the spearhead battalions to first break through the German lines.

In regard to the lead-up preparations for the battle, which involved a crossing of the Rapido River, the Surreys' Major A.W.F. Paskins said:

> A most complicated operation with boat parties, lots of signallers, engineers, tanks, gunners, medicos etc, all to be slotted in together with our own troops. Colonel Thompson showed endless patience and tact, welding these separate units with different attitudes into a smooth, cohesive and efficient force. On a personal note I count myself fortunate to have served under him, for he taught me a great deal, particularly about human behaviour.

During pursuit of the German Army north of Cassino, at around 7.00am on 7 June 1944 close to Tivoli and Rome, Colonel Thompson's jeep was blown up on a mine, and he was killed.

In a letter informing Colonel Thompson's wife of his death, Brigadier S.H. Shoesmith of 10 Infantry Brigade wrote:

> His loss was an irreparable tragedy to his regiment and to me. I would like to tell you how magnificently your husband fought, and commanded his battalion ever since we came to Italy. He was worshipped by his officers and men who would, and literally did, go through hell for him. I personally have lost a most gallant and able officer, and a most loyal and true friend. 'Tommy' was universally admired and loved by all with whom he came into contact. His unfailing cheerfulness and his delightful sense of humour, will always be remembered by his friends and every man in his regiment.

For his fine leadership of the 1/6th Surreys, Lieutenant Colonel Thompson was awarded the DSO.

Acknowledgement: QRS Museum, and Robert Thompson de Gavre (son of Colonel Thompson).

Colonel C.G.S. 'Jock' McAlester MC OBE
June 1944 to February 1945

Charles G.S. McAlester, known as 'Jock', was born on 26 February 1906. In February 1926 he was commissioned in The King's Own Scottish Borderers, with whom he served in China from 1935 to 1938, and in France 1940, where he was awarded the MC.

On the death of Lieutenant Colonel Thompson, he took over command of 1/6th Surreys until February 1945, when he was posted to a staff appointment in Crete. In November 1945 he was Mentioned in Despatches, and in December 1945 appointed OBE.

He retired from the Army in June 1949.

Lieutenant Colonel A.G.H. Culverhouse MBE
March 1945 to August 1945
Graham Culverhouse, born in 1907, was commissioned in 1/6th Surreys in 1939. He served with 1/6th Surreys in France, where he was wounded and evacuated from Dunkirk. In Italy he served as Brigade Major in 11 Brigade of 78th Division, and on the staff at HQ Eighth Army. After a period as second in command of 1st Buffs, he rejoined the 1/6th Surreys in full command in March 1945 held until August 1945.

Lieutenant Colonel Culverhouse retired from the Army in 1954, and died on 8 August 1993.

... And the Commanding Officer who got away: Colonel T.A. 'Tom' or 'Buck' Buchanan DSO MC ERD
Colonel Buchanan, known either as 'Tom' or 'Buck', was a legendary character, both during and after the Second World War. Through his personality, leadership and exploits he seemed to be known everywhere. Although he did not command a Surreys' battalion during the war, he was a company commander in 1st Surreys in Tunisia. Appointments then followed as commanding officer of 5th Northamptons and 1st Royal Fusiliers in the Italian campaign and, after the war, 2nd and 6th Surreys.

Thomas Alfred Buchanan was born on 27 August 1908. After gaining degrees in both Science and Psychology at London University, he became a teacher with Surrey County Council. In 1931 Buchanan joined the Supplementary Reserve, and in 1939 was posted to 1st Surreys to command B Company in France. Following the Dunkirk evacuation, he was a tower of strength in the rebuilding of 1st Surreys, and also spent time as Chief Instructor at the 78th Division Battle School.

Buchanan led B Company of 1st Surreys in Operation TORCH and into the Tunisian campaign. In the ill-fated first offensive to take Tunis the Allies were repulsed at Tebourba. Buchanan showed outstanding leadership as B Company beat off an elite German battlegroup, then he led a counter-attack in which he was wounded, for which he was awarded the MC.

Soon after recovery and on rejoining the Surreys, he was posted as second in command of the 5th Northamptons, with whom he gained full command in April 1943. Buchanan led 5th Northamptons in Sicily, where he was severely wounded.

Once again he made a full recovery, upon which he was appointed to command 1st Royal Fusiliers in Italy. In late 1943 in the battle for the River

Sangro, where the 1st Fusiliers suffered heavy losses, Buchanan was instrumental in blending 200 reinforcements from the 12th Cameronians into a cohesive unit of Scots and Londoners. At Cassino in May 1944 in the crossing of the River Garigliano, he was typically in the forefront, and awarded the DSO. Again he was wounded. Only a month later Buchanan was back for the battle of Ripa near Assisi, only to be wounded once more.

He returned in July 1944 to lead the 1st Fusiliers through the winter battles for the Gothic Line, and then into the victorious final victories in April and May 1945 for the Argenta Gap and the River Po. A fellow officer said of Buchanan, 'his coolness and bravery were legenday, and his leadership inspired all ranks. When he walked round after a battle, tired men's faces would light up after a word from him.'

After the German surrender Buchanan returned to the UK to take command of the rebuilding of the 2nd Surreys, who had ceased to exist after the Malayan campaign. He then took 2nd Surreys to Palestine in counter-terrorism operations. In November 1947 he returned to the UK and took up a senior position in education, then in 1953 became the principal of a new technical college at Ewell. In parallel he also rejoined the East Surreys TA, and became Lieutenant Colonel of 6th Surreys, 1950–54.

Somehow he was never lost for time or energy. In 1964 he became Deputy Lieutenant for the County of Surrey. From 1967 to 1968 he was Colonel of the 6th Battalion of the Queen's (Queen's Surreys) Regiment, and also became Surrey County Commandant of the Army Cadet Force. In 1970 Buchanan was appointed OBE for services to Education, and in 1973 married Kay Kendall.

Colonel Buchanan seemed to be universally liked and was one of the Surreys' most charismatic COs. Besides his extraordinary life of achievement, both in Education and a distinguished military career, he will always be remembered above all as a true and steadfast friend. He died in November 1997.

Acknowledgements: *The Times* Obituary 25 November 1997, and the QRS Museum.

Postscript

The Cost in Lives – Casualties of the East Surreys
The statistics below tell their own story. On their arrival in Tunisia the 1st Surreys comprised 796 men, and a similar number in 1/6th Surreys. By war's end the total combined casualties of the two battalions was 2,153.

1st Surreys

Campaign	Killed	Wounded	Missing	Total
Tunisia				
Officers	12	16	5	33
Other ranks	132	287	229	648
Total	144	303	234	681
Sicily				
Officers	–	2	–	2
Other ranks	9	70	–	79
Total	9	72	–	81
Italy				
Officers	11	21	2	34
Other ranks	82	370	63	515
Total	93	391	65	549
All Campaigns				
Officers	23	39	7	69
Other ranks	223	727	292	1,242
Total	**246**	**766**	**299**	**1,311**

1/6th Surreys

Campaign	Killed	Wounded	Missing	Total
Tunisia				
Officers	5	2	1	8
Other ranks	51	143	34	228
Total	56	145	35	236
Sicily				
Officers				
Other ranks				
Total				
Italy				
Officers	14	25	4	43
Other ranks	123	393	47	563
Total	137	418	51	606
All Campaigns				
Officers	19	27	5	51
Other ranks	174	536	81	791
Total	**193**	**563**	**86**	**842**

1st and 1/6th Surreys (combined totals)

All Campaigns	Killed	Wounded	Missing	Total
Total	**439**	**1,329**	**385**	**2,153**

What is not revealed by the figures is the mental strain on the families of those lost, and on those men who survived. For many they would continue to struggle with the war's legacy – what we now term 'post-traumatic stress syndrome'. Their lives were changed forever, and what they did changed the world for the better.

Bibliography and Sources

1. Official Records and Publications

Daniell, David Scott, *The History of the East Surrey Regiment, Volume IV*, Ernest Benn Ltd, London, 1957.

Imperial War Museum, HM Forces, *The 78th Division in the Final Offensive in Italy – The battle for, and leading up to, Lungurella (1st Battalion the East Surrey Regiment)*, Imperial War Museum, Department of Printed Books, Lambeth Road, London SE1 6HZ.

Linklater, Eric, *The Campaign in Italy*, His Majesty's Stationery Office, London 1951.

Manning, H.C., *Operations of the 1st Battalion the East Surrey Regiment in the 1939/45 War* (ESR/2/15/6/7), Surrey History Centre, 130 Goldsworth Road, Woking, Surrey, GU21 6ND.

Ray, Cyril, *Algiers to Austria, a History of 78 Division in the Second World War*, Eyre and Spottiswoode, London, 1951, (originally only for sale to members of the 78th Division Association).

Smith, Lieutenant Colonel H.B.L., *Operations of 1 Battalion The East Surrey Regiment 1939–45, Part II North Africa, Sicily and Italy* – Imperial War Museum, Ref 02(41)662, Department of Printed Books, Lambeth Road, London SE1 6HZ.

Smith, Lieutenant Colonel H.B.L., and associates, *The Cassino Battles*, the Queen's Royal Surreys' Association Museum, Clandon Park, West Clandon, Guildford GU4 7RQ.

Squire, Lieutenant Colonel G.L.A., and Hill, Major Peter, *Algiers to Tunis, The 1st and 1/6th Battalions The East Surrey Regiment in North Africa 1942–43*, The Queen's Royal Surreys' Association Museum, November 1993, Clandon Park, West Clandon, Guildford GU4 7RQ.

Squire, Lieutenant Colonel G.L.A., and Hill, Major Peter, *The Surreys in Italy 1943–45*, The Queen's Royal Surrey Regiment Museum, March 1992, Clandon Park, West Clandon, Guildford GU4 7RQ.

Surrey History Centre, 130 Goldsworth Road, Woking, Surrey, GU21 6ND – The East Surrey Regiment Records, Battalion documents and personal papers.

Taylor, Major R.C., *Seven Sunrays, One Morning in Tunisia, Return Visit to Tunisia*, Imperial War Museum, Department of Documents, Lambeth Road, London SE1 6HZ.

Woodhouse, Lieutenant Colonel J.W., *Memoirs*, unpublished (Ref: Michael Woodhouse).

2. Veterans' Sources

A wide use of Surreys' and other veterans' stories has been made, drawn from references throughout the bibliography. I am especially grateful for eyewitness accounts drawn from books, diaries, documents, articles, conversations, letters and emails, of the following veterans of the East Surrey Regiment, who served in the Second World War: Chaffer, Jack; Hill, Major P.G.E.; Gage, Frank; Manning, H.C.; Mumford, John; Oram, Major Frank; Skilton, Harry; Smith, Lieutenant Colonel H.B.L.; Squire, Lieutenant Colonel G.L.A.; Thornton, George; Taylor, Major R.C. 'Toby'; Weston, Frank; Wilson, George; Woodhouse, Lieutenant Colonel John.

3. Other Combatants in the Tunisia, Sicily and Italy Campaigns:

Besides official records and publications pertaining to the Surreys, and veterans' accounts referred to above, the research has also focused heavily on other eyewitness accounts by those who served in the three campaigns.

Alexander, Field Marshal, Earl Alexander of Tunis, *The Alexander Memoirs 1940–45*, Cassell & Co Ltd, London, 1961.

Bowlby, Alex, *Countdown to Cassino – The Battle of Mignano Gap, 1943*, Leo Cooper, London, 1995.

Carver, Field Marshal Lord, *The War in Italy 1943–1945*, Imperial War Museum Book, Pan Books, London, 2002.

Clark, General Mark, *Calculated Risk*, Harper & Brothers, New York NY, 1950.

Cunningham, Admiral Viscount Cunningham of Hyndhope, *A Sailor's Odyssey*, Hutchinson & Co. (Publishers) Ltd, London, 1951.

Eisenhower, Dwight D., *Crusade in Europe*, Heinemann, London, 1948.

Harpur, Brian, *The Impossible Victory*, William Kimber & Co Ltd, London, 1980.

Kesselring, Albert, *The Memoirs of Field Marshal Kesselring*, William Kimber, London, 1953.

Lewis, Norman, *Naples '44* , William Collins & Sons Ltd, London, 1978.

Majdalaney, Fred, *Monte Cassino, Portrait of a Battle*, Longmans, Green and Co Ltd, 1957.

Montgomery, Field Marshal the Viscount Montgomery of Alamein, *Memoirs*, Collins, London, 1958.

Montgomery, Field Marshal the Viscount Montgomery of Alamein, *El Alamein to the Sangro*, Collins, London 1958.

Orgill, Douglas, *The Gothic Line, The Autumn Campaign in Italy 1944*, William Heineman Ltd, London, 1967.

Owen, Roderic, *The Desert Air Force*, Hutchinson & Co Ltd, London, 1948.

Peniakoff, Lt Col Vladimir, *Private Army*, Jonathan Cape, London, 1950.

Pöppel, Martin, *Heaven and Hell, the War Diary of a German Paratrooper*, Spellmount Ltd, Staplehurst, 1988.

Rommel, Field Marshal Erwin, *Rommel and his Art of War*, edited by Dr John Pimlott, Greenhill Books, London, 2003.

Summersby, Kay, *Eisenhower Was My Boss*, T. Werner Laurie Ltd, London, 1949.

Woodruff, William, *Vessel of Sadness*, Abacus, London, 2004.

4. General Bibliography

Annussek, Greg, *Hitler's Raid to Save Mussolini*, Da Capo Press, New York NY, 2006.

Atkinson, Rick, *An Army at Dawn: The War in North Africa, 1942–43*, Henry Holt and Co., New York NY, 2002

Atkinson, Rick, *The Day of Battle: The War in Sicily and Italy 1943–1944*, Henry Holt and Co., New York NY, 2007

Clark, Lloyd, *Anzio*, Headline Publishing Group, London, 2006.

d' Este, Carlo, *Eisenhower, A Soldier's Life*, Henry Holt, New York NY, 2002.

d' Este, Carlo, *Bitter Victory, The Battle for Sicily 1943*, Aurum Press Ltd, London, 2008.

Doherty, Richard, *Eighth Army In Italy, 1943–45: The Long Hard Slog*, Pen & Sword Books Ltd, Barnsley, 2007.

Ellis, John, *Cassino, the Hollow Victory*, Aurum Press, London, 2003.

Fenby, Jonathan, *Alliance*, Simon & Schuster UK Ltd, London.

Follain, John, *Mussolini's Island*, Hodder and Stoughton, 2006.

Ford, Ken. *Battleaxe Division*, Sutton, Stroud, 1999.

Hamilton, Nigel, *Monty – The Battles of Field Marshal Bernard Montgomery*, Hodder & Stoughton, London, 1994.

Holland, James, *Together We Stand – North Africa 1942–43: Turning the Tide in the West*, Harper Collins, London, 2003.

Infield, Glen B., *Skorzeny: Hitler's Commando*, St Martin's Press, New York, 1981.

Liddell Hart, B.H., *The Rommel Papers*, Collins, London, 1953.

Macintyre, Ben, *Operation Mincemeat*, Bloomsbury Publishing Plc, London, 2010.

Montagu, Ewen, *The Man Who Never Was*, The Camelot Press Ltd, 1953.

Moorehead, Alan, *African Trilogy*, Hamish Hamilton, London, 1944.

Moorehead, Alan, *Eclipse*, The Text Publishing Co, 1997.

Moorehead, Alan, *Montgomery*, Hamish Hamilton, 1946.

Neillands, Robin, *Eighth Army, From the Western Desert to the Alps, 1939–1945*, John Murray (Publishers), Hodder Headline, London, 2004.

Parker, Mathew, *Monte Cassino*, Headline Book Publishing, London, 2003.

Roberts, Andrew, *Masters and Commanders*, Penguin Books Ltd, London, 2009.

5. Travel Sources

Over recent years, I have made a number of visits to Tunisia, Sicily and Italy. In addition recourse was made to a wide range of historical, geographical and travel sources on those countries, which included the following:

Tunisia

Eyewitness Travel Guide, E & A Lisewscy, *Tunisia*, Dorling Kindersley Ltd 2005.

Diana Darke, *Traveller's Tunisia*, Thomas Cook Publishing, 2005.

Tomkinson, Michael, *Tunisia*, Michael Tomkinson Printing, 2006.

Sicily

Benjamin, Sandra, *Sicily, Three Thousand Years of Human History*, Steerforth Press, 2006.

Eyewitness Travel Guide, *Sicily* , Dorling Kindersley Ltd, 2007.

Insight Guide, *Sicily*, Discovery Publications, 2007.

Italy

Eyewitness Travel Guide, *Italy* , Dorling Kindersley Ltd 2007.

Insight Guide, *Italy*, Discovery Publications, 2007.

Morton, HV, *A Traveller in Italy*

Morton, HV, *A Traveller in Southern Italy*

Publicazioni Cassinesi, *The Abbey of Montecassino*, Montecassino 2005.

Index

237

238

240